Everlasting Love

God's Greatest Gift

with

Study Guide

Patricia Marlett

Scriptures from the King James Bible

Printed in the United States of America

Published by High Tower Publications

First Edition - 2014   ISBN 978-0-9854059-1-5

Second Edition - 2015   ISBN 978-0-9854059-4-6

The God of my rock; in him will I trust: he is my shield, and the horn of my salvation, my High Tower, and my refuge, my savior; thou savest me from violence. 2 Samuel 22:3

"I cannot do great things alone,

but *God* will do great things through me."

....Patricia

Acknowledgment

I will always and forevermore acknowledge and give thanks to God. I honor, praise, and give the glory to my heavenly Father for it is by His grace that I am blessed. With the gift He has bestowed upon me, I write in His honor to glorify His name.

Also, deep appreciation to my husband, Mark, for the unwavering love and support he gives as I pursue my passion. You are my rock, I love you.

Dedication

This book is dedicated to all who desire an

intimate relationship with the Father.

For I am persuaded, that neither death, nor life, nor angels, nor principalities, nor powers, nor things present, nor things to come; Nor height, nor depth, nor any other creatures, shall be able to separate us from the love of God, which is in Christ Jesus our Lord.

Romans 8:38-39

The Greatest Commandment

Jesus was challenged by the Pharisees for His teachings, and a lawyer attempted to trick Him by asking Jesus which is the greatest commandment in the law. Christ replied as follows:

But when the Pharisees had heard that he had put the Sadducees to silence, they were gathered together. Then one of them, which was a lawyer, asked him a question, tempting him, and saying, Master, which is the greatest commandment in the law? Jesus said unto him, Thou shalt love the Lord thy God with all thy heart, and with all thy soul, and with all thy mind. This is the first and great commandment. And the second is like unto it, Thou shalt love thy neighbor as thyself. On these two commandments hang all the law and the prophets.

Matthew 22:34-40

Table of Contents

Part III ~ Trinity of the Kingdom: Mercy, Grace, and Faith

Part IV~ Spiritual Topics

Part V ~ Companion Study Guide

Part VI ~ Scriptures

Note from the Author

If any man speak, let him speak as the oracles of God; if any man minister, let him do it as of the ability which God giveth: that God in all things may be glorified through Jesus Christ, to whom be praise and dominion for ever and ever. Amen.

1 Peter 4:11

It is with honor and glory to our heavenly Father that I take great pleasure in presenting this book to share the truth of God's Word as taught in the Scriptures, and to assure each person who reads the content on the following pages that everything God created and provided is for you. It has always been about you when God established the foundation of all His creation as we read in the Bible and continues throughout eternity. I hope you gain insight of how much you are truly loved, and how desirous the Father is for you to be with Him today and forever.

God made all things possible through His Son, Jesus, when He gave man a new and better covenant. As a beneficiary of this testament, one of the many gifts is the free will to personally decide if we want a life with Him, one that is eternal. Though it is by our choice, God wants all His children to come home to the Kingdom of Heaven. We can be with our Father this very moment, spiritually, if we become one in spirit with Christ. The first step is a desire to have a relationship with God and become a born-again child of the Father. In Christ, we are changed from a sinner to a saint and secured as a joint heir through Jesus in the Kingdom.

I pray you are inspired to seek God and accept His Word as the guidepost for your life and maintain a relationship with your heavenly Father. Not simply know of Him, but fall in love with Him, learn His nature and understand what He has done for you and what He expects of you, His child. As a child to the parent, we should want our Father's love and a close bond with Him more than anything, ever. Only God can heal a broken body whether it is physical or emotional, only God can supply for personal and professional prosperity, and only God can give us eternal life. There is absolutely nothing permanent on this planet as this earthen place will one day be made anew to receive the New Jerusalem which will be the eternal home of every believer.

God's love, mercy, and grace are forever present and will always protect and provide for His children. We are His most precious creation, made in His likeness, for His pleasure, never forgotten or forsaken. Promises, blessings, gifts, and power are within His Kingdom, and we are personally responsible to acquire the knowledge that God has set forth in His Word, so that we may partake of these Kingdom treasures. It is important to understand the role of Christ and His purpose in fulfilling the Father's plan and to accept the Holy Spirit as our tutor who teaches all things of God and is our advocate in the Kingdom. This is crucial to living in the spirit and receiving all that He has prepared for us.

This book is divided into three sections of the trinity of God; the Father, the Son, and the Holy Ghost; the trinity of man as spirit, soul, and body; and the Kingdom of Heaven which operates with mercy, grace, and faith. There may, periodically, appear a redundancy as the trinities are both separate and one; God is the Father, He is the Son, and He is the Holy Ghost. A conscious effort has been made to keep the repetitiveness to a minimum. With forethought, many Scriptures are appropriately placed to serve as a reference to what God's Word says as the focus is on His truth.

Also in this second edition of the book, I have included a study guide which may be beneficial for an individual study or group participation. In talking about God, Christ, and the Holy Spirit there will be an unavoidable repetition in the study materials as it brings the knowledge of the trinity to further enlightenment.

Our relationship with our heavenly Father is defined in our belief, trust, and unwavering faith. We are not lost souls wandering aimlessly and helpless throughout this life, but saints made righteous and holy in Christ for the Father. Claim your rightful position as an heir of the Kingdom of Heaven and choose life secured and sealed in God's *everlasting love.*

Introduction

In contemplating how God established His Kingdom, we learn there is a mathematical equation at the foundation of the creation. The numbers seven and three are paramount in the Kingdom of Heaven with seven being God's revered, or holy number as taught in His Word. In both the Old and New Testaments, these numbers are paralleled to time, events, commands, warnings, and deeds most often prophesied as a foretelling of the future. Though there are other references such as the numbers twelve, thirty, and forty; seven and three remain dominant.

Beginning with the first reference to the number seven, we find it in the onset of creation. *And on the seventh day God ended his work which he had made; and he rested on the seventh day from all his work which he had made. And God blessed the seventh day, and sanctified it: because that in it he had rested from all his work which God created and made. These are the generations of the heavens and of the earth when they were created, in the day that the Lord God made the earth and the heavens.* Genesis 2:2-4 On the seventh day, God sealed His works and proclaimed it finished, for nothing would ever need to be added or changed.

Fast-forward to Jesus on the cross at Calvary and He said: "It is finished." Christ fulfilled the Father's oracles on earth. In the beginning with God, and in the end with Christ, all comes full circle. God ordained it and Jesus fulfills it. God and His Son, the Living Word, created and manifested everything man would ever require in this lifetime and eternally.

The number seven not only represents finality but perfection. In all that God created, it is perfect. *The words of the Lord are pure words: as silver tried in a furnace of earth, purified seven times.* Psalm 12:6 Seven is a ruling, or commanding number of authority and power. *Wherefore, brethren, look ye out among you seven men of honest report, full of the Holy Ghost and wisdom, whom we may appoint over this business.* Acts 6:3 God established seven Covenants: Adam, Noah, Abraham, Moses, David, Messiah (Christ's first appearance on earth), and Peace (Christ's second coming to earth; the Kingdom of Peace).

An example of the number seven is taught through Noah. He was to gather seven animals of each breed from the land and equally seven fowls of each kind from the air that were clean, male and female to bring onto the Ark, and then bring two male and female of the unclean animals as well. *Of every clean beast thou shalt take to thee by sevens, the male and his female: and of beasts that are not clean by two, the male and his female. Of fowls also of the air by sevens, the male and the female; to keep seed alive upon the face of all the earth.* Genesis 7:2-3

In seven days from doing so, God told Noah that water would cover the earth, *For yet seven days, and I will cause it to rain upon the earth forty days and forty nights; and every living substance that I have made will I destroy from off the face of the earth.* Genesis 7:4 We learn the cleansing with the flood was because the earth had become defiled and man refused to turn from his wickedness. There is coming a day when the earth will be destroyed again and made anew for the final time but not by water, rather by fire.

Throughout biblical history there is reference to seven, and perhaps, more so in the Book of Revelation. We read of the seven churches, seven spirits, seven golden candlesticks, seven stars, seven scrolls, seven seals, seven trumpets, seven bowls, seven angels and so forth as God defines and declares what is to transpire both in the Kingdom of Heaven and on earth upon the return of Christ. The bridegroom, Christ, will come for His bride, the believers. Even the antichrist is sanctioned by God a period of seven years to rule.

In the Old Testament, there was the seventh day atonement at the holy alter and sprinkled with blood seven times to anoint it. There were seven years of famine, seven years of drought, and seven years of rest for the fields. *Behold, there come seven years of great plenty throughout all the land of Egypt: And there shall arise after them seven years of famine; and all the plenty shall be forgotten in the land of Egypt; and the famine shall consume the land; And the plenty shall not be known in the land by reason of that famine following; for it shall be very grievous.* Genesis 41:29-31

If you owned a person, they were to be released from your household in seven years to go out and establish their own home; and likewise, if a debt was owed to you it was voided and considered paid in full after the seventh year. *At the end of every seven years thou shalt make a release. And this is the manner of the release: Every creditor that lendeth ought unto his neighbour shall release it; he shall not exact it of his neighbour, or of his brother; because it is called the Lord's release.* Deuteronomy 15:1-2 Many feasts were celebrated every seven years.

The number seven is verified with the seven curses placed upon man through the first Adam to the seven crowns that will be given by the second Adam, Christ, when we stand before Him on Judgment Day. Beginning in the Garden of Gethsemane and on the pathway to Calvary, Jesus shed blood from seven places on His body representative of removing the curses. So much more of God's magnificent number seven can be read throughout the Scriptures reflecting His holiness, perfection, and commanding order of events.

Giving equal affirmation to the number three, for it is representative of

24

the personage of God; He is the Father, He is the Son, and He is the Holy Ghost. Each divinity has a specific purpose for man. Though God is all, He established the trinity as God is administration, Christ is ministry, and the Holy Ghost is power. God is the Almighty and Holy One in His Kingdom. Whether an event required seven years or three days, there is a divine methodology to God's plan for nothing is random. The numbers seven and three are predominant in the foundation and function of the Kingdom of Heaven.

With attention to the number three, the Israelites traveled three days in the wilderness once released from bondage in Egypt. Moses told them to cleanse and be prepared in three days time to stand before God at Mount Sinai when He would appear in a thick cloud. Then we have Jesus at Calvary as He hung on the cross with two criminals as Christ was placed between them making three men on three crosses. *And when they were come to the place, which is called Calvary, there they crucified him, and the malefactors, one on the right hand, and the other on the left.* Luke 23:33

Why not five or twenty-five people hanging on the cross in the field when Christ was brought forth among them on that particular day? *And one of the malefactors which were hanged railed on him, saying, If thou be Christ, save thyself and us. But the other answering rebuked him, saying, Dost not thou fear God, seeing thou art in the same condemnation? And we indeed justly; for we receive the due reward of our deeds: but this man hath done nothing amiss. And he said unto Jesus, Lord, remember me when thou comest into thy kingdom. And Jesus said unto him, Verily I say unto thee, To day shalt thou be with me in paradise.* Luke 23:39-43 The answer is these two individuals represented the saved and unsaved; belief and unbelief, which remains throughout history.

Within the trinity, we see the trilogy. In Christ's crucifixion, death, and resurrection we are given redemption, reconciliation, and righteousness. Upon His death and before ascending to the Kingdom of

Heaven to reclaim His seat at the right hand of the Father, Jesus spent three days in the heart of the earth just as Jonas spent three days in the belly of the whale. *But he answered and said unto them, An evil and adulterous generation seeketh after a sign; and there shall no sign be given to it, but the sign of the prophet Jonas: For as Jonas was three days and three nights in the whale's belly; so shall the Son of man be three days and three nights in the heart of the earth.* Matthew 12:39-40 People demanded that Jesus prove to be the Messiah and the parallel given was Jonas.

However, Jesus didn't descend to the depth of the earth to please the people, or to credit Himself. He had a purpose which was to take the keys of hell to free man from an imminent death by Satan through sin. *I am he that liveth, and was dead; and, behold, I am alive forevermore, Amen; and have the keys of hell and of death.* Revelation 1:18

In God's master plan as reflected from the beginning in Genesis to the finality with the New Jerusalem, one can only be awed by the reality of His omnipotence. *But the wisdom that is from above is first pure, then peaceable, gentle, and easy to be entreated, full of mercy and good fruits, without partiality, and without hypocrisy.* James 3:17 The Almighty King of the Kingdom of Heaven allows His children access to Him on the authority given in Christ and through an intercessor, the Holy Spirit. We can see the methodology of the trinity of God. God patiently waits for us to seek Him.

Preface

To know if we are receiving the truth of God's Word whether written or spoken, we need the Holy Spirit to interpret the teachings, separating the truth from the false as the Scriptures are written for the spirit-filled person. *But the anointing which ye have received of him abideth in you, and ye need not that any man teach you: but as the same anointing teacheth you of all things, and is truth, and is no lie, and even as it hath taught you, ye shall abide in him.* 1 John 2:27 Each born-again believer is personally responsible to obtain knowledge of His Word through the discernment of the Spirit of Truth.

It is human nature to take comfort in entrusting our understanding in someone who exemplifies authority of the Scriptures such as a pastor, preacher, priest, minister, theologian, teacher, and so forth. We depend on them with expectations of accuracy and anticipate their study habits will bring spiritual wisdom to the pulpit. *That your faith should not stand in the wisdom of men, but in the power of God.* 1 Corinthians 2:5 We must verify that their interpretation is accurate. When the Holy Spirit unveils the parables as we study the Word, we will know the truth when we hear it spoken.

God has provided knowing the time would come when we would have need of His provisions. God has done His part, but we are to learn through His Word what our Father requires of us, and know how to obtain what has been set forth before we were born. Everything rests on knowledge and understanding of Kingdom principles and applying obedience in faith to receive.

God wants everyone to partake of His heavenly gifts, promises, and power because they are meant for His children, but it is mandatory to know how the Kingdom operates. God's foundational principles are set in place and must be observed. The difference in those who receive and those who do not is the application of the Kingdom laws with the key of unwavering faith.

Walking in wisdom with faith the size of a mustard seed will solve any problem because we have the authority in Christ to call upon the power of God. One prayer will obtain results if spoken according to the truth on the provision of the Holy Spirit. *The effectual fervent prayer of a righteous man availeth much.* James 5:16 Only the truth will bring the power of God into our life. *And ye shall know the truth, and the truth shall make you free.* John 8:32 This is paramount to receiving answered prayers.

In the generations before the new covenant in Christ, priests were appointed with authority to be mediators between God and the people. They did not have redemption and reconciliation through Jesus, nor did they have the Holy Spirit as their personal intercessor, so they were without the ability to have an intimate communion with the Father. When God sent His Son to redeem man, He made it personal between Himself and each person who accepts Christ.

Upon Jesus' death and resurrection, the new covenant which was established in the Kingdom at the foundation of creation is set forth between God and man. Through Christ, we have been redeemed, sanctified, made righteous and holy, saints that we may come personally before the throne of God in prayer for healing, miracles, emotional and physical prosperity, or any need. We are no longer subject to the laws as administered by Moses, the carnal laws, but rather to the Fruit of the Spirit, for we are spirit born in Christ for the Father. *Knowing this, that the law is not made for a righteous man, but for the lawless and disobedient, for the ungodly and for sinners, for unholy and profane, for murderers of fathers and murderers of mothers, for manslayers, For whoremongers, for them that defile themselves with mankind, for menstealers, for liars, for perjured persons, and if there be any other thing that is contrary to sound doctrine.* 1 Timothy 1:9-10 God's new Spirit laws are written in our heart and mind; therefore, our prayers are personal and private, an intimate time with our heavenly Father. We are to shut out all distraction when we speak to God, for He instructs: *But thou, when thou prayest, enter into thy closet and when thou hast shut thy door, pray to thy Father which is in secret; and thy Father which seeth in secret shall reward thee openly.* Matthew 6:6

How we apply faith is critical to receiving from God. It is the key that unlocks the Kingdom door. Christ teaches that a minute amount of unwavering faith likened to a mustard seed avails much. *And Jesus said unto them, Because of your unbelief: for verily I say unto you, If ye have faith as a grain of mustard seed, ye shall say unto this mountain, Remove hence to yonder place; and it shall remove; and nothing shall be impossible unto you.* Matthew 17:20 Incorrect or misguided information can place us in unbelief, for if we are not in truth then we are in unbelief. We can be a believer and have unbelief present. There is no other category and unbelief voids belief, for it dilutes our faith.

From the beginning, God has dealt with generations lacking in knowledge of His Kingdom and cutting themselves off from His blessings. It has never been God withholding His gifts, but rather people are unprepared to have a relationship with Him. We do not know our heavenly Father as we should. We may be spirit born in Christ and have the Comforter, but if we are uneducated in the principles for living within the spirit realm, we cannot reach the Father. Man has a responsibility in a relationship with God and our ignorance, whether deliberate or not, restricts our access to His Kingdom.

Everything we will ever need today and forever is within the Kingdom of Heaven. As a child of the Father, our desire is to seek a relationship with Him through faithfulness in His Word that we may attain knowledge and understanding of the principles set forth in His Kingdom. God has made it possible for His children to approach Him, but we are required to believe, trust, and hold steadfast in unshakable faith. When we do, it will be life-altering and everlasting.

Part I

Trinity of God
Father, Son, and Holy Ghost

And whatsoever ye do in word or deed, do all in the name of the Lord Jesus, giving thanks to God and the Father, by him.

Colossians 3:17

Chapter 1 ~ Beginning in the Garden of Eden

So God created man in his own image, in the image of God created he him; male and female created he them.

Genesis 1:27

There is nothing in existence that God did not create and before the heavens and earth, before Adam and before we were in the womb yet born of flesh, we were with God. *According as he hath chosen us in him before the foundation of the world, that we should be holy and without blame before him in love; having predestinated us unto the adoption of children by Jesus Christ to himself, according to the good pleasure of his will.* Ephesians 1:4-5 Because we come from God and He is Spirit, we are spirit of His Spirit.

When Adam was given a body, it was to give a physical presence for his spirit. He was breathed a soul which is the human consciousness of man. Adam was made from earth, the place he would soon occupy. *And the Lord God formed man of the dust of the ground, and breathed into his nostrils the breath of life; and man became a living soul.* Genesis 2:7 The first man has been born of God. *This is the book of the generations of Adam. In the day that God created man, in the likeness of God made he him. Male and female created he them; and blessed them, and called their name Adam, In the day when they were created.* Genesis 5:1-2 This is the trinity of man: spirit, soul, and body.

God created the heavens and earth for man. Earth was given to Adam to be his heaven, a kingdom, whereby he had dominion over this world. God took a section of the earth and designed a special home, paradise, and called it the Garden of Eden. *And the Lord God planted a garden eastward in Eden; and there he put the man whom he had formed.* Genesis 2:8 God gave Adam authority to name the animals, for he was the ruler. *And out of the ground the Lord God formed every beast of the field and every fowl of the air; and brought them unto Adam to see what he would call them: and whatsoever Adam called every living creature that was the name thereof. And Adam gave names to all cattle, and to the fowl of the air and to every beast of the field; but for Adam there was not found a help meet for him.* Genesis 2:19-20

Adam realized that all the animals had a mate but he did not, so God made Adam a mate from one of his ribs. *And Adam said, This is now bone of my bones, and flesh of my flesh: she shall be called Woman, because she was taken out of Man.* Genesis 2:23 Adam was pleased to have a companion and named his bride. *And Adam called his wife's name Eve; because she was the mother of all living.* Genesis 3:20 We have the first man and woman of God.

Adam and Eve were God's children, and He was pleased with them. *And God blessed them, and God said unto them, Be fruitful, and multiply, and replenish the earth, and subdue it: and have dominion over the fish of the sea, and over the fowl of the air, and over every living thing that moveth upon the earth.* Genesis 1:28 They lived in the spirit and life was perfect. In the cool of the afternoon, God would visit with them. In paradise, there were no misfortunes, nor hardships until the day Satan appeared.

When we hear the telling of the serpent tempting Eve with an apple, it is almost depicted as a fairytale to the reality of the significance of what transpired between God and Adam. Satan's objective was to steal Adam's position of authority over the earth and become the ruler, and to destroy the relationship Adam had with God. Lucifer was thrown out of the Kingdom of Heaven with one-third of the angels following because he wanted to be the king of the Almighty Kingdom. Satan compromises Adam's spouse with a lie, and she succumbs to his trickery and persuades her husband to be unfaithful to God.

It was a catastrophic and cataclysmic event that affected every person born thereafter from the seed of Adam. Throughout the following generations, man is born with a sinful nature into a sin world under Satan's rule. This was not a surprise to God who already had a provision, His Son. *For if by one man's offence death reigned by one; much more they which receive abundance of grace and of the gift of righteousness shall reign in life by one, Jesus Christ. Therefore as by the offence of one judgment came upon all men to condemnation; even so by the righteousness of one the free gift came upon all men unto justification of life. For as by one man's disobedience many were made sinners, so by the obedience of one shall many be made righteous.* Romans 5:17-19 Through the disobedience of Adam, man's spiritual relationship with God was severed, but Christ reconciled man back to the Father by taking the sins of the world upon Himself.

Their act of disobedience cost them their home, and they were evicted and locked out of the garden having to labor for a living for the first time. It was a humiliating calamity for Adam to be dethroned from his position of authority to working in the fields, and laboring off the land for a living. God remained in communication with him daily, but their relationship had changed. It seems such a harsh action for God to remove them from paradise because of one indiscretion, their first and only offense towards Him. However, God could not allow sin where there is purity and holiness. God knew what would transpire with Satan.

God could have established the garden whereby Adam and Eve would not be subjected to the fruit of the forbidden trees, and yet, He didn't. We know God has a reason. In the garden, there was no scale to measure the balance of good and evil because only perfection existed as long as two trees, the Tree of Good and Evil and the Tree of Life, were undisturbed. However, that changed when Adam and Eve ate the forbidden fruit from the Tree of Good and Evil and became aware of their physical self. Seeing they were naked they covered their bodies and hid from God. Why have such a reaction, if it weren't that they were unaware of their human characteristics? Though they saw each other as being different, it wasn't thought conscious until carnality came upon them. With the knowledge of good and evil, their humanism became predominant and they were governed by the carnal rather than the spirit.

This act opened their eyes to right and wrong, something they were to never have knowledge of. But, why not? If there were trees that God specifically did not want Adam or Eve to have dominion over, why put the trees in the garden? If they must be planted in the garden, why not put an invisible shield around them prohibiting Adam and Eve's ability to have access? Why didn't God forgive this first transgression and allow Adam and Eve to remain in the home He designed for them? It would seem that without this act of disobedience, Adam and Eve would not have transitioned from a spirit person to carnality, and if not, could they have procreated? As they had no natural cognitive reasoning to see themselves other than spirit, perhaps there never would have been children born of them, and therefore, no future generations.

With their knowledge of good and evil, they could make decisions in their sinful nature which gave them a measurement of likes, dislikes, wants, desires, and so forth; things that were never a consideration in the spirit. With this newfound awareness, they could choose to eat of another tree in the garden, the Tree of Life, and in doing so, they would live forever with a sinful nature. *And the Lord God said, Behold, the man is become as one of us, to know good and evil: and now, lest he put forth his hand, and take also of the tree of life, and eat, and live forever.* Genesis 3:22 Living in sin would bring corruption, destruction, illness, and disease. They would live under these conditions eternally if they ate the fruit of this forbidden tree.

Can you imagine being stricken with a horrible, painfully degenerative disease and have to live that way forever without any hope of healing? This is what was in store for Adam and Eve, and for man if God had not removed them from the garden. God even placed angels at the four corners to prevent them from reentering and eating of this tree. He was not punishing them, but protecting them from consuming another forbidden fruit. Had Adam eaten the fruit from the Tree of Life, man would live forever in sin and sickness with no hope of returning to God, spiritually and eternally.

While in the Garden of Eden and before their transgression, there was no consideration to procreate and bring forth life. In their spirit person, they were not thought conscious to know each other intimately. It wasn't until they were in carnality and removed from the garden, that God speaks to Eve and tells her she will bear children and to Adam that he will labor for a living. *Unto the woman he said, I will greatly multiply thy sorrow and thy conception; in sorrow thou shalt bring forth children; and thy desire shall be to thy husband, and he shall rule over thee. And unto Adam he said, Because thou hast hearkened unto the voice of thy wife, and hast eaten of the tree, of which I commanded thee, saying, Thou shalt not eat of it: cursed is the ground for thy sake; in sorrow shalt thou eat of it all the days of thy life.* Genesis 3:16-17 Outside the perimeters of the garden and in their human persona, Adam was intimate with his wife and she conceived. *And Adam knew Eve his wife; and she conceived, and bare Cain, and said, I have gotten a man from the Lord.* Genesis. 4:1

If they had eaten of the fruit of the Tree of Life, after the transgression and transformation from spirit to carnal, the first generation of children, Cain, Abel, and Seth would have been born to live eternally with a sinful nature. The difference is that outside paradise, man is not subjected to a life of sin without hope and redemption. In the flesh, civilization is created. Adam is the first father, physically, of generations to come and Jesus is the second Adam, spiritually, reconciling man to our spirit self and returning us to our heavenly Father. *For as in Adam all die, even so in Christ shall all be made alive.* 1 Corinthians 15:22 The fate of man rested on Adam; however, Christ saved man from Adam's fall from the Kingdom.

It would appear these were the options. First, Adam and Eve would live in the Garden of Eden forever as spirit persons communing with God daily and life would be perfect with the exception there would be no descendants. Second, Adam and Eve would be allowed to remain in the garden after committing an act of disobedience; however, it can be presumed they would eat of the Tree of Life, conceive in their human persona and their children, and all generations thereafter would live in sin, forever. There would be no reconciliation to a spirit person with God. Last would be to remove them from their heavenly home, so there would be a way through Christ to redeem man from sin and give him a rebirth in spirit. *For he hath made him to be sin for us, who knew no sin; that we might be made the righteousness of God in him.* 2 Corinthians 5:21

It was necessary for our sakes that Adam and Eve be displaced from the garden. It was required that they leave paradise, so that future generations could have a means of returning to God and His Kingdom. This could not be accomplished in the Garden of Eden. What Satan stole from the first Adam, Christ, the second Adam, paid the price with His blood and purchased our freedom from sin and the curse whereby reconciling man spiritually to the Father. Before Adam, it was established within the Kingdom of Heaven that the Living Word would be made flesh, and Christ would come down to earth to save man. In God's sovereignty, He had a plan.

Chapter 2 ~ God is our Father

He that loveth not knoweth not God; for God is love.

1 John 4:8

Most of the world's population can attest to having heard of God. Should His name be mentioned, few people in modern civilization are without awareness of who is being spoken of. Today we are reaching third world countries making the introduction. *For thus saith the Lord that created the heavens; God himself that formed the earth and made it; he hath established it, he created it not in vain, he formed it to be inhabited: I am the Lord; and there is none else.* Isaiah 45:18

God is the Almighty, Most High, Alpha and Omega, the beginning and the end, the same yesterday, today, and tomorrow; never changing, Creator of the heavens and earth, and all thereof. He is King of kings and Lord of lords. God is love, this is His nature. *Before the mountains were brought forth, or ever thou hadst formed the earth and the world, even from everlasting to everlasting, thou art God.* Psalm 90:2 God has always been.

Many profess to know of God but not about Him, nor understanding His nature. His divine essence is love and is expressed solely for His most precious creation, you. *For all things are for your sakes, that the abundant grace might through the thanksgiving of many rebound to the glory of God.* 2 Corinthians 4:15 We are of God and belong to Him.

His love is an agape love unconditional without boundaries, manipulations or stipulations, for it has no dimension. There is no measure of depth, width, or height, nor limitations. *And we have known and believed the love that God hath to us. God is love; and he that dwelleth in love dwelleth in God, and God in him.* 1 John 4:16 Such a love greatly surpasses our carnal ability to comprehend as our human instinct places conditions on this emotion.

He is Spirit manifested in the trinity of the Father, the Son, and the Holy Ghost. *God is a Spirit: and they that worship him must worship him in spirit and in truth.* John 4:24 God presents Himself in the trinity, separately, for a specific and significant purpose in man's life. For example, the Son is sent from heaven to reconcile man to the Kingdom, and the Holy Ghost is a gift that we may have communion with God and receive His blessings. Everything has been premeditated and prepared for those who believe and established at the foundation of Creation.

Mercy and grace are always forthcoming from the Father. His blessings, promises, and gifts abound, and His power is sufficient to those who hold His truth. He gave His only begotten Son, a gift, who died that we may live because He loves us so much. *For God so loved the world that he gave his only begotten Son, that whosoever believeth in him should not perish, but have everlasting life.* John 3:16 He came down from the Kingdom of Heaven, born into flesh, lived as a man, and died for the sins of the world because He didn't want anyone to be forsaken. God wants everyone to return to Him, for we are His children.

To understand God, we need to know love. However, we do not know of His kind of love for the mere reason we are born with a sinful nature. God's love is perfect, we are not. It is so important that His first two Commandments, or instructions for man's life are to love Him and love one another. When God established the Commandments for His people, the Israelites, He was telling them of His nature. *And thou shalt love the Lord thy God with all thy heart, and with all thy soul, and with all thy mind, and with all thy strength: this is the first commandment. And the second is like, namely this, Thou shalt love thy neighbour as thyself. There is none other commandment greater than these.* Mark 12:30-31

Christ taught this to His disciples when He told them to have charity, or love as it is the most important testament. Man only understands conditional love which can be infused with performance; and yet, we are supposed to have a love as Christ did, willing to die for another. Even though we fall short, we can know with assuredness that God's love is forgiving and forever as trespasses are not held against those who love Him and His Son. The world would be a far better place if there was more thoughtfulness and compassion springing forth from an attitude of brotherly love. We should be expressing the same love God shows towards us in our relationship with others.

If not for God, we would not be here for He is our Father, and if not for His Son, the finality of this life would be death with no hope of eternity. The most important thing is to maintain a strong communion with God, and it begins by establishing one with Christ. God is a parent who loves His children. Our desire should be to love Him with all our heart and never want to be apart from His presence. *Who hath saved us, and called us with an holy calling, not according to our works, but according to his own purpose and grace, which was given us in Christ Jesus before the world began.* 2 Timothy 1:9 We were first with God. We need to understand how deeply loved we are that no matter the degree of the sin committed, God forgives with continuous mercy and grace through His enduring and *everlasting love.*

There is only one unforgivable and unpardonable offense that will affect the love God has for us and that is blasphemy against the Holy Ghost. *Wherefore I say unto you, All manner of sin and blasphemy shall be forgiven unto men: but the blasphemy against the Holy Ghost shall not be forgiven unto men.* Matthew 12:31 Ill-favored and negative vocabulary implicating God, Christ, or the Holy Ghost is a sin against the trinity because speaking against one is unfavorable to all who is God. *And whosoever speaketh a word against the Son of man, it shall be forgiven him: but whosoever speaketh against the Holy Ghost, it shall not be forgiven him, neither in this world, neither in the world to come.* Matthew 12:32 This can also be reflected in our attitude and actions just as easily as with the spoken word.

We go unchecked in our communications, freely expressing ourselves sometimes to the detriment of others' feelings. Often our words may criticize, demean, and hurt rather than encourage, uplift, and praise. Language is so natural that we do not monitor the words that flow from our lips. *If any man among you seem to be religious, and bridleth not his tongue, but deceiveth his own heart, this man's religion is vain.* James 1:26 If we profess faith but do not filter our communication, faith becomes ineffectual in the eyes of God.

Caution is required with forethought when we open our mouth to speak understanding that inappropriate verbiage can be a sin. Derogatory comments have an impact on the recipient, but simultaneously boomerangs back on the accuser, for Christ is our witness. This is why we are reminded often in His Word to guard our tongue. *For he that will love life, and see good days, let him refrain his tongue from evil, and his lips that they speak no guile.*1 Peter 3:10 We can also read in the Old Testament: *Death and life are in the power of the tongue: and they that love it shall eat the fruit thereof.* Proverbs 18:21 There is power in the spoken word be it for good or harm. *And the tongue is a fire, a world of iniquity: so is the tongue among our members, that it defileth the whole body, and setteth on fire the course of nature; and it is set on fire of hell.* James 3:6 We must monitor our communications for improper use of language is a detriment to our relationship with our heavenly Father.

God keeps no secrets from His children and shows no favoritism. We are all equally provided the treasures within the Kingdom, but we must seek them. *For there is no respect of persons with God.* Romans 2:11

Comprehending the nature of our heavenly Father and the principles of the Kingdom of Heaven prepares us to live for the glory of God. *Let a man so account of us, as of the ministers of Christ, and stewards of the mysteries of God.* 1 Corinthians 4:1

In an intimate communion with God, we can learn the plan the Father has preordained for our life. Our instructions are in the laws of His Kingdom, and we are responsible to know them. *And he said, Unto you it is given to know the mysteries of the kingdom of God: but to others in parables; that seeing they might not see, and hearing they might not understand.* Luke 8:10 Faithful in obedience to the Kingdom, we become stewards of Christ's ministry; disciples of His gospel.

When we become intimately connected with God, our will becomes His; and likewise, His becomes ours that we may glorify Him in all we say and do. His desire is to give us our desires when they align with His laws, so the things we ask in prayer may be given. *And whatsoever ye do in word or deed, do all in the name of the Lord Jesus, giving thanks to God and the Father by him.* Colossians 3:17 There is unison between the Father and His children that the will of God may be manifested through us. We have a responsibility in the relationship with our heavenly Father that we may establish our destiny unto His glory, and magnify His Kingdom with our words and deeds.

We are not to be worrisome because our needs have already been met. His mercy protects and His grace provides. There will never be a better place than enveloped in the love of God. *The blessing of the Lord, it maketh rich, and he addeth no sorrow with it.* Proverbs 10:22 When we accept that no one will ever do a more perfect job of troubleshooting a problem than God, we surrender our willfulness. Our best will always come up short to His perfection. It is when we put our complete reliance in God that we win victory over our battle, whatever it may be.

By our human weakness, we do not easily forgive. God did the very opposite and forgave us every wrongful deed, no matter the degree and instructs us to do the same by treating others as we wish to be treated. *But I say unto you, Love your enemies, bless them that curse you, do good to them that hate you, and pray for them which despitefully use you, and persecute you.* Matthew 5:44 Christ gave the example of how to love, but man is a selfish creature by default of sin. Our love has reservations.

When we truly love God and His Word abides in our heart, there is a completion to who we are in Christ and an understanding of how precious we are to our Father. Living in peace and fulfillment is to be close to Him, and showing compassion with a caring nature is a display of love. *Beloved, I wish above all things that thou mayest prosper and be in health, even as thy soul prospereth.* 3 John 1:2 God desires that our soul, the conscious and carnal aspect of our life, turns to Him so that we may prosper in all matters. As a parent, our Father wants only good things for His children.

Because of His love, God gives us Kingdom power to change our circumstances from bad to good, from poor to prosperous, from sickness to health, from death to life. Know the reality of who you belong to and that God will take care of you because He loves you. Love your Father by living as He says with peace, joy, kindness, and compassion in your heart. Fall in love with the Lord and your life will never be the same.

He will not force you into a relationship with Him. Instead, God has given each person the free will to decide and it is a choice; a decision made to live for God and want to be with Him. *I call heaven and earth to record this day against you, that I have set before you life and death, blessing and cursing: therefore choose life, that both thou and thy seed may live: That thou mayest love the Lord thy God, and that thou mayest obey his voice, and that thou mayest cleave unto him: for he is thy life, and the length of thy days: that thou mayest dwell in the land which the Lord sware unto thy fathers, to Abraham, to Isaac, and to Jacob, to give them.* Deuteronomy 30:19-20

Although this proclamation was for the children of Israel, it applies today. Our Father is commanding us to choose eternal life; otherwise, it will be the finality of death. Love your Father who loved you so much that He gave His Son to die that you may live forever. Choose life with God and His Son.

Chapter 3 ~ Jesus is our Savior

The Lord possessed me in the beginning of his way, before his works of old. I was set up from everlasting, from the beginning, or ever the earth was. When there were no depths, I was brought forth; when there were no fountains abounding with water, before the mountains were settled, before the hills was I brought forth: While as yet he had not made the earth, nor the fields, nor the highest part of the dust of the world. When he established the clouds above: when he strengthened the fountains of the deep: When he gave to the sea his decree, that the waters should not pass his commandment: when he appointed the foundations of the earth: Then I was by him, as one brought up with him: and I was daily his delight, rejoicing always before him; Rejoicing in the habitable part of his earth; and my delights were with the sons of men. Now therefore hearken unto me, O ye children: for blessed are they that keep my ways.

Proverbs 8:22-32

Jesus is God manifested as the Son of God. He is the second of the trinity of the Father, the Son, and the Holy Ghost. Christ is the Living Word, the Son of God, the Lamb of God, the Good Shepherd, the Counselor, Light of the World, and the Prince of Peace. Jesus is Lord and Savior, Messiah,

Yeshua, El Shaddai, King of kings and Lord of lords; Almighty, our mediator to the Father and our Redeemer from sin. *For there is one God, and one mediator between God and men, the man Christ Jesus.* 1 Timothy 2:5

Everything God created He spoke into existence, and as He spoke, Jesus was the Living Word fashioning the foundation of all creation. *And to make all men see what is the fellowship of the mystery, which from the beginning of the world hath been hid in God, who created all things by Jesus Christ.* Ephesians 3:9 All things were created by Him and for Him. *For by him were all things created, that are in heaven, and that are in earth, visible and invisible, whether they be thrones, or dominions, or principalities, or powers: all things were created by him, and for him: And he is before all things, and by him all things consist.* Colossians 1:16-17

Accepting the omnipresence of Christ in the Kingdom and His role on earth, we learn of the immense proclamation of what God and Jesus did for man. *For unto us a child is born, unto us a son is given: and the government shall be upon his shoulder: and his name shall be called Wonderful, Counsellor, The Mighty God, The Everlasting Father, The Prince of Peace.* Isaiah 9:6 God's entire Kingdom has been given to His Son and no one enters but through Christ.

When it was necessary for Christ to come down to earth to save man, the Living Word became flesh. *Which were born, not of blood, nor of the will of the flesh, nor of the will of man, but of God. And the Word was made flesh, and dwelt among us, and we beheld his glory, the glory as of the only begotten of the Father, full of grace and truth.* John 1:13-14 In accepting the relationship between the Father and the Son, we can see a picture that tells a story that has always been about man from the very beginning. *For through him we both have access by one Spirit unto the Father.* Ephesians 2:18

Sin separated man from God; however, Jesus reconciled man fulfilling the Father's plan that we be reunited with Him. *For he hath made him to be sin for us, who knew no sin; that we might be made the righteousness of God in him.* 2 Corinthians 5:21 Jesus' main purpose wasn't to take away man's sins which occurs when we repent. Christ's objective was to reestablish man's relationship with the Father. The spiritual connection God had with His children, Adam and Eve, was severed in the Garden of Eden.   Christ came to rectify and reconcile man to his heavenly Father. Jesus brings man full circle back to the garden before sin.

Sin had to be dealt with, removed, to achieve the primary goal of reconciliation. We can see the strategy in God's plan. *And all things are of God, who hath reconciled us to himself by Jesus Christ, and hath given to us the ministry of reconciliation; To wit, that God was in Christ, reconciling the world unto himself, not imputing their trespasses unto them; and hath committed unto us the word of reconciliation.* 2 Corinthians 5: 18-19 Our Father wanted His children and came to earth in Christ to claim them.

There is absolutely no hope without Jesus, for He is the only pathway to everlasting life. *And, having made peace through the blood of his cross, by him to reconcile all things unto himself; by him, I say, whether they be things in earth, or things in heaven.* Colossians 1:20 Because of what Jesus did at Calvary, man may be given a rebirth in spirit for a relationship with the Father. *Therefore if any man be in Christ, he is a new creature: old things are passed away; behold, all things are become new.* 2 Corinthians 5:17

God is Spirit, Christ is Spirit, and we are spirit. It is all about living a spirit life. Jesus took the sins of the world and bore them upon Himself because it was required for reconciliation. There is no other way to be with the Father but to abolish the corruptible; changing man from flesh to spirit, sinner to saint. *Having abolished in his flesh the enmity, even the law of commandments contained in ordinances; for to make in himself of twain one new man, so making peace; And that he might reconcile both unto*

God in one body by the cross, having slain the enmity thereby: And came and preached peace to you which were afar off, and to them that were nigh. For through him we both have access by one Spirit unto the Father. Ephesians 2:15-18 It is important to understand why Christ did what He did because our relationship with our heavenly Father begins with Jesus.

Man was corrupted by Adam's sin and our spirit spoiled by the lust of the flesh. We miss the reason for Christ's birth, death, and resurrection for it wasn't just about salvation. His purpose on earth was to gather the lost children and teach of our Father, so we would know of Him and desire to be with God and because of this we are given the gift of salvation. Christ came to establish the way and dealing with sin became necessary to accomplish His mission. In our return to the Father, we have eternal life. *But of him are ye in Christ Jesus, who of God is made unto us wisdom, and righteousness, and sanctification, and redemption: That, according as it is written, He that glorieth, let him glory in the Lord.* 1 Corinthians 1:30-31

Why did Christ have to be born of the flesh to accomplish this objective? Why didn't God simply speak the words to eliminate the sin in the world? Because when God, the Almighty King, set forth the precepts or laws that operate His Kingdom, He will not violate them. *Who is he that overcometh the world, but he that believeth that Jesus is the Son of God? This is he that came by water and blood, even Jesus Christ; not by water only, but by water and blood. And it is the Spirit that beareth witness, because the Spirit is truth. For there are three things that bear record in heaven, the Father, the Word, and the Holy Ghost: and these three are one. And there are three that bear witness in earth, the spirit, and the water, and the blood: and these three agree in one.* 1 John 5:5-8 Kingdom principles were put in place for man's purpose, and our destiny in Christ requires our obedience and participation.

In the Old Testament, the Israelites were without a quickened spirit. They did not have Jesus, or the Holy Spirit; therefore, there didn't exist a way for them to be reconciled, spiritually. This was the purpose for the commandments, a means of measurement to show their sins and that they could never be righteous through the law. With God giving man a better covenant through His Son, one that was preordained, we all are given an opportunity for redemption and reconciliation through Christ. Without Jesus we are nothing, lost forever and trapped in corruption that was never our Father's will. It was necessary that sin be taken out of the equation, so we may be sanctified to return to the spirit realm within the Kingdom for the Father. God's gift of a free will allow us to choose the Father.

Before the new covenant, God spoke to the Israelites when He removed them from bondage and gave them statutes, laws, and commandments to structure a lifestyle and show them how to conduct themselves. *Thou camest down also upon Mount Sinai, and spakest with them from heaven, and gavest them right judgments, and true laws, good statutes and commandments: And madest known unto them thy holy sabbath, and commandedst them precepts, statutes, and laws, by the hand of Moses thy servant: And gavest them bread from heaven for their hunger, and broughtest forth water for them out of the rock for their thirst, and promisedst them that they should go in to possess the land which thou hadst sworn to give them.* Nehemiah 9:13-15 If God had not presented the people a way to live, they would not have known how to reside as a nation. They were ill-equipped to live a civilized life from a slavery background.

God was their Lord and defined how their sins would be imputed against them according to the Commandments as administered by Moses. Without these in place, they had no means to gage sin, for there would have been no measurement of right and wrong. Rather than be obedient to the One who took them out of slavery, they became a generation defiant to His Word. *But they and our fathers dealt proudly, and hardened their necks, and hearkened not to thy commandments; And refused to obey, neither were mindful of thy wonders that thou didst among them; but hardened their necks, and in their rebellion appointed a captain to return to their bondage: but thou art a God ready to pardon, gracious and merciful, slow to anger, and of great kindness, and forsookest them not.* Nehemiah 9:16-17

God gave them freedom, destroyed their enemy, and set aside a territory where they could build their homes and prosper, but they quickly forgot His Word and fell back into the ways they understood. They accepted the surrounding pagan lifestyles with their foreign beliefs. In man's attempt to be obedient to God, he failed and regressed to a wickedness so severe that it was like an unstoppable plague. There were so few who believed in God, they became a nation blinded to the truth and refusing to accept Him. It was Sodom and Gomorrah.

They wanted a tangible object to worship and demanded that Aaron allow one to be made during the absence of Moses when he was with God for forty days. *Yea, when they had made them a molten calf, and said, This is thy God that brought thee up out of Egypt, and had wrought great provocations.* Nehemiah 9:18 It set the precedence throughout the following generations of man's need for a symbol to worship as their god, a continuous act of rebellion and disobedience. Today, there are many symbol-isms, tangible and otherwise, that become our gods and we pay homage without realizing the impact it has in our relationship with God.

The Israelites were living strictly carnal governed by their thoughts and emotions. Jesus was the shadow of things spoken of in the earlier generations who would come to establish a new covenant between God and His people. *Which are a shadow of things to come; but the body is of Christ.* Colossians 2:17 There has to be a separation of the spirit from the flesh and this is done by Christ removing one to save the other. Jesus provided the redemption for man's sinful behavior.

Jesus became like man, human, to take the sins of the world upon Himself and nailed them to the cross. That is why when we repent of our sins, we are dead to the flesh and alive in the spirit. The flesh, corrupted in sin, died on the cross with Christ, and we are resurrected in spirit with Jesus when we accept Him into our life. *For which cause we faint not; but though our outward man perish, yet the inward man is renewed day by day.* 2 Corinthians 4:16 Jesus had to be born from the womb and become flesh, just as man has a physical body because sin is ascribed to the carnal, and He put sin to death with His own.

His death destroyed sin, His blood removed the curses placed upon man by Adam, and Christ's resurrection returned Him to the Kingdom because His work on earth was finished. He came to do the Father's will, and He accomplished the assignment. Man has been given the opportunity to be reborn in spirit and live with Christ. *Hereby know we that we dwell in him, and he in us, because he hath given us of his Spirit.* 1 John 4:13 As our Lord and Savior is seated in the Kingdom of Heaven, we may call up-on His name to receive heavenly power in our time of need through our faithful obedient petitions.

To know Christ, it becomes imperative to understand the earthly role of Jesus and the significance of His sacrifice. We fail to see the enormity of what Christ did for the sole purpose of being the shepherd gathering the lost sheep to return them home. We are the lost souls, corrupted by our flesh, and wandering aimlessly without direction or purpose with death our end. Then Jesus came with the promises of the Father and everlasting life.

After Christ's three and one-half year ministry of teaching about the Father and His Kingdom, Jesus was put to death. However, He knew the end of His time on earth was man's new beginning. It was the only way for it to be accomplished. *But with the precious blood of Christ, as of a lamb without blemish and without spot: Who verily was foreordained before the foundation of the world, but was manifest in these last times for you, Who by him do believe in God, that raised him up from the dead, and gave him glory; that your faith and hope might be in God.* 1 Peter 1:19-21 He gave Himself for you. Jesus left His throne and came to earth for you.

As it began in the Garden of Eden with the first Adam, so shall it end in the Garden of Gethsemane by the second Adam, Jesus. Christ was removing the sins of the world and breaking the curses when He shed His blood from seven areas of His body. First, in the Garden of Gethsemane on the night of the last supper before He was taken, Christ sweats blood through His pores when blood vessels break beneath the skin as He prayed in agony to the Father knowing what was to come. *And being in an agony he prayed more earnestly: and his sweat was as it were great drops of blood falling down to the ground.* Luke 22:44 Second, at the whipping post where He was scourged repeatedly. Scriptures do not give an account as to the number Jesus withstood. According to Jewish law, a man was scourged no more than forty times as punishment, but not to be the means of death. *Forty stripes he may give, and not exceed: lest, if he should exceed, and beat him above these with many stripes, then thy brother should seem vile unto thee.* Deuteronomy 25:3 However, we know that Christ was whipped by the Romans who had no law for the number they could administer upon a body. Thus, we have no scriptural verification to the total number of lashes upon Jesus. What we do know is that by these very strokes upon His back man is healed in all manner. By His stripes we are healed, sickness and disease, sins and transgressions have all been removed. *Who his own self bare our sins in his own body on the tree, that we, being dead to sins, should live unto righteousness: by whose stripes ye were healed.* 1 Peter 2:24 Third, He was taken to the chief priests and a crown of thorns placed on His head. *And when they had platted a crown of thorns, they put it upon his head, and a reed in his right hand: and they bowed the knee before him, and mocked him, saying, Hail, King of the Jews!* Matthew 27:29 Though this symbolic crown was used to mock Jesus, the blood shed from the puncture wounds from the thorns represents a different meaning for man. Fourth, the palm of His hands bled from the nails piercing His flesh. *For dogs have compassed me: the assembly of the wicked have enclosed me: they pierced my hands and feet.* Psalm 22:16 Fifth, blood dripped from nailed feet. Sixth, His side was pierced by a soldier's spear after Jesus was already dead. *But one of the soldiers with a spear pierced his side, and forthwith came there out blood and water.* John 19:34 Seventh, blood bruises shown on the outside of His skin reflective of internal bleeding. Another example of the number seven in the Almighty Kingdom.

Everything that was stolen from the first Adam by Satan has been returned to the Father by the second Adam, Jesus. Christ spoke to the Father: *I have glorified thee on the earth: I have finished the work which thou gavest me to do.* John 17:4 Man has been given complete restoration by the blood of Christ.

The blood released from Jesus' body from these wounds redeems man from any curse of the law. In the Old Testament, the peoples attempt at removing their sins was with a clean, or pure sacrificial animal's blood and this is done continually. Christ shed His blood for man to set us free from bondage to the curses and gives us liberty to live under the grace of God. *For Christ also hath once suffered for sins, the just for the unjust, that he might bring us to God, being put to death in the flesh, but quickened by the Spirit.* 1 Peter 3:18

All things set forth in the Kingdom for man's redemption, reconciliation, and salvation was taken care of on the cross at Calvary. *When Jesus therefore had received the vinegar, he said, It is finished; and he bowed his head, and gave up the ghost.* John 19:30 With Jesus' final words, His work of the Father was accomplished. With His return to the Kingdom of Heaven, man is now responsible to choose life with Christ, or by default of a sinful nature, the finality of death.

This is why when we pray, we do so on the blood of Jesus. There is a purpose unto the Kingdom for every drop that flowed from Christ's body. Nothing Jesus did was without premeditation and carried a price He willingly paid for man to be reconciled to the Father. It was established between the Father and the Son at the foundation and the plan was put into action upon the birth of Jesus. Christ was willing to save man. When we believe on the name of Jesus, knowing the punishment He withstood in our place and ask for forgiveness of our sins, we are sanctified. *And that ye put on the new man, which after God is created in righteousness and true holiness.* Ephesians 4:24

As we are one in spirit with Christ, our body is the physical temple of God who dwells within each faithful believer as the Holy Spirit. No longer are we entrapped in bondage to the flesh, but live under the reign of Christ as sons and daughters of the Father. *But now being made free from sin, and become servants to God, ye have your fruit unto holiness, and the end everlasting life.* Romans 6:22

Our recorded transgressions are erased from the Book of Life. Christ claims ownership of each person and all things are possible in Him. *Jesus said unto him, If thou canst believe, all things are possible to him that believeth.* Mark 9:23 We are not human first with a small inconsequential spirit, but rather we are a spirit person who lives in a physical body. Our spiritual life begins the day we accept Christ and are reborn in spirit. We have it completely backwards to the way it really is, and once we understand this it changes the dynamics of how we live. *That which is born of the Spirit is spirit.* John 3:6 Living in the spirit is the only way to receive authority and power through Christ.

Christ will judge us for our heavenly crowns when we stand before Him. There are seven categories and based on the accountability of how we lived this earthen life, and what we have accomplished in discipleship to the Kingdom will determine which crowns we receive. *For we must all appear before the judgment seat of Christ; that every one may receive the things done in his body, according to that he hath done, whether it be good or bad.* 2 Corinthians 5:10

The necessity of Christ in our life becomes very clear. God loves us so much that He sent His Son to earth, and Jesus loves us so much that He was willing to come and die for man that we may have everlasting life with the Father and the Son. How can we live a single day without thanksgiving to Jesus and glorifying our Father for His love of someone so unworthy, and yet, forgiven? Jesus said: *I am the way, the truth and the life: no man cometh unto the Father, but by me.* John 14:6 This declaration takes on a new meaning once we understand Jesus.

Chapter 4 ~ The Holy Ghost is our Tutor

Likewise the Spirit also helpeth our infirmities: for we know not what we should pray for as we ought: but the Spirit itself maketh intercession for us with groanings which cannot be uttered.

Romans 8:26

We are a society that prides ourselves on learning and placing a value system on ranks attained towards an education to master a specific skill, or profession. Our success is often measured by this platform, and likewise, promotions in the workplace are scored accordingly. Classroom participation is mandatory throughout our youth; however, procurement of degrees in specialized education is by choice. Thus, we are influenced by our piers based upon such a protocol.

There is another learning environment which should be taken far more seriously, and it is the classroom of life. There is a life-altering education to be obtained in studying the Word of God, and the school book is the Bible. In this book, we are given lessons about God and His Kingdom, and how to live a spirit-filled life even though we continue our physical and temporary residency on earth. Our thoughts, words, actions, and deeds must align with the Holy Spirit's teachings on the Word. Within the Scriptures is the key to living an abundant life today with the promise of an eternal homeland in the New Jerusalem.

However, there is one stipulation. This treasured book is written in two languages with only one being for the spirit-filled person. *And he said unto them, Unto you it is given to know the mystery of the kingdom of God: but unto them that are without, all these things are done in parables: That seeing they may see, and not perceive; and hearing they may hear, and not understand; lest at any time they should be converted, and their sins should be forgiven them.* Mark 4:11-12 The Bible can be read with a carnal mind which is our intellectual comprehension, or with spiritual discernment.

Accepting the prophetic writings at face value, or simply as written is reading from a human perspective whereby the truth will be lost to the reader. It is possible to be a born-again believer and read with carnal awareness. To those with a quickened spirit, God's Word is revealed through the interpretation of the Holy Spirit. Jesus spoke to His disciples: *Therefore speak I to them in parables: because they seeing see not; and hearing they hear not, neither do they understand.* Matthew 13:13

The Holy Spirit is the third in the trinity and is sent on the authority of Christ that each born-again person may have an intimate communion with the Father. He is our tutor, intercessor, and advocate before the Lord. We are virtually helpless to receive anything from the Kingdom without the Holy Spirit, for heavenly gifts and power come through the Spirit of Truth who is God. Jesus teaches: *And I will pray the Father, and he shall give you another Comforter, that he may abide with you forever; Even the Spirit of truth; whom the world cannot receive, because it seeth him not, neither knoweth him: but ye know him; for he dwelleth with you, and shall be in you.* John 14:16-17 This is why Jesus told His disciples He must go, but would send a Comforter knowing the need man would have for the Holy Ghost. *Who hath also sealed us, and given the earnest of the Spirit in our hearts.* 2 Corinthians 1:22 What Jesus spoke to His disciples remains effectual today. As Jesus is our Savior and mediator, the Holy Spirit is our intercessor and advocate within the Kingdom of Heaven. We can understand the trinity of God as Christ, and as the Holy Spirit, for His

Kingdom purpose in reuniting man for a relationship with Himself as it once was with Adam.

The Holy Spirit knows what is in our heart and mind, so when we pray He renders our prayerful petitions to be acceptable and appropriate to the Kingdom. If not for the Holy Spirit's intercession, our prayers would not be translated from carnal thought to spiritual interpretation. *And he that searcheth the hearts knoweth what is the mind of the Spirit, because he maketh intercession for the saints according to the will of God.* Romans 8:27 God hears our prayers; however, the channel of communication to God is through the Holy Ghost.

To personally receive the Holy Spirit, we must first be reborn into the spirit person we were created, and we already know to do so with a repentance prayer. Christ comes into our life and God sends the Comforter. Think about what must transpire when we ask to be received, spiritually, into the Kingdom. It is an awesome occurrence and so joyous that angels sing because another child has returned to the Father. *Likewise, I say unto you, there is joy in the presence of the angels of God over one sinner that repenteth.* Luke 15:10

Many doctrines teach that baptism of the Holy Spirit is received simultaneously when we repent of our sins and accept Christ as our Lord and Savior. We are given the gift of the Comforter; however, baptism requires action on our part. Like someone handing you a present, but you have yet to open the box to see what is inside. *If ye then, being evil, know how to give good gifts unto your children: how much more shall your heavenly Father give the Holy Spirit to them that ask him?* Luke 11:13

As a born-again child, we have the Comforter but if not active, His power will be limited because of our restrictions. There is much within the Kingdom that we have been given entitlement on the authority in Christ, but we receive these gifts through the Holy Spirit. As John the Baptist said: *I indeed have baptized you with water: but he shall baptize you with the Holy Ghost.* Mark 1:8 It is crucial to ask God for the quickening or awakening of the Holy Spirit. Here's an analogy that may help. If someone gives you a bank card as a gift, and you hold onto it without calling the number on the back to activate the card, but instead place it in your wallet, or throw it into a drawer, there are no benefits from the gift. The card is useless in making purchases. Likewise, this is true of the Holy Spirit.

In our request to be a spirit-filled person with privileges in the Kingdom, it is important to understand our role to the divinity of the trinity of God. We are required to establish a relationship with Christ first, and then the Holy Spirit, for the sole preparation of our complete communion with God, the Father. Without Christ, there is no Holy Spirit, and without the Holy Spirit there is no channel to God.

The baptism of the Holy Spirit can be accomplished with a brief prayer right where you are at this moment. It doesn't require anyone else, only you praying to the Father. An example is: *Father, thank you for sending your Son to free me from the bondage of sin, and as I am reborn in Christ, I am also thankful for the gift of the Holy Spirit. I come before you asking that the Holy Ghost be awakened within me, so that I may live and serve according to your Word. On the name of Christ and the blood He shed at Calvary for me, I pray, Amen.* Now you are prepared for the Holy Spirit to have an active role in your life.

We must present ourselves with belief, trust, and faith confident in our relationship with the Father, the Son, and the Holy Ghost. When we do, there are spiritual gifts from the trinity. The Holy Spirit gifts are of power which is why it is vital to have the Holy Spirit quickened that we may receive what God has set forth for us. The Holy Spirit's gifts are wisdom, knowledge, faith, healing, miracles, prophecy, discerning of spirits, speaking in tongues, and interpretation of tongues. *But the manifestation of the Spirit is given to every man to profit withal.For to one is given by the Spirit the word of wisdom; to another the word of knowledge by the same Spirit; To another faith by the same Spirit; to another the gifts of healing by the same Spirit; To another the working of miracles; to another prophecy; to another discerning of spirits; to another divers kinds of tongues; to another the interpretation of tongues: But all these worketh that one and the selfsame Spirit, dividing to every man severally as he will.* 1 Corinthians 12:7-11 Notice that healing and miracles are forthcoming from the Holy Spirit. The gifts of the Father and the Son are administration and ministry.

The Holy Spirit will discern and administer the gifts according to the desire of our heart in appropriation for the glory of the Kingdom. He knows which gifts we will ask for, and we are to exemplify the ability to apply our gift correctly. For example, just because your twelve year child wants the keys to the car to drive around the block, doesn't mean he or she is knowledgeable in the operation of the vehicle to trust them with the use of the car.

Another example, we may ask for the gift of healing. If we are requesting a healing for ourselves, or namely someone specific, the gift may be given to use accordingly. However, if we claim the gift so that we may attempt to perform random acts of healing, this is not Holy Spirit empowerment but rather man's ambition. Not only does the Holy Spirit grant the gifts, but tells us when to apply them. It is His provision of power that flows through us to heal, or for whatever the requirement. We are merely the vessel God can use.

We may be given more than one gift for the Holy Spirit *divides to every man severally as He wills.* Asking for God's gifts benefits our life and those around us because of the Holy Spirit. He empowers us to live fully within God's grace that we may receive miraculous blessings because it is the Father's will to give gifts to His children. If only we understood the magnitude of what God has done, we would not be without the presence of the Holy Spirit.

Now that we have the Holy Spirit, our new life begins. We don't feel any different, and yet, we are a completely new person in Christ even though our reflected image shows the same person in the mirror. The Holy Spirit will teach us as likened to a kindergartener and carry us through to maturation in the Word.

Our prayers petitioned on the authority of Christ are fulfilled through the Holy Spirit when we ask according to His Word. *And whatsoever ye shall ask in my name, that will I do, that the Father may be glorified in the Son. If ye ask any thing in my name, I will do it.* John 14:13-14 This is not a name it and claim it mindset. There is a stipulation not only for how we pray, but also what we pray for that it be in accordance to the principles set forth. Therefore, *If ye abide in me, and my words abide in you, ye shall ask what ye will, and it shall be done unto you.* John 15:7 Praying for a yacht because it would be wonderful to have one isn't a prayer in alliance with the Kingdom. Our prayers should be concentrated with knowledge of His precepts whereby in our quest for His provisions, we automatically give God praise and glory as we manifest His Kingdom on earth.

Many individuals are seeking God for a healing whether for a long-term illness, a devastating disease, an accident that presents a physical challenge, mending a relationship, removing emotional bondage, or overcoming addictions. No matter the circumstance that overwhelms our lives, God has already provided the remedy. He has given us the means to triumph, so we may be free of whatever holds us captive. He put your need in His plan at the foundation of creation and accomplished it through His Son. It is His will that we live happy, healthy, and productive lives.

The Holy Spirit dwells within our heart and when we hear from God, the communion is of the heart before His Word takes hold in our mind as a thought. Logically, it would seem a thought would appear in our mind before the heart's discernment, but not so. *For this is the covenant that I will make with the house of Israel after those days, saith the Lord; I will put my laws into their mind, and write them in their hearts: and I will be to them a God, and they shall be to me a people.* Hebrews 8:10 Therefore,

Let us draw near with a true heart in full assurance of faith, having our hearts sprinkled from an evil conscience, and our bodies washed with pure water. Hebrews 10:22 When a thought enters our mind before the heart's conception, it would be our own self effort. We should listen carefully to not miss what the Holy Spirit is teaching us.

We must be able to differentiate between the Holy Spirit giving us wisdom and our soul's persuasion through emotions and the senses. The words we speak, the way we conduct ourselves, and how we handle situations all must be a good and positive reflection of the Kingdom of Heaven. Sadly, many are unaware of what is amiss in their life because they take direction from the carnal with expectation of supernatural power. *Be not carried about with divers and strange doctrines. For it is a good thing that the heart be established with grace: not with meats, which have not profited them that have been occupied therein.* Hebrews 13:9 We forget that the natural world and the spirit realm do not mix. We need the supernatural power of God to overcome the negative circumstances of this earthen life, but to receive it we must step away from carnal interference and remain fervent in the spirit that the power of God may be manifested.

The Holy Spirit provides clarity as we gain understanding and knowledge. We can take charge of our circumstances and handle matters that confront us with confidence and forthrightness. *Ye have not chosen me, but I have chosen you, and ordained you, that ye should go and bring forth fruit, and that your fruit should remain: that whatsoever ye shall ask of the Father in my name, he may give it you.* John 15:16 Our fruit is the example we present by living in obedience to His Word.

As a faithful child of God, our spirit is sealed with everlasting life. Our world is no longer earthen but heavenly, and we can call upon the Father through the Holy Spirit to supply for all our needs. While living with mercy and grace, we have His blessings, gifts, and power for our life that we may overcome adversities. It requires our trust in the Holy Spirit, allowing Him to teach and direct our daily walk in faith.

Approach the Father's throne with perseverance so that what you ask in prayer gives honor to God, and the Holy Spirit will give you an expected response. The Holy Spirit is God and He does not go against Himself, for what the Father promises, He always provides.

Part II

Trinity of Man
Body, Soul, and Spirit

For ye are bought with a price: therefore glorify in your body, and in your spirit, which are God's.

1 Corinthians 6:20

Chapter 5 ~ Who is Man?

For thou hast possessed my reins: thou hast covered me in my mother's womb. I will praise thee; for I am fearfully and wonderfully made: marvelous are thy works; and that my soul knoweth right well. My substance was not hid from thee, when I was made in secret, and curiously wrought in the lowest parts of the earth. Thine eyes did see my substance, yet being unperfect: and in thy book all my members were written, which in con-tinuance were fashioned, when as yet there was none of them. How precious also are thy thoughts unto me, O God! How great is the sum of them!

Psalm 139:13-17

Man was given two births. One is referred to as a horizontal birth, or physically born of a man and woman, and there is a birth which is vertical, a spirit birth from God down to man on earth. There are two aspects to our personage; carnal and spirit. *That which is born of the flesh is flesh; and that which is born of the Spirit is spirit.* John 3:6 The flesh will perish to the dust of the earth from where it was formed, but the spirit, reconciled to the Kingdom of Heaven, will live eternally. There is a trinity to man which is spirit, soul, and body.

The important question is which are you living, a carnal life or spirit led? The carnal person responds to this earthen world while the spirit person answers to the Kingdom. We are to separate the carnal from the spirit and not accept the misconception that we can live a worldly life and be in the spirit, simultaneously. Reborn in Christ, we should yearn for the things of the spirit realm. *For they that are after the flesh do mind the things of the flesh; but they that are after the Spirit the things of the Spirit.* Romans 8:5 It is against the Kingdom to attempt to mix carnal willfulness with the spirit realm, for the natural and the spirit are governed by two entirely different ruling powers.

In fact, they fight one another for supremacy. *For the flesh lusteth against the Spirit, and the Spirit against the flesh: and these are contrary the one to the other: so that ye cannot do the things that ye would.* Galatians 5:17 God tells us to beware of the conflict that arises between the two and remain staunch in the spirit. This is critical concerning our relationship with God. *But put ye on the Lord Christ, and make not provision for the flesh, to fulfill the lusts thereof.* Romans 13:14

It is human nature to default to the carnal, or natural, without consideration of the spirit, but God emphasizes the difference. *It is sown a natural body; it is raised a spiritual body. There is a natural body, and there is a spiritual body.* 1 Corinthians 15:44 Conducting our life according to the spirit person we are in Christ begins the day we accept Jesus as our Savior, for He absolved us of our sins and sinful nature at the cross. Now we initiate our study of God's Word.

Unmistakably, there is an innate comfort in the natural, and we trust ourselves and others based on what we see, hear, touch, taste, and smell. What is tangible to our human person is far more real than anything we cannot apply our senses. When we are reborn in spirit in Christ, we have chosen to live as a spirit person for God and not be persuaded by our carnality. We choose faith over the senses. In not making this distinction and transition and continuing to rely on the natural, we are cutting ourselves off from the Father. God declares: *No man can serve two masters: for either he will hate the one, and love the other; or else he will hold to the one, and despise the other. Ye cannot serve God and mammon.* Matthew 6:24 The results we experience are determined by whom we serve. In living a carnal life, our servitude is to man and not God which is man's downfall to receiving Kingdom power.

In our modern culture, we are exposed to a multitude of media information used to persuade our thinking and structure our lifestyle. We follow the fads, fashions, and trends striving to have the best. In theory, these things are meant to make our life easier; however, in reality the object of our desires does the opposite. It causes overconsumption or greed, manipulation of our time and money, placing people in bondage under various addictions from debt to gambling to physical destruction and so much more. With this constant inundation, we are bombarded and our mind is overloaded which makes it almost impossible to give any thought to God. This is a deliberate distraction by the ruler of this world, so that we may not receive our Kingdom inheritance.

Our heavenly Father should be the first person we think of when we open our eyes in the morning, the One we commune with throughout the day, and the last One we give praise and glory to before we fall asleep. *Whosoever denieth the Son, the same hath not the Father:(but) he that acknowledgeth the Son hath the Father also. Let that therefore abide in you, which ye have heard from the beginning. If that which ye have heard from the beginning shall remain in you, ye also shall continue in the Son, and in the Father. And this is the promise that he hath promised us, even eternal life. These things have I written unto you concerning them that seduce you. But the anointing which ye have received of him abideth in you, and ye need not that any man teach you: but as the same anointing teacheth you of all things, and is truth, and is no lie, and even as it hath taught you, ye shall abide in him. And now, little children, abide in him; that, when he shall appear, we may have confidence, and not be ashamed before him at his coming. If ye know that he is righteous, ye know that everyone that doeth righteousness is born of him.* 1 John 2:23-29

For the individuals who have made a conscious choice to live in the natural with no interest in a relationship with God, they do not live according to the Kingdom laws nor by faith, and He is not present in their life. Their interest remains self-serving. They want instant gratification and follow the dictates of the world accepting the present day as the substance of life. *Love not the world, neither the things that are in the world. If any man loves the world, the love of the Father is not in him. For all that is in the world, the lust of the flesh, and the lust of the eyes, and the pride of life, is not of the Father, but is of the world.* 1 John 2:15-16 God is very explicit.

The atheist does not believe in God and concludes that man evolved into a human form. In this line of thinking, evolutionists believe man's earliest manifestation began with fish larva first detected on the ocean's bed of coral rock and through time and numerous transformations elevated into a mammal, the ape, and then a human. Of course, this is after the great cataclysmic energy explosion in space, thus, creating the universe and all its components. This is far removed from God's Kingdom without any forethought, or validation to creation as a whole. They also live without God's presence.

For the person who chooses to live a spirit life with a rebirth in Christ, they are children of the Father and seek His Kingdom. The spirit realm, or unseen, becomes more real than what the natural declares. *There is therefore now no condemnation to them which are in Christ Jesus, who walk not after the flesh, but after the Spirit.* Romans 8:1 A child of God inclines his heart towards the truth of his Father's Word. *Who by him do believe in God that raised him up from the dead, and gave him glory; that your faith and hope might be in God.* 1 Peter 1:21 God's children understand they are cleansed by the blood of Jesus and made righteous, holy, and sanctified as an heir in the Father's Kingdom. They stay focused in faithful obedience to His Word.

However, the majority of the Christian population falls somewhere in between. They believe in God but also in their human capabilities and lack the willingness to surrender the things of the flesh. They claim faith in Christ but continue to place trust in the wisdom of men even when God explicitly instructs against it. *That your faith should not stand in the wisdom of men, but in the power of God.* 1 Corinthians 2:5 They have not made the separation. This is where God says we can't have it both ways. We cannot live, figuratively speaking, with one foot in the Kingdom and the other grounded in the world. Either we commit to establishing a relationship with God and live by the governing principles of His Kingdom, or we put our attention on the world relying on our instinctive nature and the wisdom of others.

If we conduct our life according to the carnal, or natural, we should not expect supernatural power. God's spiritual laws apply. *Let no man deceive himself. If any man among you seemeth to be wise in this world, let him become a fool, that he may be wise. For the wisdom of this world is foolishness with God. For it is written, He taketh the wise in their own craftiness.* 1 Corinthians 3:18-19 The attempt to combine the two worlds, carnal and spirit, violates Kingdom laws; therefore, we are responsible for blocking God's power from entering our life. It depends on which we are living as to the results obtained, earthen or heavenly.

We wonder why we aren't receiving a miracle or healing, mending an estranged relationship, or obtaining satisfaction in a financial or emotional crisis. We question if God is even listening to our plea. God has not changed, nor has His Kingdom moved, you are not forgotten or forsaken, so what is the reason for not hearing from God? By not knowing how His Kingdom functions, we have inadvertently distanced ourselves from our Father. What we thought was entitlement through our belief has prevented closeness to Him because we lack knowledge with diligent application of faithful obedience. *And be not conformed to this world: but be ye transformed by the renewing of your mind that ye may prove what is that good, and acceptable, and perfect will of God.* Romans 12:2

We are responsible to learn how the Almighty King of His Kingdom rules, and submit ourselves before Him in unwavering faithfulness. Mixing the natural with the spirit is not in alignment with His laws. This is one of the reasons Adam and Eve could not remain in the Garden of Eden.

When we are born into the spirit realm, we are to shed the old carnal ways and put on the armor of Christ and live as He lived, holy and righteous. We renew our mind continuously that we may be accurate in our thoughts, words, and deeds according to His Word. *And be renewed in the spirit of your mind; And that ye put on the new man, which after God is created in righteousness and true holiness.* Ephesians 4:23-24 When we live by God's precepts and not our own perception, we gain knowledge, understanding, and wisdom found in His Word which sets us apart from the world. It is when we are fully vested in God, that we may expect His power to flow in our life, for we are positioned by our faithfulness to receive His blessings and gifts. *By whom we have received grace and apostleship, for obedience to the faith among all nations, for his name.* Romans 1:5

A serious issue is that man isn't prone to see himself as the problem. Instead, he places the fault on God with such misunderstandings as He is a sovereign God in charge of everything; therefore, it must be His will that such and such happened. Beware for the wrath of God will come down on you to teach you a lesson. We forget that we are living with a new covenant of grace, not wrath. God does not put bad things in our life, nor is it His will to allow negative occurrences. We live in a fallen world, and if anyone is causing bad things to happen, we should consider the ruler of earth as the culprit. *For we wrestle not against flesh and blood, but against the rulers of the darkness of this world, against spiritual wickedness in high places.* Ephesians 6:12 Satan sets out to kill, steal, and destroy as many of God's children as he can for he knows his time is limited.

We fail to give credence to the spiritual warfare that is ongoing behind the scenes. This is a major factor that affects the events and circumstances we find ourselves dealing with whether illness, disease, heartache, destitution, etc. Satan doesn't want us to have knowledge of the power that is within our reach because this eliminates him and voids his destruction in our life. The only way Satan can deceive is through our thoughts. When we renew our mind and stay focused on God's Word, Satan has no inlet.

When there is reference to the wrath of God, it is for the sinners and unbelievers, the corrupt and defilers. *For the wrath of God is revealed from heaven against all ungodliness and unrighteousness of men, who hold the truth in unrighteousness; because that which may be known of God is manifest in them; for God hath showed it unto them.*Romans 1:18-19 God's anger was expressed during the generations living under the first covenant because the people refused to be obedient. God dealt with the soul of man, his carnal nature. In this covenant before Christ, there was performance associated with the law. Obedience was defined by doing something. For example, the sacrifice of a healthy animal taken to the alter to be slain for its blood for man's sins. There was always an action required to show God their faithfulness.

With the new covenant in Christ, God gives grace. He is no longer angry, but is gracious to His people. Performance is not required in grace. Born of Christ, we are pardoned by His blood whereby we are not subjected to wrath as a child of the Father. *Much more then, being now justified by his blood, we shall be saved from wrath through him.* Romans 5:9 God tells us that our sins and iniquities He will remember no more.

In the new covenant, we live under grace for God has made it personal, communing with each believer individually who comes before Him in unwavering faith. The communication is in the spirit realm, our spirit to the Father through the intercession of the Holy Spirit. With Christ, our obedience is no longer to the letter of the law, but is in our faith to His Word. *But now we are delivered from the law, that being dead wherein we were held; that we should serve in newness of spirit, and not in the oldness of the letter.* Romans 7:6

Absolutely God is sovereign, but He isn't the one who is making you unhappy by directing misfortunes to occur to you, or your loved ones. He isn't wishing you well and providing you mercy and grace with promises of blessings and gifts while slapping you with negative obstacles leaving you disappointed and discouraged. God takes the bad and turns it into good. He doesn't cause it, He corrects it. *And we know that all things work together for good to them that love God, to them who are the called according to his purpose. For whom he did foreknow, he also did predestinate to be conformed to the image of his Son, that he might be the firstborn among many brethen. Moreover whom he did predestinate, them he also called: and whom he called, them he also justified: and whom he justified, them he also glorified. He that spared not his own Son, but delivered him up for us all, how shall he not with him also freely give us all things?* Romans 8:28-32 We live in a fallen world with the ruler of this earthen place constantly striving to destroy us but even in his attempts, he cannot touch the faithful children of the Almighty King when we profess our faith. Whatever Satan throws in our path, God will turn it to good for He is protective of His children.

God dwells in each believer first through Christ and second as the Holy Spirit. Why would He place harm upon Himself? He isn't, for the least of reasons it would be counterproductive. *Every good gift and every perfect gift is from above, and cometh down from the Father of lights, with whom is no variableness, neither shadow of turning.* James 1:17 He would be going against the very essence of His nature of love to render illness and disease, or anything that is detrimental to His children.

It is not our Father's intention that anyone should suffer, or die prematurely. Faithful children of the Father live under the provision of grace whereby wrath is not expressed in grace. It is important to understand and separate the covenants realizing that after Jesus came and died for us, everything changed for man. Our relationship with God is not the same as the Israelites because we have Christ.

In believing God gives, or allows the circumstance that we seek Him in prayer for restitution, why should He answer when He has been accused and found guilty? If someone charged you with a hideous incident, how willing would you be to give that person your blessings? When we believe that our loving Father gives us diseases and hardships, we have in reality rejected His love, His Word.

We obstruct Kingdom power by allowing our carnal thinking to get in the way of our spiritual relationship with the Father. By human nature, man tends to gravitate towards the familiar and accept our security in one another, and consequently, not turning to the only One who provides the promises and power. We get out of sync with God. *Because the carnal mind is enmity against God: for it is not subject to the law of God, neither indeed can be. So then they that are in the flesh cannot please God.* Romans 8:7-8

Carnal influence voids answered prayers. There can be no combining man's intellect with Jesus' authority and come up with a whole new belief, one that suits our lifestyle. Family, friends, colleagues, and professionals may give advice and guidance, but it is our responsibility to take their recommendations to the Word and see what God says and then obey His command. Therefore, *Beware lest any man spoil you through philosophy and vain deceit, after the tradition of men, after the rudiments of the world, and not after Christ.* Colossians 2:8

We are stepping out of grace without realizing the ramifications of our actions, like walking out of a dome of light that holds powerful influence and finding ourselves stranded in the dark, ill-equipped to handle what life presents. *But ye are a chosen generation, a royal priesthood, an holy nation, a peculiar people; that ye should show forth the praises of Him who hath called you out of darkness into his marvelous light.* 1 Peter 2:9 God's grace is always apparent, but we can find ourselves without the benefits. *And God is able to make all grace abound toward you: that ye, always having all sufficiency in all things, may abound to every good work.* 2 Corinthians 9:8

God tells us not to waver in our faith for if we do, we have severed our ability to connect to the Kingdom. Our faith must be inexorable and consistent in all matters. When we mix worldly influences with our soulful reasoning, faith becomes diluted and ineffectual. *But let him ask in faith, nothing wavering. For he that wavereth is like a wave of the sea driven with the wind and tossed.* James 1:6 It shows instability which reflects a lack of trust and places doubt in our belief. God has given us a place in His Kingdom as an heir in Christ. We are His children. *And if children, then heirs; heirs of God, and joint-heirs with Christ; if so be that we suffer with him, that we may be also glorified together.* Romans 8:17 With a lack of knowledge and misplacement of our faith, we can miss the marvelous blessings, gifts, and power of the Father. We must not allow the carnal to affect our daily walk with Christ. *But of him are ye in Christ Jesus, who of God is made unto us wisdom, and righteousness, and sanctification and redemption; That, according as it is written, He that glorieth, let him glory in the Lord.* 1 Corinthians 1:30-31

Show God how much you love Him by living according to the truth in His Word with the obedience of unwavering faith. Shed the carnal thinking and take up the cross with Christ and become the spirit person whom God created you to be. *Therefore we are buried with him by baptism into death: that like as Christ was raised up from the dead by the glory of the Father, even so we also should walk in newness of life.* Romans 6:4 There will be no greater decision than this one, for it is everlasting.

Chapter 6 ~ The Body of Man

And the Lord said, My spirit shall not always strive with man, for that he also is flesh: yet his days shall be an hundred and twenty years.

Genesis 6:3

Purpose: Temple of God, Earthen Vessel

God made all the creatures of the air, land, water, and man from the dust of the earth. He made the animals to give habitation to the planet just as He dressed it with vegetation. God put His Spirit within man and breathed a soul into the body He had formed giving him a conscience. This is the creation of man before the following generations were born of the flesh.

In the conception of man, we have two components: Adam and Christ. Adam is our soul, and Christ our spirit. *And so it is written, the first Adam was made a living soul; the last Adam was made a quickening spirit.* 1 Corinthians 15:45 We are from the seed of Adam, and his sin is upon man throughout all generations as we are born with a sin nature and into a sin environment. Man does not choose to be born of flesh, but we do choose to be born of the spirit in Christ.

God designed the body of man for two purposes; first, to be the home of the spirit person we are in His likeness; and second, to be His temple on earth, a vessel for the accomplishment of His Kingdom work through our physical presence. *But the Lord said unto him, Go thy way: for he is a chosen vessel unto me, to bear my name before the Gentiles, and kings, and the children of Israel.* Acts 9:15 Whether in the Old or New Testaments, God has His chosen people to be vessels for the fulfillment of His plan. Today, those in Christ who are faithful to His Word are His people.

We accept being born-again as adding another dimension to life which is salvation. When we make the transition from sinner to saint, we agree with Christ that our body becomes the temple of the Holy Spirit just as a brick and mortar house is a tangible place of residency. *Know ye not that ye are the temple of God, and that the Spirit of God dwelleth in you? If any man defile the temple of God, him shall God destroy; for the temple of God is holy, which temple ye are.* 1 Corinthians 3:16-17 We are responsible for the wellbeing of the temple.

Our spirit and soul coexist within the framework of our body with only one in charge, and it should always be the spirit of man guided by the Spirit of Truth. *I beseech you therefore, brethren, by the mercies of God, that ye present your bodies a living sacrifice, holy, acceptable unto God, which is your reasonable service.* Romans 12:1 Before Christ, the temple of God was a geographic landmark, a location with an alter that only the appointed priest could enter. In Christ, we are the temple. *That every one of you should know how to possess his vessel in sanctification and honour.* Thessalonians 4:4

The flesh cannot perform independently. It makes no decision and has no opinion but requires direction from either the soul, or the spirit. *For I know that in me (that is, in my flesh), dwelleth no good thing: for to will is present with me; but how to perform that which is good I find not. For the good that I would I do not: but the evil which I would not, that I do. Now if I do that I would not, it is no more I that do it, but sin that dwelt in me.* Romans 7:18-20 Whichever leads, the body will oblige. *I thank God through Jesus Christ our Lord. So then with the mind I myself serve the law of God; but with the flesh the law of sin.* Romans 7:18-20 Commonly, we rely on the senses and the body will respond and express through our thoughts and emotions.

We are on earth for a season and a reason, a time and a purpose. When we fail to realize the significance of presenting our body as God's vessel, we can miss our opportunity in servitude to His Kingdom. *If a man therefore purge himself from these, he shall be a vessel unto honor, sanctified, and meet for the master's use, and prepared unto every good work.* 2 Timothy 2:21

God has a plan for everyone's life whether we live it or not, for it has been established at the foundation. We see only the forgiveness of sins and salvation without pursuance of the duty we have when we ask to be reborn in spirit. *Wherefore come out from among them, and be ye separate, saith the Lord, and touch not the unclean thing; and I will receive you. And will be a Father unto you, and ye shall be my sons and daughters, saith the Lord Almighty.* 2 Corinthians 6:17-18 God has done His part, and now we have a role in the relationship that reunites us to the Kingdom of Heaven.

We should live believing in the things we do not see to be more real than what our senses tell us for truth and power is in the spirit, not in the visible. *For the invisible things of him from the creation of the world are clearly seen, being understood by the things that are made, even his eternal power and Godhead; so that they are without excuse: Because that, when they knew God, they glorified him not as God, neither were thankful; but became vain in their imaginations, and their foolish heart was darkened. Professing themselves to be wise, they became fools, And changed the glory of the uncorruptible God into an image made like to corruptible man, and to birds, and fourfooted beasts, and creeping things. Wherefore God also gave them up to uncleanness through the lusts of their own hearts, to dishonour their own bodies between themselves: Who changed the truth of God into a lie, and worshipped and served the creature more than the Creator, who is blessed for ever. Amen.* Romans 1:20-25

Needs, wants, and desires have already been met for those who walk in stewardship to God's Kingdom. There is nothing we cannot ask that our Father has not already provided. *Therefore I say unto you, Take no thought for your life, what ye shall eat, or what ye shall drink; nor yet for your body, what ye shall put on. Is not the life more than meat, and the body than raiment?* Matthew 6:25 As the Father has supplied, we must petition in wisdom and have faith to receive.

Our desire should be to live a life in Christ whereby all things are sufficient for all we do in His name, for there is no greater achievement than to succeed in God's plan. There will come a time when we will stand before Christ to give account of our earthen work and surely we want to hear Him say, "Well done, my child."

Chapter 7 ~ The Soul of Man

And the Lord God formed man of the dust of the ground, and breathed into his nostrils the breath of life; and man became a living soul.

Genesis 2:7

Purpose: Destiny in Christ, Free Will

When God created man, He had a plan. He did not form Adam of dust and Eve of his rib, and place them on earth without a purpose for every person born of his seed. Our destiny has been established at creation, and it becomes our responsibility to know it once we are reborn into the spirit realm. Whether we fulfill our Father's predestined role depends on our accepting our heritage.

We are all born with a soul tainted with sin and a spirit waiting to be awakened. God has given us the gift of a free will to decide how we will conduct our life: by our soul, or by the spirit; therefore, of the world, or of the Kingdom. Man can live by default with the inherited sins of Adam, or by the Spirit of God as a saint. *The first man Adam was made a living soul; the last Adam was made a quickening spirit. Howbeit that was not first which is spiritual, but that which is natural; and afterward that which is spiritual. The first man is of the earth and the second is the Lord for heaven.* 1 Corinthians 15:45-47

Often for the born-again believer, this transition is not made for we do not completely sever the influences of the world. Even as a child of the Father, we can be living without His Almighty blessings and promises. When God gave man a free will, it was that he would choose the Kingdom of Heaven.

Our soul is influenced by the natural, or what our senses reveal through hearing, seeing, and touching the tangible things of the world. Our soul is the essence of who we are as a person in this carnal life. It is what makes us human. Through the soul we express desires, opinions, and emotions with our unique personality and characteristics. It exemplifies our attitudes, attributes, and aptitude. We give no thought to who we are in the natural, for it is clearly seen and understood. Often, our spirit within receives little, if any, attention going unnoticed and unnourished in God's Word.

The soul cannot accomplish God's preordained plan. When we are tuned-in more to the world through our self efforts, we are unable to achieve our destiny for God. *It is better to trust in the Lord than put confidence in man.* Psalm 118:8 Many are missing wonderful blessings and gifts merely for lack of separating the soul from the spirit.

There are doctrines that teach the soul and spirit are the same, so when speaking of the soul we are also referring to the spirit and vice versa, intertwining them as one. To highlight the separation, we can verify in the book of Thessalonians the soul from the spirit. *And the very God of peace sanctify you wholly; and I pray God your whole spirit and soul and body be preserved blameless unto the coming of our Lord Jesus Christ.* 1 Thessalonians 5:23 We have verification of the trinity of man.

God did not create man to be a robot, but fashioned him with the ability to think. He wants man to freely return to the Kingdom without coercion which is the reason man was given a free will. He instructed Adam and Eve to not eat of a certain tree within the garden, and it was their free will that enabled them to choose to be obedient, or not. Without the free will, God would be a dictator and man His slave.

Man continues life as though nothing has changed; however, everything should be new for the believer as the Holy Spirit teaches how to live a spirit-filled life. *Teaching us that, denying ungodliness and worldly lusts, we should live soberly, righteously, and godly, in this present world.* Titus 2:12 God is instructing each child to step out of the corrupt world, out of unbelief and all things unclean, away from our narcissism, and live with Him in spirit.

Society has taught us to name it and claim it, go for it, obtain a quick fix to whatever ails us on a personal level. We adhere to the same attitude in our prayers to God. We expect an instantaneous answer in our time of need and become disillusioned when one is not immediately forthcoming. However, if we have an intimate relationship with our Father, we would know this is not the way to communicate with Him. It may be our carnal attempt at reaching God, but it leaves us discouraged and without a response.

Our unwavering prayer of faith should always begin and end in thanksgiving and praise giving glory to the Father and His Son with an absolute and unshakable trust in the knowledge that what we ask to be manifested in the natural has already been established in the spirit realm. We are merely calling what is in the Kingdom of Heaven down to earth.

It is through our soul that we experience happiness, laughter, and joy or fear, depression, and anger. Likewise, it is through the soul, we perceive and experience physiological issues such as illness, injury, emotional pain, and so forth. If we allow our thoughts to command the body and not listen to our heart, we become submissive to the world even though we have a rebirth in Christ. *Only take heed to thyself, and keep thy soul diligently, lest thou forget the things which thine eyes have seen, and lest they depart from thy heart all the days of thy life: but teach them thy sons, and thy sons' sons.* Deuteronomy 4:9 It can be a challenge to relinquish ones own willfulness.

We have learned in the Old Testament how God dealt with the soul of people, their carnality, because they did not have Christ. They had a spirit as every person does; however, there wasn't the manifestation of a quickening of their spirit, or a baptism with the Holy Spirit as Jesus had not yet come as the Savior. Therefore, the people lived strictly in the natural, and it is how God communicated with them and dealt with their disobedience. *And now, Israel, what doth the Lord thy God require of thee, but to fear the Lord thy God, to walk in all his ways, and to love him, and to serve the Lord thy God with all thy heart and with all thy soul, To keep the commandments of the Lord, and his statutes, which I command thee this day for thy good?* Deuteronomy 10:12-13

In the New Testament, the Living Word was made flesh and Christ came to earth and taught all things of the Spirit. His disciples and followers often struggled to comprehend what He was teaching, so Jesus performed miracles and healing to exemplify there is another world, and it was from where He came, a place other than what the eye can see. He taught about the Father of all creation and an eternal life to those who accepted His truth. God was communicating with man through his soul while Christ brought the Spirit of God to man. We have to forget about ourselves and lean completely on Him placing our trust in His Word. God is not withholding His greatness, but rather we are limiting ourselves by our own stubbornness.

There are many things that obstruct our ability to reach God. First to consider is sin. Do our thoughts, actions, and deeds reflect goodness, kindness, and compassion? Do we strive to be like Jesus as He is our example? What we consider as living a sin free life perhaps according to God, we may not be. Even though we are reborn in Christ, and our sins are forgiven, we can still be inclined towards a sinful nature because of our human characteristics.

Second to consider is wavering. Do we hold to God's Word with resoluteness, or are there times when we waver in our faith wanting to combine man's wisdom with a desire for God's power? Is there doubt that God may not answer? If we question God, then we do not know Him as we should because we are to have certainty in the knowledge that He has already provided. Sinning and wavering can go undetected and both are in direct violation of Kingdom laws.

When man's soul is in control, the spirit is not. There will always be worldly manipulations attempting to integrate into our thoughts, steering us in a direction away from the Kingdom. The spirit is directly obedient to the Word; therefore, we should not allow our soul, self thought, to get in the way of a relationship with the Father. We will never be wiser than the One who created us, for the child is not smarter than the parent. *The disciple is not above his master, nor the servant above his lord.* Matthew 10: 24

Nothing is greater or more satisfying than living for God, so apply the gift of a free will and choose life in the spirit. Take to heart the laws of the Kingdom and be faithful to your heavenly Father. There is immense reward to those who choose wisely.

Chapter 8 ~ The Spirit of Man

But we all, with open face beholding as in a glass the glory of the Lord, are changed into the same image from glory to glory, even as by the Spirit of the Lord.

2 Corinthians 3:18

Purpose: Child of God, Eternal Life

The trinity of God is for man's purpose; likewise, the trinity of man is for God's plan. When we accept the body is the temple of the Holy Spirit, the soul is our free will to choose the Father, and the spirit is the eternal life of man for a relationship, then man is complete for a life for God. If we concentrate only on the body and the soul, we miss the spirit; the most important aspect of our existence. *God is a spirit and they that worship him must worship him in spirit and in truth.* John 4:24 Christ prepared man to be an heir in Him for the Father, and all things in the Kingdom became attainable that we may be equipped to live a productive life in servitude to God.

Let's look at it from a different perspective. Christ purchased a home (body) for the Holy Spirit to live in while on planet earth. God personally furnishes it (vessel) with all the treasures in heaven (gifts) to make the home pleasant and comfortable (spirit). There is no limitation in equipping this new home with all the daily necessities. Just as God made a paradise in the garden for Adam and Eve; today, we are His earthen residency and he has supplied the dwelling place abundantly. There will be no future requirements or additions, for nothing is missing. The treasures of blessings, gifts, and power we know to be in the Kingdom are also in earth nestled within every born-again faithful child of the Father. How do we know this? God places Himself as Christ and the Holy Spirit within each person who chooses a life for Him. That is, two parts of the trinity of God dwell on the inside of each believer. Where there is the presence of God also would be His blessings and power.

In unison, God, Christ, and the Holy Ghost have prepared the believer to live in spirit for the Father's plan. *Now we have received, not the spirit of the world, but the spirit which is of God; that we might know the things that are freely given to us of God.* 1 Corinthians 2:12 When we understand the dynamics of the trinities both of God, and of man, it becomes clear for the role of each believer reborn in spirit. We become the beneficiaries of all the treasures in the storehouse. *But we have this treasure in earthen vessels, that the excellency of the power may be of God, and not of us.* 2 Corinthians 4:7

Because man is so removed to understand the operation of the trinities, we miss what is right in front of us, or more accurately speaking, inside of us. These wonderful gifts are to benefit our life, and more so, available in serving God. So how do we bring forth what we seek knowing it is within reach, and yet, seemingly so unattainable? We have to think differently, renew our mind to God's Word, and know His ways. See the things of the Kingdom to be more real than what our eyes tell us in the natural. Believe in Him, solely, as it should be and as God expects of us.

We are a student of His Word as our tutor brings all things in heaven to our awareness. Jesus spent time with His disciples and the multitudes who gathered to listen to Him teach, so now are we to do the same. *And be not conformed to this world: but be ye transformed by the renewing of your mind, that ye may prove what is that good, and acceptable, and perfect, will of God.* Romans 12:2 We should focus on the important matters of God rather than the temporary things of the world. As we study the scriptures, the Holy Spirit will give us knowledge and understanding of the Kingdom of Heaven.

Man has a propensity to do the opposite and seek the natural with little regard to God. When we pray and don't see evidence of an answer, we have a tantrum with illegitimate accusations towards the Father. We do this because we don't understand. We aren't connected to Him. God set His Kingdom with rules and unwavering faithful obedience to these laws is the key that releases His supernatural power. A prayer spoken in wisdom and allegiance to God will cause the Holy Spirit to unlock the storehouse.

As the physical body needs food, water, and oxygen to sustain life, so does the spirit of man require a special diet found in the Word. In the Scriptures, we learn of everything we need. *Which things also we speak, not in the words which man's wisdom teacheth, but which the Holy Ghost teacheth; comparing spiritual things with spiritual.* 1 Corinthians 2:13 Like an infant, we are without wisdom but as we mature, we learn what is required to live in the spirit realm. Once we do, we will know how to rely on the Holy Spirit with the authority Christ has given in appropriation to the laws of the Kingdom.

There are three reasons to be without blessings. First, we are not living in the spirit with faithful obedience; second, we mix carnal thinking with supernatural expectations; and third, we are not focusing on the Kingdom. If our faith is tainted with unbelief, we have disqualified ourselves to receive. As mentioned previously, we can have belief and unbelief at the same time, and anything not solidly committed in faith falls into the second category. *If we live in the Spirit, let us also walk in the Spirit.* Galatians 5:25 We must train our thoughts from the natural, or what our senses confirm. It requires diligence that our reliance is strictly on God.

We need to troubleshoot our knowledge of the functionality of the Kingdom. Do we live in the spirit, are we in truth to His Word, and are our prayers petitioned accurately to release His power? *For what man knoweth the things of a man, save the spirit of man which is in him? Even so the things of God knoweth no man, but the spirit of God.* 1 Corinthians 2:11 If you are not releasing His abundant heavenly treasures, then seek to understand why and identify what needs to be addressed, so that you may live with the riches the Father has furnished. *Charge them that are rich in this world, that they be not highminded, nor trust in uncertain riches, but in the living God, who giveth us richly all things to enjoy.* Timothy 6:17 Trust not in the world, but in God.

An analogy is likened to an egg. There is the white and yellow parts of an egg. The whole egg may be used in recipes, but the nutritional value is in the small yellow center and not in the white of the egg. In this analogy, man is similarly no different. The carnal thinking, flesh, is the white and the spirit person within is the yolk; thus, it is the spirit that holds the value of man's life. We struggle in making this distinction.

Remember the divine trinity; God is Spirit, Christ is Spirit, the Holy Ghost is Spirit, the Kingdom of Heaven operates in the spirit, and man is made spirit. We were created to be a part of the Kingdom. Children of the Father are well-equipped with everything in Christ and the Holy Spirit. God's gifts are given that we use them for His Kingdom purpose, and in doing so, we reap the rewards.

Faithfulness is the key to unlock the storehouse of treasures in the Kingdom of Heaven, prominent to the obedient child. *By whom we have received grace and apostleship, for obedience to the faith among all nations, for his name.* Romans 1:5 This is where the life of man begins, in the spirit, and lives on with the Father and His Son, eternally.

Part III

Trinity of the Kingdom
Mercy, Grace, and Faith

But seek ye first the kingdom of God, and his righteousness; and all these things shall be added unto you.

Matthew 6:33

Chapter 9 ~ The Kingdom of Heaven

How great are his signs! and how mighty are his wonders! his kingdom is an everlasting kingdom, and his dominion is from generation to generation.

Daniel 4:3

Within the Scriptures, we are given a vivid description of heaven as a magnificent kingdom somewhere in the distant unknown where God and His Son live and whereby we have the hope of eternal salvation. *For we know that if our earthly house of this tabernacle were dissolved, we have a building of God, an house not made with hands, eternal in the heavens. For in this we groan, earnestly desiring to be clothed upon with our house which is in heaven.* 2 Corinthians 5:1-2

We have been taught through various doctrines that our arrival in heaven is immediate upon departure from our earthen home. We take comfort in believing that our loved ones, who have preceded us in leaving this world, are in the presence of God. In this thinking, there is a major oversight for God's Almighty Kingdom is not for man's occupancy. We know God to be the beginning and the end; therefore, we accept that His Kingdom has always been. *I am Alpha and Omega, the beginning and the ending, saith the Lord, which is, and which was, and which is to come, the*

Almighty. Revelation 1:8 The Kingdom of Heaven is God's throne and cannot be our final destination. Though there is evidence in the Bible of specific individuals brought straight forth into His Kingdom, we know it was an act of God for His purpose in prophecy. Our heaven, the New Jerusalem, will come down from God's Kingdom upon the earth to be our eternal home.

In the Book of Genesis, God details His creation beginning with the earth. *In the beginning God created the heaven and the earth. And the earth was without form, and void; and darkness was upon the face of the deep. And the Spirit of God moved upon the face of the waters.* Genesis 1:1-2 God made the earth on the first day. *And God made the firmament, and divided the waters which were under the firmament from the waters which were above the firmament: and it was so. And God called the firmament Heaven. And the evening and the morning were the second day.* Genesis 1:7-8

God created two heavens, or kingdoms for man; one for the *carnal* man, Adam, and one for the *spirit* man by the second Adam, Christ. The first Adam was given earth and the second Adam, Christ, is King of the New Jerusalem, our everlasting home. As there are two Adams, there exist two kingdoms within God's Almighty Kingdom of Heaven. *These are the generations of the heavens and of the earth when they were created, in the day that the Lord God made the earth and the heavens.* Genesis 2:4 Notice the plural for heavens. *Thus the heavens and the earth were finished, and all the host of them.* Genesis 2:1

When God created Adam and placed him in Heaven on Earth, He gave him authority, or jurisdiction over all the inhabitants. Adam was king of the earth with his personal throne the Garden of Eden. Adam's obedience was only to God as the Almighty King of all creation. In succumbing to Satan's deceit, Adam lost his ruling privilege forfeiting his kingdom. Earth was no longer heaven for Adam and Eve, nor would be for future descendants.

God knew this earthen heaven would be defiled requiring a second heaven which would be forever upon Christ's return. *And I saw a new heaven and a new earth: for the first heaven and earth were passed away; and there was no sea.* Revelation 21:1 The new heaven is the New Jerusalem where all God's children will live eternally with Christ, not in God's Almighty Holy Kingdom, but in the heaven that will be of His Kingdom. *Him that overcometh will I make a pillar in the temple of my God, and he shall go no more out: and I will write upon him the name of my God, and the name of the city of my God, which is New Jerusalem, which cometh down out of heaven from my God: and I will write upon him my new name.* Revelation 3:12

To believe there is only one heaven is a one-dimensional viewpoint. First is the Kingdom of Almighty God; second, the Kingdom of Earth as given to Adam, and the third eternal kingdom, the New Jerusalem, which is Christ's Kingdom. *And there was given him dominion, and glory, and a kingdom, that all people, nations, and languages, should serve him: his dominion is an everlasting dominion, which shall not pass away, and His kingdom that which shall not be destroyed.* Daniel 7:14 Our heavenly home is in the New Jerusalem with Christ as our King, and not in God's Almighty Kingdom of Heaven though God's Kingdom encompasses all.

We are not qualified to enter before the throne of God. What we have been given is cleansing of our unrighteousness and sanctified by the blood of Jesus to be called children of God with the privilege to seek our Father, personally, and not through an appointed priest as in generations past. *This is the covenant that I will make with them after those days, saith the Lord, I will put my laws into their hearts, and in their minds will I write them; And their sins and iniquities will I remember no more.* Hebrews 10:16-17

There is a distinct difference between entering God's holy Kingdom and having the means of communing with Him. It is with Christ's authority as He sits at the right hand of the Father, and the Holy Spirit as our advocate and intercessor, that each faithful believer may have assess to

God through prayer. We do not enter into the sacred Kingdom of God; however, God made a way for His children to approach Him until the time comes and we live with Christ as our King.

We partake of a resurrection just as Jesus was resurrected from death, and our resurrection is in Christ upon His return. As Christ died, resurrected, and ascended into the Kingdom of Heaven, so when man dies he also must have a resurrection unto eternal life in the New Jerusalem. *In a moment, in the twinkling of an eye, at the last trump: for the trumpet shall sound, and the dead shall be raised incorruptible, and we shall be changed.* 1 Corinthians 15:52 As Christ conquered death, so has He done for the believers giving us a new body for our new life.

There is a period of a thousand years, the Kingdom of Peace (Millennium), when the saints will live with Christ as He prepares us for our new, eternal home. It is also during this time that those who have not known of God are given the opportunity of everlasting life. *But the rest of the dead lived not again until the thousand years were finished. This is the first resurrection: on such the second death hath no power, but they shall be priests of God and of Christ, and shall reign with him a thousand years.* Revelation 20:5-6

When we die, our spirit awaits for the Lord to call us forth from the grave. *For if we believe that Jesus died and rose again, even so them also which sleep in Jesus will God bring with him. For this we say unto you by the word of the Lord, that we which are alive and remain unto the coming of the Lord shall not prevent them which are asleep. For the Lord himself shall descend from heaven with a shout, with the voice of the archangel, and with the trump of God: and the dead in Christ shall rise first: Then we which are alive and remain shall be caught up together with them in the clouds, to meet the Lord in the air: and so shall we ever be with the Lord.* 1 Thessalonians 4:14-17

God's Kingdom functions in a very succinct and orderly manner. Laws are in place and we are expected to honor them. All nations have governments or parliaments with legislations that the people are required to adhere to. God's Kingdom is no different and when we lack wisdom or misunderstand His principles, we do not benefit. *For the kingdom of God is not in word, but in power.* 1 Corinthians 4:20

As King and our Father, God has given instructions on how we may communicate with Him in the example of the Lord's Prayer. *And when thou prayest, thou shalt not be as the hypocrites are: for they love to pray standing in the synagogues and in the corners of the streets, that they may be seen of men. Verily I say unto you, they have their reward. But thou, when thou prayest, enter into thy closet, and when thou hast shut thy door, pray to thy Father which is in secret; and thy Father which seeth in secret shall reward thee openly. But when ye pray, use not vain repetitions, as the heathen do: for they think that they shall be heard for their much speaking. Be not ye therefore like unto them: for your Father knoweth what things ye have need of, before ye ask him. After this manner therefore pray ye: Our Father which art in heaven, Hallowed be thy name. Thy kingdom come. Thy will be done in earth, as it is in heaven. Give us this day our daily bread. And forgive us our debts, as we forgive our debtors. And lead us not into temptation, but deliver us from evil: For thine is the kingdom, and the power, and the glory, for ever. Amen.* Matthew 6:5-13 This does not mean that we recite the Lord's Prayer, but to see the methodology by which we are to approach our Father in His Kingdom. God presents the keynotes of what is required.

This is our commandment of prayer and is very simple. God tells us to seek Him, privately, make it very intimate and personal. He already knows what we will ask of Him, but requires that we not be prideful in our petitions. He teaches that whatever He has established within His Kingdom is available to His children on earth. If at any time, we waver, hold doubt, or question His ability, we have voided the prayer because our prayer is the example of our faith. Therefore, should we lack in the application of our faith, it will not release Kingdom power for the Holy

Spirit only responds to the truth in God's Word. We have not lost our salvation, but we are unprepared to live a bountiful life as our Father intended and overcome the adversities of living in a fallen world.

God's Kingdom treasures are spiritual, and we know them to be love, forgiveness, mercy, grace, faith, praise, goodness, kindness, glory, belief, trust, blessings, promises, healing, compassion, miracles, prosperity, prophesy, power, authority, and eternal life. *Again, the kingdom of heaven is like unto treasure hid in a field; the which when a man hath found, he hideth, and for joy thereof goeth and selleth all that he hath, and buyeth that field.* Matthew 13:44 These treasures are foundational for our spirit life.

We should never forget that we are the sons and daughters of the Almighty King and all that is established within His Kingdom is for His children. *Thy kingdom is an everlasting kingdom, and thy dominion endureh throughout all generations.* Psalm 145:13 Nothing would please God more than the acceptance of our inheritance. It becomes imperative that we conduct ourselves as the rightful heirs we are in Christ for the King, our Father.

Chapter 10 ~ The Mercy of God

*But God, who is rich in mercy, for his great love wherewith he love*d us.

Ephesians 2:4

Living in the mercy of God is likened to an insurance policy; however, there is no better life insurance, health coverage, or retirement benefits than with God. His provisions never expire, and we are guaranteed physical and emotional healing, provided prosperity, and given eternal life. We are far greater than the angels, for we are God's children. *Keep yourselves in the love of God, looking for the mercy of our Lord Jesus Christ unto eternal life.* Jude 1:21 His Kingdom operates in the trinity of mercy, grace, and faith. Mercy and grace are an apparent part of God, and it is faith that enables man to receive of the Father. Before we talk about our part, let's begin with God's mercy.

What is mercy, exactly? Webster's dictionary defines mercy as the compassionate or kindly forbearance shown towards an offender, an enemy, or other person under one's influences; an act of kindness or favor, something that gives evidence of divine favor; blessing. This is precisely what God gives to us. *Blessed be the God and Father of our Lord Jesus Christ, which according to his abundant mercy hath begotten us again unto a lively hope by the resurrection of Jesus Christ from the dead.* 1 Peter 1:3 Notice this verse says, 'again'. We are reunited for a second time through the death and resurrection of His Son because of the mercy our Father has towards a people He loves, even with our disobedience. *In a little wrath I hid my face from thee for a moment; but with everlasting kindness will I have mercy on thee, saith the Lord thy Redeemer.* Isaiah 54:8 It is because of God's compassionate nature that man is given mercy.

To understand God's mercy is to see it as the love and patience He expresses continuously to man. His mercy is constant without degree or dimension. It is always in place, a perfect expression of love. *For the Lord is good; his mercy is everlasting; and his truth endureth to all generations.* Psalm 100:5 To have mercy or compassion towards someone who has done an injustice is a remarkable act of kindness.

We would find it difficult to do so by our human nature. If someone commits a wrong against us, our immediate reaction is to retaliate and seek restitution for the assault. However, when we do wrong before our Father, He shows mercy and forgives us. *But I say unto you, That ye resist not evil: but whosoever shall smite thee on thy right cheek, turn to him the other also.* Matthew 5:39 A lesson we are required to learn from the example in Christ.

From the beginning of man's existence with Adam and Eve in the garden, God has displayed mercy towards disobedience with the patience of a parent to a child. Though they disobeyed, God showed mercy and continued communicating with them daily even through the necessity of removing them from the home He prepared for them. There are many ways that God reveals His love for His children.

When God was dealing with the Israelites after releasing them from a life of slavery, it was a display of mercy towards a wayward people that He took care of them in the desert by supplying manna from heaven to feed them. *And when the children of Israel saw it, they said one to another,*

It is manna: for they wist not what it was. And Moses said unto them, This is the bread which the Lord hath given you to eat. Exodus 16:15 And when they complained of thirst, God supplied water. *Behold, I will stand before thee there upon the rock in Horeb; and thou shalt smite the rock, and there shall come water out of it, that the people may drink. And Moses did so in the sight of the elders of Israel.* Exodus 17:6 Their clothing and sandals never wore out. They were a lost generation, arrogant and unfaithful; and yet, God showed love, He showed mercy. It was never God's plan for His people to live forty years in the wilderness. Man did that to himself by refusing to accept God as their Lord.

Fast-forward and we have a nation ill-equipped in the knowledge of heavenly things and unprepared for a relationship with God because we do not know our Father as we should. When it comes to the application of God's Word, we fall short due to lack of knowledge. In our modern society, the interest seems to be more on attaining the tangible things of the world rather than procuring time with God. Even so, God continues to have mercy and patience for a people that fail miserably at expressing love for Him.

His mercy is upon us even when we do not deserve it, for it remains constant. *And he said, I will make all my goodness pass before thee, and I will proclaim the name of the Lord before thee; and will be gracious to whom I will be gracious, and will show mercy on whom I will show mercy.* Exodus 33:19 Whether we do right or wrong, God's mercy never changes; it never falters or fades. *O give thanks unto the Lord; for he is good; for his mercy endureth for ever.* 1 Chronicles 16:34

God's mercy is not handed out by a performance of good deeds, for God is not a respecter of persons, there is no favoritism. *For there is no respect of persons with God.* Romans 2:11 Mercy is upon the sinners and the saints; however, it is the saints who will reap the benefits when we understand the mercy of God.

Another aspect of mercy is forgiveness. If not for God's mercy, how could we be forgiven our sins and transgressions towards Him and others? By what means would He apply forgiveness if He first did not have compassion. When we repent, we know our sins are forgiven. We take this transformation from sinner to saint far too lightly without consideration of the enormity of what has transpired through God and His Son.

We want all God has to offer with an unconditional expectation but are reluctant to reciprocate. It takes a desire to want to know Him and an earnest longing to be with Him. Just as we seek and fall in love with another person, we should more so desire to be with our heavenly Father. It is far more crucial that we be committed to God than any person on earth, for it is forever.

Perhaps an analogy of the trinity can be expressed in the ingredients for baking a pie. First, you have the crust or the foundation, then you add the filling, and last the topping. The filling is the substance of the pie, grace; finishing with the topping, faith. All are necessary for the making of a good dessert. Though we may eliminate the topping (faith), the crust and filling still makes a substantial pie, just as mercy and grace are always in place by the very nature of God. The point of this illustration is to show that God remains loyal in mercy and grace, never changing even when we are nonparticipants. He is the same yesterday, today, and tomorrow, always constant.

God's mercy sets the foundation for grace, and grace is where He supplies for our needs. We are protected by mercy and provided for by grace with both harmoniously given by the Father in caring for His children.

Chapter 11~ The Grace of God

*Grace be with you, mercy, and peace, from God the Father,
and from the Lord Jesus Christ, the Son of the Father, in truth
and love.*

2 John 1:3

It could probably be said that very few people give thought to God's grace, and if we did, would we truly understand the magnificence of such an undeserving gift? Should someone ask you to define grace, how would you answer? Simply stated, grace is unmerited favor, leniency, or special courtesy towards a person. We do not earn grace, for grace is a gift. *But not as the offence, so also is the free gift. For if through the offence of one many be dead, much more the grace of God, and the gift by grace, which is by one man, Jesus Christ, hath abounded unto many.* Romans 5:15 Grace was in the Garden of Eden, but with the offense of Adam grace was lost to man until Christ restored it. Grace is upon man through Christ.

God's mercy is always present as we see in how He cared for the Israelites, but grace was not given to a disrespectful and disobedient people. Where sin is present, grace is not. Even during His short time on earth, Jesus followed the laws changing nothing of the Father, for it wasn't His mission to change anything, but to carry out God's will that all things set at the foundation of creation may occur. It took the death of Jesus to release the promises within the new covenant, whereby grace exists.

It was a matter of timing when Christ would journey to earth and be born of the flesh. *And the Word was made flesh, and dwelt among us, (and we beheld his glory, the glory as of the only begotten of the Father), full of grace and truth. John bare witness of him, and cried, saying, This was he of whom I spake, He that cometh after me is preferred before me: for he was before me. And of his fulness have all we received, and grace for grace. For the law was given by Moses, but grace and truth came by Jesus Christ.* John 1:14-17 Upon Jesus' death and resurrection, God's new covenant is present to those reborn into the Kingdom. As a child of God, we are no longer subject to the carnal laws as the generations living under the old covenant, but have the gift of grace when we abandon our sinful nature and live a righteous life in Christ.

In the new covenant, grace is reestablished as it was with Adam and Eve. *For sin shall not have dominion over you: for ye are not under the law, but under grace.* Romans 6:14 This is such an immense proclamation for the mere magnitude of what the Father and the Son have done for an unworthy people. God's *everlasting love* in all His magnificence is shown to man through His grace. Gifts, blessings, and power are given because of grace. *And God is able to make all grace abound toward you; that ye, always having all sufficiency in all things, may abound to every good work.* 2 Corinthians 9:8 This is not to say that God's wrath will not be witnessed again to all the unbelievers as there will be a finality to this corrupt world, but for the believers, we live in His grace.

Some Christians believe in adhering to the carnal laws, the Commandments, but also think they have the merit of grace not realizing that the law and grace do not go together, for one is of an old covenant and the other a new one. The first covenant reflects the anger of God while the second exemplifies the goodwill; one tells of an offense taken and the other of a pardon given. *A new covenant, he hath made the first old. Now that which decayeth and waxeth old is ready to vanish away.* Hebrews 8:13 The second covenant brought to man by Christ replaces the first one; therefore, those wanting to live by the old ordinances are impeding the benefits of grace. Born in Christ, the grace of God is given in the new covenant and does not mix with the old. *For if they which are of the law be heirs, faith is made void, and the promise made of none effect: because the law worketh wrath: for where no law is, there is no transgression.* Romans 4:14-15 Holding onto the old covenant while attempting to live in the new one severely hampers a relationship with God. As believers living in the new covenant of grace, it is not a dismissing of the Commandments, but rather accepting that they are the measurement for sin held against the unbeliever. Thus, we are no longer governed in sin by the old covenant laws.

Such individuals will be the first to fault God when things do not go as they expect, viewing Him as having wrath and metering out punishment to teach a lesson. If this were true, no one would receive a miracle, a healing, or blessings in this lifetime for we all would come up short. There is plenty man does that angers God, but instead He gives us grace and not wrath. *For the Lord God is a sun and shield: the Lord will give grace and glory: no good thing will he withhold from them that walk uprightly.* Psalm 84:11 To believe God is angry after His Son has come to satisfy the judgment on the sins of the world, who redeemed and reconciled man to the Father, is to not accept the glorious blessings of His new covenant.

Grace is a gift of pardon and forgiveness. It is because of grace that we may acquire God's many gifts. *But unto every one of us is given grace according to the measure of the gift of Christ.* Ephesians 4:7 We should want to live within the boundaries of grace which far exceed the old covenant laws of performance. We have grace by our faith and not because of a deed done. *For by grace are ye saved through faith; and that not of yourselves: it is the gift of God: Not of works, lest any man should boast.* Ephesians 2:8-9 God's loving and forgiving nature as shown in His mercy presents grace. We cannot earn it.

It is important to know how to allocate faith to release grace like a combination to a lock. The wrong set of numbers will not open the lock just as misguided information will not release grace. *Let us therefore come boldly unto the throne of grace that we may obtain mercy, and find grace to help in time of need.* Hebrews 4:16 This is a truth we must understand, so that we may apply our faith to receive the gift of grace. God's grace is omnipresent, but we can obstruct its function in our life.

God's continuous love, forgiveness, mercy, and grace provides blessings, gifts, promises, and power. God has provided, Christ has scarified, and we are the recipients for whom it is given. *And the grace of our Lord was exceeding abundant with faith and love which is in Christ Jesus.* 1 Timothy 1:14 Like water flowing over a waterfall, so is God's grace, forever plentiful. Everything of the Father is in perfect harmony in His Kingdom for our benefit; however, we are required to know how to release grace into our life. Though His grace is always present, we can inadvertently position ourselves to be without God's grace if our faith is lacking.

It has never been God's will that we should live in hardship, sickness, disease, and disarray struggling to survive. These issues are a part of living in a fallen world, but through God's grace, we have a means to be free of the elements that hold us in bondage. God has been protecting and providing for His children since Adam and Eve and remains doing so today.

It is God's will that we all live abundant and prosperous lives with good health and longevity. His mercy and grace have made this possible. *Grace be to you, and peace, from God our Father, and from the Lord Jesus Christ.* Ephesians 1:2 Let the measure of your faith be according to His Kingdom, so that you may receive a sufficient supply of grace for all your needs.

Chapter 12 ~ The Faith of Man

For we walk by faith, not my sight.

2 Corinthians 5:7

As we live spiritually within the Kingdom, we know it is the gift of faith that enables us to have a relationship with God and to receive His blessings in our life. Understanding that God's mercy and grace is upon His children, so must our faith be just as prevalent towards our Father. *Without faith it is impossible to please God.* Hebrews 11:6 It should become our desire to be an obedient child with wisdom in His Word. In doing so, we gain the knowledge and understanding of how to walk by faith.

When Jesus spoke to the disciples and the multitude of followers that gathered to hear His teachings, He was also speaking to all generations henceforth. Faith is God's gift, it is not something of our own making, nor is it required that we earn it. *Therefore being justified by faith we have peace with God through our Lord Jesus Christ: By whom also we have access by faith into this grace wherein we stand, and rejoice in hope of the glory of God.* Romans 5:1-2 This gift comes with instructions. If we begin to use our gift of faith without knowing the many facets of its functionality, we can miss out on valuable benefits.

An analogy would be likened to a cell phone. If we have not taken the time to read the manual that came with the new device, but instead continue to operate the phone based on our perception of how it works, we can miss many of its features. Just because we haven't made ourselves privy to various preprogrammed applications, doesn't mean they aren't accessible on the phone. Same holds true with faith. We receive the gift and are expected to study the manual, the Bible, to learn how faith operates in the Kingdom, so we will not be without the many blessings that come through faith.

As previously stated, believers can have faith and be in unbelief at the same time. You may think this is not possible, but revisit the disciples scenario. They questioned why their faith was not rendering a healing when it came to the boy who was dealing with seizures. Why couldn't they do the same as Christ because they had experienced the power of faith before, but in this particular incident it did not work? *And when they were come to the multitude, there came to him a certain man, kneeling down to him and saying, Lord, have mercy on my son: for he is a lunatic, and sore vexed: for ofttimes he falleth into the fire, and oft into the water. And I brought him to thy disciples, and they could not cure him. Then Jesus answered and said, O faithless and perverse generation, how long shall I be with you? how long shall I suffer you? bring him hither to me. And Jesus rebuked the devil; and he departed out of him: and the child was cured from that very hour. Then came the disciples to Jesus apart, and said, Why could not we cast him out? And Jesus said unto them, Because of your unbelief: for verily I say unto you, If ye have faith as a grain of mustard seed, ye shall say unto this mountain, Remove hence to yonder place; and it shall remove; and nothing shall be impossible unto you.* Matthew 17:14-20 What did Jesus say to His disciples? He told them their faith was ineffectual because it was mixed with unbelief, and unbelief voided the power.

It isn't the quantity of faith that we should strive to obtain because there is no such thing. God gives every believer the same measure of faith.

For I say, through the grace given unto me, to every man that is among you, not to think of himself more highly than he ought to think; but to think soberly, according as God hath dealt to every man the measure of faith. Romans 12:3 One person does not obtain more faith than another, nor do we receive faith by degrees of performance, the better I serve the Lord the more faith He will pour into my life. Faith is administered the same to all children of the Father.

Our faith has to be pure, unadulterated, not diluted with unbelief. There must be absolute assuredness, unequivocal and unwavering faith. Many believe they have such faith, but do not understand why their faith isn't rendering God's power in their life. Check for unbelief. How do I know if I am in unbelief? What do I look for? The answer is simple when we begin to consider the definition of unbelief.

Again, in recalling the story of the boy with seizures, the father took his son to Jesus. *And one of the multitude answered and said, Master, I have brought unto thee my son, which hath a dumb spirit; And wheresoever he taketh him, he teareth him: and he foameth, and gnasheth with his teeth, and pineth away: and I spake to thy disciples that they should cast him out; and they could not. He answereth him, and saith, O faithless generation, how long shall I be with you? how long shall I suffer you? bring him unto me. And they brought him unto him: and when he saw him, straightway the spirit tare him; and he fell on the ground, and wallowed foaming. And he asked his father, How long is it ago since this came unto him? And he said, Of a child. And ofttimes it hath cast him into the fire, and into the waters, to destroy him: but if thou canst do any thing, have compassion on us, and help us. Jesus said unto him, If thou canst believe, all things are possible to him that believeth. And straightway the father of the child cried out, and said with tears, Lord, I believe; help thou mine unbelief.* Mark 9:17-24 Desperate for a healing for his child, the father said: "Lord, I believe; help thou mine unbelief." He openly admitted to Jesus that he believed, and begged Christ to remove any unknown unbelief. The father did not want to hinder a healing for his son should he be harboring unbelief. At first glance, you may interpret the father speaking to Jesus when he said: "But if thou canst do any thing, have compassion on us and help us." as a statement of unbelief, but not so. Typically, when the word "if" is applied it denotes doubt. However, the father wasn't questioning Jesus' *ability* to heal his son, but rather would He be *willing* to do so. This is another distinction in understanding this scripture. When he replied to Jesus' question, the father said: "Lord, I believe; help thou mine unbelief." which shows his belief, but again, if there was anything that would be unknown to him that would block the healing for his son, he wanted Jesus to remove it.

Another thought to this scripture is that Jesus addressed the father or parent of the child, and not the child directly. Interestingly, perhaps it was because the child was under the age of thirteen which is recognized to be the official rite of passage into manhood for the Jewish males. We do not know if the father was Jew or Gentile, but we understand that Jesus would show no partiality. Also, note that when Jesus first set out to do His Father's works, He was twelve. *And when he was twelve years old, they went to Jerusalem after the custom of the feast.* Luke 2:42 It was here that Jesus remained behind and was later found by His parents in the temple sitting among the doctors. *And it came to pass, that after three days they found him in the temple, sitting in the midst of the doctors, both hearing them, and asking them questions. And all that heard him were astonished at his understanding and answers.* Luke 2:46-47

This scripture also reveals to us that parents are responsible for their children in their physical upbringing but also in nurturing them into a relationship with God. In Christ's authority and with the Holy Spirit, we may pray over our children with expectations of heavenly power in a time of need. However, a person must be wise in the truth of the principles of God's Kingdom.

Unbelief is a lack of trust. It's like saying to Christ: "I hear you, and I think I know what you are teaching me; however, my thoughts and feelings are leading me in another direction." We put our own human twist on the matter, and it weakens our faith in God's Word. We stagger and falter in His truth, unbelief. Then we make excuses with such traditional statements as, "It must be God's will.", or "It is what it is, can't do anything about it." which shows faith is not present. Excuses are merely another means of unbelief and will keep a person stagnant in their circumstance. When unbelief is present, it voids the power that comes through faith.

To identify how we fall into the trap of unbelief is to look at the human character. We slip out of our spirit person and listen to our soul, and consequently, we get out of sync with God's truth. When we are confronted with adversities such as a health crisis, or a financial matter, loss of employment, and so forth, our first reaction is fear. We look inward to ourself, "What am I going to do?" Fear immediately takes hold. Remember, fear is a negative emotion governed by the senses and is not a Fruit of the Spirit for our spirit-filled life.

Fear takes our thoughts in a direction away from God's Word. Fear grows until it is the only emotion we respond to, and we begin to question that His Word isn't going to hold true and present a solution. All the attention is focused on the negative circumstance rather than the power Christ has vested into each believer through faith. *For God hath not given us the spirit of fear, but of power, and of love, and of a sound mind.* 1 Timothy 1:7 We must hold strong and allow our faith to command over fear.

With fear, worry becomes the aura that surrounds and binds us in unbelief. Our problem is constantly in the forefront, for we think, talk, study, question, and dwell on the matter until we are in complete bondage to the negative situation. Loving and happy thoughts are a distant memory as we concentrate on our crisis. In the midst of the affliction, we gravitate to the negative instead of standing firm in faith. What became of our faith? It only requires the unwavering faith of a mustard seed, "Ye of so little faith."

In our hour of need, we become just like the disciples before Jesus. Our measure of faith is overridden by our unbelief, and we have nothing to combat and counter an illness, a monetary crisis, a disparaging emotional problem, or any other situation. We must be mature in wisdom of our Father's Word, so we may be secure in truth to handle events that arise. *For ye have not received the spirit of bondage again to fear; but ye have received the Spirit of adoption, whereby we cry, Abba, Father.* Romans 8:15 Give praise to the Lord for the gift of faith and hold to your faith with complete trust that God's Kingdom power will be effectual in your life.

An analogy in understanding how faith works would be as to the keys on a key ring. Most of us have several keys on a ring, but only the right one will unlock the door to our home. Likewise, only the correct key called Faith will unlock the door to the Father's Kingdom. *And I will give unto thee the keys of the kingdom of heaven: and whatsoever thou shalt bind on earth shall be bound in heaven: and whatsoever thou shalt loose on earth shall be loosed in heaven.* Matthew 16:19 Where our faith is will be what is reflected in the Kingdom of Heaven just as what is lost on earth by our lack of knowledge or directive will also be lost in the Kingdom. The connection that exists between the Kingdom and earth is based on our belief and faith. Whatever our need may be on earth, so is it understood in heaven; therefore, what we receive is by faith.

When Jesus taught His disciples, He explained the connection between heaven and earth, but because they were human and having not yet received the Holy Spirit it was difficult for them to comprehend His teachings. Though the men were eager to listen and accept His words, they still faltered with the understanding, for He spoke of things they had not heard of before and could not verify. Desperate as they were to believe and maintain faith, they often failed. Again, Christ would remind them of having so little faith and continue to teach them the lessons they needed to know before He left them.

It is no different today. The same lessons are being taught, but if we aren't listening with a discerning heart as we study the scriptures, we will be like the disciples stumbling in our faith. We must be absolute in our knowledge and strong to not waver.

Just as we are unable to measure mercy or grace, neither can we put a boundary on faith. These are spiritual gifts operating in the spirit realm of our Father's Kingdom. Faith is not a physical expression of our human senses. We attempt to evaluate faith and categorize it with an emotion by placing a natural application to it. Faith does not involve any emotional, or sensory mechanism. *Now faith is the substance of things hoped for, the evidence of things not seen.* Hebrews 11:1 Faith is what carries our trust in whatever we may ask of our Father as our belief remains intact and undiluted until the unseen, spiritual or supernatural, becomes the seen, natural or physical. If we have the understanding of how to reach the Kingdom, we can bring forth on earth heavenly power by our faith. *If ye shall ask anything in my name, I will do it.* John 14:14 Christ has given us authority on His name to call upon the Father with the key of faith.

It is not a complex matter. If our faith is not in direct alignment with God's Word, it will not gain us answered prayers, healing, and miracles. To move the mountain in our life, whatever it may be, we must maintain an unshakable faith that no matter what our senses tell us, or our eyes show us, we know the truth that comes only in trusting God's Word.

Perhaps you have prayed and wondered why you didn't receive an answer. You pray more diligently hoping an answer will soon be forthcoming, but when there is no manifestation you begin to question if God heard your plea, or is He merely not going to supply for your need? Neither is the case. God knows all, and He hears our petitions and provided the answer long before the time came that we would seek Him. God is not withholding, but we have not come before Him in absolute faith without unbelief.

Everyone needs God in their life, whether they are accepting of this realization or not; and not only for salvation, but for all the blessings, promises, and gifts He desires to bestow upon His faithful children. *And Jesus looking upon them saith, With men it is impossible, but not with God: for with God all things are possible.* Mark 10:27

Each person is responsible for a relationship with the Father. We have been given the authority in Christ and with the Holy Spirit to approach the Almighty King within His Kingdom. God established the trinity for man, for those who seek Him in truth with the gift of faith. Be a child of God and walk by faith, not by sight. It is for today and forever.

Always and forever, we give praise, thanksgiving, honor, and glory to our heavenly Father; Christ, the Son; and the Holy Ghost who are all God, for His *everlasting love.* Glory to God in the Kingdom of Heaven.

Amen and Amen!

Part IV

Spiritual Topics

And I will give unto thee the keys of the kingdom of heaven and whatsoever thou shalt bind on earth shall be bound in heaven: and whatsoever thou shalt loose on earth shall be loosed in heaven.

Matthew 16:19

The Power of Prayer

The Power of Prayer

And all things, whatsoever ye shall ask in prayer, believing, ye shall receive.

Matthew 21:22

We should consider our prayer before we speak, for there is an incorrect method of communicating with our heavenly Father. We pray in churches, synagogues, at weddings and funerals, and even at mealtime each in a group or congregational gathering. Some believe prayer is more powerful when performed among others. *And when thous prayest, thous shalt not be as the hypocrites are: for they love to pray standing in the synagogues and in the corners of the streets, that they may be seen of men.* Matthew 6:5 It can be comforting and beneficial to participate in joint worship; however, God requires we come to Him personally.

Prayer is a very intimate time with God, and He has given the Holy Spirit for our communion. The Holy Spirit is our intercessor and advocate before the Lord and presents our prayer. God hears our prayers, but the response we receive from the Kingdom is dependent upon the Holy Spirit. The Holy Spirit will render our prayer spiritually acceptable according to Kingdom laws, and the answer forthcoming is based on our unwavering faith and trust.

There is never a circumstance that God does not know about and has a provision in place for our need. *Be not ye therefore like unto them; for your Father knoweth what things ye have need of, before ye ask him.* Matthew 6:8 Do we truly understand the value of a prayer, and how important it is that our petitions are accurate to God's Word that we may receive an expected answer?

We refresh our knowledge of what God declares: *But when ye pray, use not vain repetitions, as the heathen do: for they think that they shall be heard for their much speaking.* Matthew 6:7 It is a common mistake to take certain biblical scriptures, memorize them and repeat often. This according to God is not praying, and He says beware of doing such. We have His example in the Lord's Prayer. It seems when we want to pray to our Father, we turn to this prayer and recite it verbatim. In doing so, we believe we have covered all the bases and prayed as God intended. The Lord's Prayer is given to teach what we are to take into account.

Simply reciting this prayer when convenient does not constitute praying. Let's break it down, so that we may understand what God is teaching. *Our Father which are in heaven, Hallowed be thy name, Thy kingdom come, Thy will be done in earth, as it is in heaven. Give us our daily bread. And forgive us our debts, as we forgive our debtors. And lead us not into temptation, but deliver us from evil: For thine is the kingdom, and the power, and the glory, for ever. Amen.* Matthew 6:9-13 God is telling us how to pray.

We begin our prayer acknowledging our Father with honor, praise, and thanksgiving. What God has established within His Kingdom for man can and should be accomplished on earth as He has met our every need. Give us our daily bread is His provision for our life that our faith and trust rest in Him. For God says we are not to be concerned for what we eat, wear, or where we live for He provides for His children. We ask forgiveness of our sins and as we know ourselves to be forgiven in Christ, we are to forgive others that do us harm. God tells us to turn our cheek the other way in forgiveness, and if harm persists, we are to walk away. *But I say unto you, That ye resist not evil: but whosoever shall smite thee on thy right cheek, turn to him the other also.* Matthew 5:39 Also, those that take from you, rather than fight for your possessions, give to them freely. *And unto him that smitten thee on the one cheek offer also the other; and him that taketh away thy cloak forbid not to take thy coat also.* Luke 6:29 We seek His guidance and ask for protection from the evil of this fallen world. Most importantly, we are to affirm that our faith is always in Him, His heavenly Kingdom, for it is forever.

Remember, whatever we may bring to God has already been provided for, so it is by faith we pray, for our benefit, not His. It is with obedience to His Word that our prayer releases in the Kingdom the resolution that we may receive on earth. The blessings will manifest into the natural, or physical realm, when we hold with conviction in belief with the faith of a mustard seed. Therefore, pray to the Father with thanksgiving, seek Him always, and rely only on Him for an effectual, fervent prayer avails much.

Prayer to the Father

Even unto them will I give in mine house and within my walls a place and a name better than of sons and of daughters: I will give them an everlasting name, that shall not be cut off.

Isaiah 56:5

Dear Father,

I come to you knowing my life is not as you meant for it to be, and I bear the responsibility of allowing worldly influences to dictate and dilute my thoughts, separating me from your presence and plan. I repent of my sins and transgressions and ask forgiveness for being unfaithful to you. Through my weakness, pride, and self-righteousness, I did not accept your Word, nor seek you for understanding and completion of who I am.

I present myself before you to be reborn into the spirit person you created me to be. I choose life with your Son, Christ, and accept the gift of the Holy Ghost. You gave your Son, Jesus, that I may have salvation, but I also receive His death at Calvary for my wellbeing, healed by His stripes.

I believe:

- You love me so much, you left your Kingdom and came to earth in Christ to claim me as your own; giving your Son to die for me.

- You have a plan for my life before I was in the womb, not yet born.

- Jesus has given me a rebirth in spirit fusing His Spirit to mine, and I am reunited to you, my Father. With the authority of Christ and the gift of the Holy Spirit, I am adopted and become your child, made a saint and heir in the Kingdom of Heaven.

- The Holy Spirit will teach me all things of the Kingdom, so that I may receive knowledge, understanding, wisdom, and discernment of your Word. He will be my intercessor, tutor, and advocate before you.

- Through the Holy Spirit, I may come before your throne in prayer and receive your heavenly gifts and power that I may live in honor and glory to you, my heavenly Father and Almighty King.

- As my Father, I know you will be there for me. I am forgiven and never forsaken, and your mercy and grace are always present.

- In faith, I will be obedient and hold the truth in your Word.

- I have everlasting life with you and your Son.

- I am your creation, held accountable to you, and one day I will live with you as my heavenly Father and King.

I know my prayers will be answered because your Word is a Living Word and responds to the Holy Spirit for the glory of your Kingdom. Thank you, Father, for loving me, forgiving me, and providing for my life. I praise, glorify, and give thanksgiving to you always. On the blood of your Son, Jesus, and through the Holy Spirit, I pray, Amen.

A Relationship with God

A Relationship with God

There is one body, and one Spirit, even as ye are called in one hope of your calling; One Lord, one faith, one baptism, One God and Father of all, who is above all, and through all, and in you all. But unto every one of us is given grace according to the measure of the gift of Christ.

Ephesians 4:4-7

There is an orderly manner to a relationship with God.

1. Be born-again - Become a child of God by accepting His Son, Jesus. Christ fuses His Spirit to your spirit giving you a rebirth into the Kingdom of Heaven.

2. Receive the Holy Spirit - God gives the gift of the Holy Spirit to those who are reborn in Christ for the Father.

3. Baptism of the Holy Spirit - Ask God to quicken the Holy Spirit. This is an important step for the Holy Ghost to be actively present in your life.

4. Feed the Spirit - Study God's Word which is nourishment to your spirit as the Holy Spirit interprets the Scriptures.

5. Fruit of the Spirit - Live with love, peace, joy, kindness, goodness, long suffering, temperance, faith, meekness, and gentleness in your heart.

6. Walk in Spirit - Your daily journey is that of a spirit-empowered person for you are a child of the King.

7. Led by the Spirit - The Spirit of Truth, the Holy Spirit, is your tutor, intercessor, and advocate to all things of the Kingdom. He will guide your life through faithfulness.

8. Live in the Spirit - Learn to live in the spirit realm and not be influenced by the world. It is living a daily life in complete surrender to God that you may fulfill your destiny for the glory of His Kingdom.

9. Spirit-Filled Person - Remain in obedient faithfulness to the principles of God's Kingdom. The authority of Christ and the Holy Spirit makes it possible to receive heavenly promises and power.

10. Speaking in Tongues - Speaking in tongues is the most intimate expression of faith when the Holy Spirit speaks directly to God in a heavenly language, unknown to man. It is not mandatory, but a priceless gift for the asking.

Gifts of the Trinity

Gifts of the Father

Gifts of the Son

Gifts of the Holy Ghost

Spirit Gifts

Now concerning spiritual gifts brethren, I would not have
you ignorant.

1 Corinthians 12:1

There are gifts from the holy trinity of God, the Father; Christ, the Son; and the Holy Ghost. The gifts of God are all encompassing and divided among Christ and the Holy Spirit. God's gifts are administrative in the function of His Kingdom. Christ's gifts are for the continuation of His ministry. Though He is no longer a physical presence on the earth, Christ lives within each believer, and we are to be disciples of His ministry. The gifts of the Holy Spirit are for interpretation of God's Word, so we may learn of the Kingdom, have a relationship with the Father, and do His will. With the ability to receive heavenly gifts and power through the Holy Spirit, we may live a spirit-filled life for the glory of God's Kingdom.

Now there are diversities of gifts, but the same Spirit. And
there are differences of administrations, but the same Lord.
And there are diversities of operations, but it is the same
God which worketh all in all.

1 Corinthians 12:4-6

Gifts of God - **Administration**

Apostles	Prophets
Teachers	Miracles
Healing	Helps
Governments	Diversities of Tongues

Now ye are the body of Christ, and members in particular. And God hath set some in the church, first apostles, secondarily prophets, thirdly teachers, after that miracles, then gifts of healings, helps, governments, diversities of tongues. Are all apostles? Are all prophets? are all teachers? are all workers of miracles? Have all the gifts of healing? do all speak with tongues? do all interpret? But covet earnestly the best gifts: and yet show I unto you a more excellent way.

1 Corinthians 12:27-31

God's gifts are established within His Kingdom and dispensed through the trinity of Christ and the Holy Ghost according to His purpose for man.

Gifts of Christ - **Ministry**

Apostles	Prophets
Evangelists	Pastors
Teachers	

Now that he ascended, what is it but that he also descended first into the lower parts of the earth? He that descended is the same also that ascended up far above all heavens, that he might fill all things. And he gave some, apostles; and some, prophets; and some, evangelists; and some, pastors and teachers; For the perfecting of the saints, for the work of the ministry, for the edifying of the body of Christ.

Ephesians 4:9-12

Christ's gifts are for the ministry of the Kingdom of Heaven. We have many individuals professing the gospel of Christ, but it should be noted that Jesus chooses who will be the true apostles of His ministry, for He knows their heart is pure with obedience to receiving and edifying His Word. Though, it should be stated that each faithful believer in truth to His Word and directed by the Spirit of Truth is a joint disciple of the gospel of Christ.

Gifts of the Holy Spirit - **Power**

Wisdom	Knowledge
Faith	Healing
Miracles	Prophecy
Discerning of Spirits	Speaking in Tongues
Interpretation of Tongues	

But the manifestation of the Spirit is given to every man to profit withal. For to one is given by the Spirit the word of

wisdom; to another the word of knowledge by the same Spirit;
To another faith by the same Spirit; to another the gifts of
healing by the same Spirit; To another the working of
miracles; to another prophecy; to another discerning of
spirits; to another divers kinds of tongues; to another the
interpretation of tongues: But all these worth that one
and the selfsame Spirit, dividing to every man severally as
he will.

1 Corinthians 12:7-11

Notice the Holy Spirit gives the most gifts. In the Holy Spirit, God has provided all that we will need in this lifetime. The Holy Spirit gives us our education in God's Word and teaches the principles of the Kingdom. He grants us the ability to interpret the truth from inaccurate teachings, helps in the appropriation of our faith that we may receive the Father's gifts and supernatural power, and that we edify God in the most intimate manner by speaking in a heavenly, spiritual language.

We can be given more than one gift, but we should understand that with the gifts also is the Holy Spirit providing the utterance of when to apply them. We are not presented a gift and left on our own merit because in reality we wouldn't use it properly. There would be the natural inclination to apply our personal perception and preference. Spiritual gifts are pure and holy requiring guidance to make them effectual. It is supernatural power, and we are the vessels it flows through.

Having then gifts differing according to the grace that is
given to us, whether prophecy, let us prophesy according
to the proportion of faith; Or ministry, let us wait on our

ministering: or he that teacheth, on teaching; Or he that exhorteth, on exhortation: he that giveth, let him do it with simplicity; he that ruleth, with diligence; he that showeth mercy, with cheerfulness.

Romans 12:6-8

It is noteworthy that the gifts are administered according to grace. Though we may ask for certain gifts, the Holy Spirit will determine if we are mature in faith with appropriate discernment to receive them.

The Covenants

Old Testament Covenant in Adam

New Testament Covenant in Christ

Covenants of God

Covenant with Adam

And the Lord said unto Moses, Thus thou shalt say unto the children of Israel, Ye have seen that I have talked with you from heaven.

Exodus 20:22

Though many covenants were established between God and His appointed people such as with Adam, Abraham, Moses, Noah, Jonah, David, Isaac, Jacob, and so forth, there are two primary covenants which were for the generations that existed before Christ as reflected in the Old Testament and after Christ in the New Testament. All covenants begin with Adam and end with Christ. Adam is the beginning of life for man (carnal), and Christ is the end of life for man (spirit).

God's first covenant to the people as a nation is the Ten Commandments written on a tablet of stone, a tangible document, and given to Moses to administer. The second covenant is through the blood of Jesus, and is written in the heart of each person reborn in Christ, a spiritual covenant. In Christ, the first covenant becomes old, replaced with the new one. Christ brings a better testament.

Under the first covenant when God removed His chosen people, the Israelites from bondage in Egypt, He came down from heaven in a cloud at Mount Sinai and spoke to them and commanded Moses to enforce His laws, statutes, and judgments. The Ten Commandments were considered the law and breaking them was a sin against God.

Ten Commandments

The Carnal Law

And God spake all these words, saying:

- I am the Lord thy God, which have brought thee out of the land of Egypt, out of the house of bondage. Thou shalt have no other gods before me.

- Thou shalt not make unto thee any graven image, or any likeness of any thing that is in heaven above, or that is in the earth beneath, or that is in the water under the earth.

- Thou shalt not take the name of the Lord thy God in vain; for the Lord will not hold him guiltless that taketh his name in vain.

- Remember the Sabbath day, to keep it holy.

- Honor thy father and thy mother: that thy days may be long upon the land which the Lord thy God giveth thee.

- Thou shalt not kill.

- Thou shalt not commit adultery.

- Thou shalt not steal.

- Thou shalt not bear false witness against thy neighbour.

- Thou shalt not covet thy neighbour's house, thou shalt not covet thy neighbour's wife, nor his manservant, nor his maidservant, nor his ox, nor his ass, nor any thing that is thy neighbour's.

Exodus 20:1-17

Covenant with Christ

For this is the covenant that I will make with the house of Israel after those days, saith the Lord; I will put my laws into their mind, and write them in their hearts: and I will be to them a God, and they shall be to me a people.

Hebrews 8:10

A new covenant, he hath made the first old. Now that which decayeth and waxeth old is ready to vanish away.

Hebrews 8:13

But now we are delivered from the law, that being dead wherein we were held; that we should serve in newness of spirit, and not in the oldness of the letter.

Romans 7:6

Generations pass, and God comes down from His Kingdom as Christ to give the people a new and better covenant. We have the Old Testament of how God dealt with the people. With the New Testament in Christ, we have a greater covenant and He spent three and one-half years teaching of God and His Kingdom. *For this is my blood of the new testament, which is shed for many for the remission of sins.* Matthew 26:28 We are no longer under the carnal laws, the Commandments, as the generations preceding Christ. As a believer and child of the Father, we live above the carnal laws in righteousness through Christ. However, to those who are not reborn in spirit, they remain under the carnal laws which defines their sins against them.

When we accept Christ, who took away the sins of the world, we are forgiven our sins and iniquities and given grace. We are spiritually reborn to live by the Fruit of the Spirit. *For then must he often have suffered since the foundation of the world: but now once in the end of the world hath he appeared to put away sin by the sacrifice of himself. And as it is appointed unto men once to die, but after this the judgment: So Christ was once offered to bear the sins of many; and unto them that look for him shall he appear the second time without sin unto salvation.* Hebrews 9:26-28 God's spiritual laws are written in the heart, not on stone. Our obedience is no longer to the letter of the law, but to faith.

By whom we have received grace and apostleship, for obedience to the faith among all nations, for his name.

Romans 1:5

144

Fruit of the Spirit

The Spirit Law

But the fruit of the Spirit is love, joy, peace, longsuffering, gentleness, goodness, faith, meekness, temperance: against such there is no law.

Galatians 5:22-23

Born into the Kingdom, sanctified and made holy in Christ for the Father, we are His children who live under the new covenant. As a child cleansed of sin and made righteous by the blood of Christ, we may experience the second covenant blessings. We live above the carnal laws with the Fruit of the Spirit in our heart. The law of the Spirit is what we proclaim and profess in our daily life.

Love   Joy
Peace   Longsuffering
Gentleness   Goodness
Faith   Meekness
Temperance

God's Seven Covenants

Between the first and last covenants, Adam to Christ, there are five additional covenants. God's creation is seven days and He established seven covenants that correlate with these days. Each covenant (contract) has a symbol (representation) and a seal (confirmation). As we know, seven days equates to seven thousand years. The first four covenants are of the Old Testament (four thousand years) and the last two covenants are of the New Testament (two thousand years). We are living in the last days of the sixth day of creation, or the six thousand years to be followed by the final one thousand year reign of Christ in the Kingdom of Peace.

These covenants are as follows:

1) ADAM

Symbol - Ground of the earth
Seal - The skin of the animals for a covering for Adam and Eve
Note: Man was made from the dust of the earth, and the flesh will return to dust of the earth.

2) NOAH

Symbol - Rainbow
Seal - Noah sacrifices one of every clean animal
Note: God promises to not judge man again with a flood of water.

3) ABRAHAM

Symbol - Stars
Seal - Circumcise of the foreskin of males; Changing Abram's name
to Abraham
Note: God tells Abraham for the number of stars in the sky, so will he
be the father of as many children.

4) MOSES

Symbol - Tablets of Stone (Ten Commandments)
Seal - Broken by Moses (rewritten)
Note: God met with the Israelites at Mount Sinai and gave the people
statutes, ordinances, judgments, and laws. God imposed a
covenant administered by Moses.

5) DAVID

Symbol - House of David (Israel)
Seal - The sacrifices on the alter in the temple (Jerusalem)
Note: King David's son, Solomon, (appointed by God) built a temple
to honor God. The temple is called Jerusalem, and the Israelites
brought their sacrifices to this alter to worship God.

6) MESSIAH

Symbol - Christ

Seal - Cup of wine and bread at the Last Supper, representative of the body and blood of Jesus

Note: Christ spoke to His disciples at the Last Supper and made a covenant using wine and bread as representation of His body broken for man. The covenant was He would send the Holy Spirit, empowering them (and generations thereafter) with wisdom to continue teaching His gospel.

7) PEACE

Symbol - Christ

Seal - The word Shalom (peace) split into two words in the Scriptures

Note: Christ returns for the saints and we live with Him, our King, in the Kingdom of Peace for one-thousand years before entering our final home, the New Jerusalem.

The Will of God

The Will of God

Jesus saith unto them, My meat is to do the will of him that sent me, and to finish his work.

John 4:34

God and the Living Word set forth at creation what will transpire both in the Kingdom of Heaven and on earth. The plan was established that a time would come and Christ would need to come to earth to save man. When Jesus came, He only did what the Father had preordained, not changing anything but rather fulfilling the plan. What Christ has lived in the flesh, so must man do also. As Jesus was persecuted for teaching of the Father, and the disciples for continuing His gospel, so shall the believers succumb to a tribulation period. As Christ was buried and resurrected, so shall the believers be brought forth to live in the spirit with new bodies.

Just as Jesus had a purpose in coming to earth, we also have been given a destiny of the Father to fulfill. Webster's dictionary defines destiny as to set apart for a particular use, purpose, design, or intent; to appoint or ordain beforehand. We have been preordained to be vessels with a preplanned role. One of the responsibilities in accepting Christ as our Lord and Savior is that we have become qualified to be a disciple, or steward for the Father. It isn't all about what God can do for us, but what we are required to do for God. *For it is God which worketh in you both to will and to do of his good pleasure.* Philippians 2:13 When we ask to learn of His plan for our life, and work diligently to achieve it, this is when God shows favor upon us. Not favoritism, but favor, blessings, equipping us with all the heavenly gifts we need to succeed.

Many today are so busy with life's struggles, we are not taking the time to be still and listen to what the Father wants to tell us. No thought is given to what God's plan is for our life while others do not know how to acquire it. Everything we do in life is a choice and requires a decision. Even not making a decision is making one; it is a decision to do nothing. Our choices set us on a path towards success, or failure. As a society, we monitor progress by worldly achievements; however, we should be measuring our accomplishments according to the Kingdom, for the rewards are of far greater value and everlasting. Things of this world are temporal.

Whether we use our time for helping others or our own gratification, a selfish life or a selfless one, we are subject to the results of our actions. At the end of the day, there is a tally for the twenty-four hours and we are accountable be it profitable for man, or productive to God. We will all have our turn before Christ on Judgment Day and give a report of our earthen works. Do we want to stand before our King and say our efforts were for self satisfaction, or address ourselves as good stewards of His ministry?

When we see the pieces of a puzzle spread across a table, it is daunting at first to think of putting it together. So much effort and time is spend finding the right piece to insert into the correct slot to have a finished scene. In many ways, our life is like a puzzle. Each day we orchestrate events, people, places, and the next day we do the same routine again. This goes on and the puzzle of life is never quite complete because of delays, obstructions, unexpected changes, and so forth. It is not important what we aim to accomplish for ourselves, but what are we doing for the Father's work? We are given a reasonable time on this planet and are to know that we are not here randomly. Therefore, it becomes important to learn of our purpose, or destiny, and desire to accomplish it for the glory of the Kingdom of God.

Are you waiting for God to reveal His plan for your life? Have you silenced the world around you and listened to what He is saying to you? Those who either ignore, or wait, may never know what the Father has planned for them. What we choose to do, to become, and how we conduct ourselves makes the fabric of our life. The key to achieving our destiny for God is to know that our duties are always in direct alignment with His Word, for the sole purpose that God is acknowledged and His Word is spread among the people.

Blood of Christ

Blood of Christ

For Christ also hath once suffered for sins, the just for the unjust, that he might bring us to God, being put to death in the flesh, but quickened by the Spirit.

1 Peter 3:18

Christ shed blood from seven areas of His body to release man from the curses placed by the first Adam. These wounds represent a purpose in the Kingdom that man may be redeemed for reconciliation with the Father.

1) GARDEN OF GETHSEMANE

In the Garden of Gethsemane on the night of the Last Supper before He was taken, Christ sweats blood through His pores when blood vessels break beneath the skin. Alone, He prayed in agony to the Father knowing what was to occur.

And being in an agony he prayed more earnestly: and his sweat was as it were great drops of blood falling down to the ground. Luke 22:44

2) WHIPPING POST

Jesus was scourged an unaccountable number at the whipping post for all manner of healing. Infirmities, whether physical or emotional, have been dealt with along with our sins and transgressions.

> *Who his own self bare our sins in his own body on the tree,*
> *that we, being dead to sins, should live unto righteousness:*
> *by whose stripes ye were healed.* 1 Peter 2:24

3) CROWN OF THORNS

He was taken to the chief priests and elders, and a crown of thorns was made and placed on His head to make a mockery of Jesus.

> *And when they had platted a crown of thorns, they put it upon*
> *his head, and a reed in his right hand: and they bowed the knee*
> *before him, and mocked him, saying, Hail, King of the Jews!*
> Matthew 27:29

4) NAILS IN THE HANDS

The palm of His hands bled from the nails that pierced His skin.

> *For dogs have compassed me: the assembly of the wicked*
> *have enclosed me: they pierced my hands and my feet.*
> Psalm 22:16

5) NAILS IN THE FEET

Blood dripped from His feet as they were nailed to the cross.

Behold my hands and my feet, that it is I myself: handle me, and see; for a spirit hath not flesh and bones, as ye see me have. And when he had thus spoken, he showed them his hands and his feet. Luke 24:39-40 (after Christ's resurrection)

6) SPEAR IN THE SIDE

Jesus was pierced in the side by a soldier's spear after He died.

But one of the soldiers with a spear pierced his side, and forthwith came there out blood and water. John 19:34

7) INTERNAL BLEEDING AND BRUISING

Blood bruises on the outside of His skin reflective of internal bleeding.

I have glorified thee on the earth: I have finished the work which thou gavest me to do. John 17:4

And when Jesus had cried with a loud voice, he said, Father, into thy hands I commend my spirit: and having said thus, he gave up the ghost. Luke 23:46

Glory to Almighty God, Most High!

Seven Final Words

of Jesus

Seven Final Words of Jesus on the Cross

As Jesus hung on the cross at Calvary, He spoke seven final statements before succumbing to His death. Notice the holy number, seven.

THE FIRST WORD

Then said Jesus, Father, *forgive them; for they know not what they do.* Luke 23:34

THE SECOND WORD

Jesus speaks to the man on the cross beside him. And he said to Jesus, Lord, remember me when thou comest into thy kingdom. And Jesus said unto him, *Verily, I say to unto thee, to day shalt thou be with me in paradise.* Luke 23:42-43

THE THIRD WORD

When Jesus therefore saw his mother, and the disciple standing by, whom he loved, he saith unto his mother, *Woman, behold thy son!* Then saith he to the disciple, *Behold thy mother!* And from that hour that disciple took her unto his home. John 19:26-27

THE FOURTH WORD

And about the ninth hour, Jesus cried with a loud voice, saying, *Eli, Eli, lama sabachthani?* That is to say, *My God, my God, why have you forsaken me?* Matthew 27:46; Mark 15:34

THE FIFTH WORD

Jesus cried out in a loud voice, *Father, into your hands I commend my spirit.* Luke 23:46

THE SIXTH WORD

After this, Jesus knowing that all things were now accomplished, that the scripture might be fulfilled, saith, *I thirst.* John 19:28

THE SEVENTH WORD

Now there was set a vessel full of vinegar: and they filled a sponge with vinegar, and put it upon hyssop, and put it to his mouth. When Jesus therefore received the vinegar, he said, *It is finished*: and he bowed his head, and gave up the ghost. John 19:29-30

The Trinity in Christ

The Trinity in Christ

In studying and understanding the Trinity of God, we witness the relevance of God's creation and all God fashioned at the foundation was defined in His Son, Jesus; the Living Word. *For by him were all things created, that are in heaven, and that are in earth, visible and invisible, whether they be thrones, or dominions, or principalities, or powers: all things were created by him, and for him: And he is before all things, and by him all things consist.* Colossians 1:16-17 We can see the trinity Through the nature, position, and works of Christ.

The Nature of Christ

CHIEF CORNERSTONE – Jesus is the cornerstone of the building which is His church. He cements together Jew and Gentile, male and female; all saints from all ages and places into one structure built on faith in Him which is shared by all. *And are built upon the foundation of the apostles and prophets, Jesus Christ himself being the **chief corner stone**; In whom all the building fitly framed together groweth unto an holy temple in the Lord.* Ephesians 2:20-21

FIRSTBORN OVER ALL CREATION – Not the first thing God created, but that Christ occupies the rank and preeminence of the firstborn over all things, that He sustains the most exalted rank in the universe. He is preeminent above all others; He is at the head of all things. *Who is the image of the invisible God, the **firstborn** of every creature: For by him were all things created, that are in heaven, and that are in earth, visible and invisible, whether they be thrones, or dominions, or principalities, or powers: all things were created by him, and for him: and he is before all things, and by all things consist.* Colossians 1:15-16

HEAD OF THE CHURCH – Jesus Christ, not a king or a pope, is the only supreme, sovereign ruler of the Church. *And hath put all things under his feet, and gave him to be the head over all things to the church, Which is his body, the fulness of him that filleth all in all.* Also, *For the husband is the head of the wife, even as Christ is the **head of the church**: and he is the saviour of the body.* Ephesians 1:22-23; 5:23

HOLY ONE – Christ is holy, both in His divine and human nature, and the fountain of holiness to His people. By His death, we are made holy and pure before God. *But ye denied the **Holy One** and the Just, and desired a murderer to be granted unto you; And killed the Prince of life, whom God hath raised from the dead; whereof we are witnesses.* Also, *For thou will not leave my soul in hell; neither wilt thou suffer thine **Holy One** to see corruption.* Acts 3:14; Psalm 16:10

JUDGE – The Lord Jesus was appointed by God to judge the world and to dispense the rewards of eternity. *And he commanded us to preach unto the people, and to testify that it is he which was ordained of God to be the **Judge** of quick and dead.* Also, *Henceforth there is laid up for me a crown of righteousness, which the Lord, the righteous **Judge**, shall give me at that day: and not to me only, but unto all them also that love his appearing.* And, *And hath given him authority to execute judgment also, because he is the Son of man; For the Lord is our **Judge**, the Lord is our* *lawgiver, the Lord is our king; he will save us.* Acts 10:42; 2 Timothy 4:8; John 5:27

KING OF KINGS AND LORD OF LORDS – Jesus is King and has dominion over all authority on the earth, over all kings and rulers of this world. *Which in his times he shall show, who is the blessed and only Potentate, the **King of kings, and Lord of lords**.* Also, *And he hath on his vesture and on his thigh a name written, **King of kings, and Lord of Lords**.* 1 Timothy 6:15; Revelation 19:16

LIGHT OF THE WORLD – Jesus came into a world darkened by sin and shed the light of life and truth through His work and His words. *Then spake Jesus unto them, saying, I am the **light of the world**: he that followeth me shall not walk in darkness, but shall have the light of life.* John 8:12

PRINCE OF PEACE – Jesus came to bring peace to the world and remove the sin that came between God and man. He died to reconcile sinners to a holy God. *For unto us a child is born, unto us a son is given: and the government shall be upon his shoulder: and his name shall be called Wonderful, Counsellor, The mighty God, The everlasting Father, **The Prince of Peace**.* Isaiah 9:6

SON OF GOD – Jesus is the only begotten of the Father and, therefore, is the Son of God. This is revealed throughout the New Testament. *And the angel answered and said unto her, The Holy Ghost shall come upon thee, and the power of the Highest shall overshadow thee: therefore also that holy thing shall be born of thee shall be called the **Son of God**.* Also, *For God so loved the world, that he gave his only begotten Son, that whosoever believeth in him should not perish, but have everlasting life; And we know that the **Son of God** is come, and hath given us an understanding, that we may know him that is true, and we are in him that is true, even in his Son Jesus Christ. This is the true God, and eternal life, Nathanael answered and saith unto him, Rabbi, thou art the **Son of God**;*

thou art the King of Israel. And, *And the Word was made flesh, and dwelt among us, (and we beheld his glory, the glory as of the only begotten of the Father), full of grace and truth.* Luke 1:35; John 3:16; John 1:14; 1:49; 1 John 5:20

SON OF MAN – Son of God and Son of Man are personages of Jesus Christ. Son of Man affirms the humanity of Christ in His divinity as the Son of God. It depicts His all encompassing authority of man. *For the Father hath life in himself; so hath he given to the Son to have life in himself; And hath given him authority to execute judgment also, because he is the **Son of man**.* John 5:27

WORD – The Word is the second person, Jesus Christ, of the trinity of God, who spoke all things out of nothing in the first creation, who was in the beginning with God the Father, and was God, and by whom all things were created. *In the beginning was the **Word**, and the **Word** was with God, and the **Word** was God. Also, For there are three that bear record in heaven, the Father, the **Word**, and the Holy Ghost: and these three are one. And there are three that bear witness in earth, the Spirit, and the water, and the blood: and these three agree in one.* John 1:1; 1 John 5:7-8

WORD OF GOD – This is the name given to Christ that is unknown to all but Himself. It denotes the mystery of His divine person. *His eyes were as a flame of fire, and on his head were many crowns; and he had a name written, that no man knew, but he himself. And he was clothed with a vesture dipped in blood: and his name is called The **Word of God**.* Revelation 19:12-13

WORD OF LIFE – Jesus not only spoke words that would give us eternal life, but He is the very words of life. *That which was from the beginning, which we have heard, which we have seen with our eyes, which we have looked upon, and our hands have handled, of the **Word of life**.* 1 John 1:1

ALPHA AND OMEGA – We know God and Christ to be as One in the trinity. God is Christ and Jesus is God. As One deity, they are the Alpha and Omega of all creation. *I am the **Alpha and Omega**, the beginning and the end, saith the Lord, which is, and which was, and which is to come, the Almighty.* Also, *I am the **Alpha and Omega**, the beginning and the end, the first and the last.* And, *And he said unto me, It is done. I am **Alpha and Omega**, the beginning and the end, I will give unto him that is athirst of the fountain of the water of life freely.* Revelation 1:8; 22:13; 21:6

EMMANUEL – God came to earth in the second person of the trinity, Christ, born of flesh to live among His people. *Behold, a virgin shall be with child, and shall bring forth a son, and they shall call his name **Emmanuel**, which being interpreted is, God with us.* Matthew 1:23

I AM – We can see the deity of God and Christ as One. Both God and Jesus declare to the people their omnipresence. *And God said unto Moses, **I am** that **I am**: and he said, Thus shalt thou say unto the children of Israel, **I am** hath sent me unto you.* Also, *Jesus said unto them, Verily, verily, I say unto you, Before Abraham was, **I am**.* Exodus 3:14; John 8:58

LORD OF ALL – Jesus is King over all things. The Father gave all creation to His Son. *The word which God sent unto the children of Israel, preaching peace by Jesus Christ (he is **Lord of all**:) That word, I say, ye know, which was published throughout all Judaea, and began from Galilee after the baptism which John preached; How God anointed Jesus of Nazareth with the Holy Ghost and with power: who went about doing good, and healing all that were oppressed of the devil; for God was with him.* Acts 10:36-38

TRUE GOD – God and Jesus are One Divinity, for God came to earth as Christ, and God is Jesus. In the personage of Christ, God reveals a part of His nature. *And we know that the Son of God is come, and hath given us an understanding, that we may know him that is true, and we are in him that is true, even in his Son Jesus Christ. This is the **true God**, and eternal life.* 1 John 5:20

Christ's Work on Earth

AUTHOR AND PERFECTER OF OUR FAITH – Eternal life is accomplished through the faith that is the gift of God, and Jesus is the founder of our faith and the finisher of it as well. From first to last, He is the source and sustainer of the faith that saves us. *Looking unto Jesus **the author and finisher of our faith**; who for the joy that was set before him endured the cross, despising the shame, and is set down at the right hand of the throne of God.* Also, *For by grace are ye saved through faith; and that not of yourselves: it is the gift of God. Not of works, lest any man should boast.* Hebrews 12:2; Ephesians 2:8-9

BREAD OF LIFE – Just as bread sustains life in the physical sense, Jesus is the bread that gives and sustains eternal life. God provided manna in the wilderness to feed His people, and He provided Jesus to give us eternal life through His body, broken for us. *And Jesus said unto them, I am the **bread of life,** he that cometh to me shall never hunger, and he that believeth on me shall never thirst.* Also, *I am the **bread of life.** Your fathers did eat manna in the wilderness, and are dead. This is the bread which cometh down from heaven, that a man may eat thereof, and not die. I am the living bread which came down from heaven: if any man eat of this bread, he shall live for ever: and the bread that I will give is my flesh, which I will give for the life of the world.* John 6:35; 6:48-51

BRIDEGROOM – Christ is the Bridegroom and the faithful saints are His bride. We are bound to Jesus in a covenant of grace that sets us apart as we wait for our bridegroom to come for us. *And Jesus said unto them, Can the children of the bride chamber mourn, as long as the **bridegroom** is with them? But the days will come, when the **bridegroom** shall be taken from them, and then shall they fast.* Also, *Then shall the kingdom of heaven be likened unto ten virgins, which took their lamps, and went to meet the **bridegroom**; And at midnight there was a cry made, Behold, the **bridegroom** cometh; go ye out to meet him.* Matthew 9:15; 25: 1; 25:6

DELIVERER – Just as the Israelites needed God to deliver them from bondage to Egypt, so Christ is our Deliverer from the bondage of sin. *And so all Israel shall be saved: as it is written, There shall come out of Sion the **Deliverer**, and shall turn away ungodliness from Jacob: For this is my covenant unto them, when I shall take away their sins.* Romans 11:26-27

GOOD SHEPHERD – A good shepherd is willing to risk his life to protect his sheep from predators. Jesus laid down His life for His sheep to gather us to Him in faith. He provides and protects us from worldly predators. *I am the **good shepherd**: for the **good shepherd** giveth his life for the sheep.* Also, *I am the **good shepherd**, and know my sheep, and am known of mine.* John 10:11; 10:14

HIGH PRIEST – The Jewish high priest entered the temple once a year to make atonement for the sins of the people. Jesus did this once for all at the cross. *Wherefore, holy brethren, partakers of the heavenly calling, consider the Apostle and **High Priest** of our profession, Christ Jesus.* Also, *Seeing then that we have a great **high priest**, that is passed into the heavens, Jesus the Son of God, let us hold fast our profession.* And, *For verily he took not on him the nature of angels; but he took on him the seed of Abraham. Wherefore in all things it behoved him to be made like unto his brethren, that he might be a merciful and faithful in things pertaining to God, to make a reconciliation for the sins of the people; Whither the forerunner is for us entered, even Jesus, made an **high priest** for ever after* *the order of Melchisedec.* Hebrews 3:1; 4:14; 2:16-17; 6:20

LAMB OF GOD – God's law called for the sacrifice of a spotless, unblemished lamb as an atonement for sin. Jesus became that lamb showing His patience in His sufferings and His readiness to die for His own. *The next day John seeth Jesus coming unto him, and saith, Behold the **Lamb of God**, which taketh away the sin of the world.* Also, *And looking upon Jesus as he walked, he saith, Behold the **Lamb of God**.* John 1:29; John 1:36

MEDIATOR – A mediator is one who goes between two parties to reconcile them. Christ is the one and only mediator who reconciles man to God. *For there is one God, and one **mediator** between God and men, the man Christ Jesus; Who gave himself a ransom for all to be testified in due time.* Also, *But now hath he obtained a more excellent ministry, by how much also he is the **mediator** of a better covenant, which was established upon better promises*; *For this cause he is the **mediator** of the new testament, that by means of death, for the redemption of the transgressions that were under the first testament, they which are called might receive the promises of eternal inheritance*; *And to Jesus the **mediator** of the new covenant, and to the blood of sprinkling, that speaketh better things than that of Abel.* 1 Timothy 2:5-6; Hebrews 8:8; 9:15; 12:24

ROCK – As life-giving water flowed from the rock Moses struck in the wilderness, Jesus is the Rock from which flows the living waters of eternal life. He is the Rock upon whom we build our spiritual house. *And did all drink the same spiritual drink: for they drank of that spiritual **Rock** that followed them: and that **Rock** is Christ.* 1 Corinthians 10:4

RESURRECTION AND LIFE – Jesus is the means to resurrect sinners to eternal life, just as He was resurrected from the grave. Our sin is buried with Him nailed at the cross, and we are resurrected to walk in newness of life. *Jesus said unto her, I am the **resurrection, and the life**: he that believeth in me, though he were dead, yet shall he live.* Also, *And with* *great power gave the apostles witness of the resurrection of the Lord Jesus: and great grace was upon them all.* John 11:25; Acts 4:33

SAVIOUR – Jesus is Lord and Saviour. He saved His people by dying to redeem them, by giving the Holy Spirit to renew them by His power, by enabling them to overcome their spiritual enemies, by sustaining them in tribulation and in death, and by raising them up at the last day. *And she shall bring forth a son, and thou shalt call his name Jesus: for he shall save his people from their sins.* Also, *For unto you is born this day in the city of David a **Saviour**, which is Christ the Lord.* And, *Thou shalt also suck the milk of the Gentiles, and shalt suck the breast of kings: and thou shalt know that I the Lord am thy **Saviour** and thy Redeemer, the mighty One of Jacob.* Matthew 1:21; Luke 2:11; Isaiah 60:16

TRUE VINE – Jesus is the true vine who supplies to the branches (believer). Our life is in Christ, and He furnishes all we need in this lifetime and our new eternal life. *I am the **true vine**, and my Father is the husbandman.* John 15:1

WAY, TRUTH, LIFE – Jesus is our mediator and only pathway to the Father. There is no other means of securing a relationship with God and obtaining eternal life with the Father and His Son, but by Christ. *Jesus saith unto him, I am **the way, the truth, and the life**: no man cometh unto the Father, but by me.* John 14:6

Names and Titles

of Jesus

Names and Titles of Jesus Christ

There are over two hundred names and titles in the Bible for Jesus Christ. The specific names given to Christ, and the numerous titles he held depicts that everything God created was by and for the Living Word, Christ. Throughout the generations spanning six thousand years from the Book of Genesis to the final book of Revelation, the language and teachings are a reflection of the life of Christ. It has always been about the Son of God when He was spoken of as "a shadow of things to come" in the Old Testament to His time on earth taught in the New Testament, and soon Christ will return again for a final appearance.

ADAM: And so it is written, The first man **Adam** was made a living soul; the last **Adam** was made a quickening spirit. 1 Corinthians 15:45

ADVOCATE: My little children, these things write I unto you, that ye sin not. And if any man sin, we have an **advocate** with the Father, Jesus Christ the righteous. 1 John 2:1

ALMIGHTY: I am Alpha and Omega, the beginning and the ending, saith the Lord, which is, and which was, and which is to come, the **Almighty**. Revelation 1:8

ALPHA AND OMEGA: I am **Alpha** and **Omega**, the beginning and the ending, saith the Lord, which is, and which was, and which is to come, the Almighty. Revelation 1:8

AMEN: And unto the angel of the church of the Laodiceans write; These things saith the **Amen**, the faithful and true witness, the beginning of the creation of God. Revelation 3:14

APOSTLE OF OUR PROFESSION: Wherefore, holy brethren, partakers of the heavenly calling, consider the **Apostle** and High Priest **of our profession**, Christ Jesus. Hebrews 3:1

ARM OF THE LORD: Awake, awake, put on strength, O **arm of the Lord**; awake, as in the ancient days, in the generations of old. Art thou not it that hath cut Rahab, and wounded the dragon? Who hath believed our report? And to whom is the arm of the Lord revealed? Isaiah 53:1; and Isaiah 51: 9

AUTHOR AND FINISHER OF OUR FAITH: Looking unto Jesus **the author and finisher of our faith**; who for the joy that was set before him endured the cross, despising the shame, and is set down at the right hand of the throne of God. Hebrews 12:2

AUTHOR OF ETERNAL SALVATION: And being made perfect, he became the **author of eternal salvation** unto all them that obey him. Hebrews 5:9

BEGINNING OF CREATION OF GOD: And unto the angel of the church of the Laodiceans write; These things saith the Amen, the faithful and true witness, the **beginning of the creation of God**. Revelation 3:14

BELOVED SON: Behold my servant, whom I have chosen; my **beloved**, in whom my soul is well pleased: I will put my spirit upon him, and he shall show judgment to the Gentiles. Matthew 12:18

BLESSED AND ONLY POTENTATE: Which in his times he shall show, who is the **blessed and only Potentate**, the King of kings, and Lord of lords. 1 Timothy 6:15

BRANCH: In that day shall the **branch** of the Lord be beautiful and glorious, and the fruit of the earth shall be excellent and comely for them that are escaped of Israel. Isaiah 4:2

BREAD OF LIFE FROM HEAVEN: Then Jesus said unto them, Verily, verily, I say unto you, Moses gave you not that **bread from heaven**; but my Father giveth you the true **bread from heaven**. John 6:32

CAPTAIN OF SALVATION: For it became him, for whom are all things, and by whom are all things, in bringing many sons unto glory, to make the **captain of their salvation** perfect through sufferings. Hebrews 2:10

CHIEF SHEPHERD: And when the **chief Shepherd** shall appear, ye shall receive a crown of glory that fadeth not away. 1 Peter 5:4

CHRIST OF GOD: He said unto them, But whom say ye that I am? Peter answering said, The **Christ of God**. Luke 9:20

CONSOLATION OF ISRAEL: And, behold, there was a man in Jerusalem, whose name was Simeon; and the same man was just and devout, waiting for the **consolation of Israel**: and the Holy Ghost was upon him. Luke 2:25

CHIEF CORNERSTONE: The stone which the builders refused is become the head stone of the corner. And are built upon the foundation of the apostles and prophets, Jesus Christ himself being the **chief corner stone**; In who all the building fitly framed together groweth unto a holy temple in the Lord. Psalm 118:22; Ephesians 2:20-21

COUNSELLOR: For unto us a child is born, unto us a son is given: and the government shall be upon his shoulder: and his name shall be called Wonderful, **Counsellor**, The Mighty God, The Everlasting Father, The Prince of Peace. Isaiah 9:6

CREATOR: All things were made by him; and without him was not any thing made that was made. Who is the image of the invisible God, the firstborn of every creature: For by him were all things **created**, that are in heaven, and that are in earth, visible and invisible, whether they be thrones, or dominions, or principalities, or powers: all things were **created** by him, and for him: and he is before all things, and by all things consist. Colossians 1:15-16; John 1:3

DAYSPRING: Through the tender mercy of our God; whereby the **dayspring** from on high hath visited us. Luke 1:78

DELIVERER: And so all Israel shall be saved: as it is written, There shall come out of Sion the **Deliverer**, and shall turn away ungodliness from Jacob. Romans 11:26

DESIRE OF THE NATIONS: And I will shake all nations, and the **desire of all nations** shall come: and I will fill this house with glory, saith the Lord of hosts. Haggai 2:7

DOOR: Then said Jesus unto them again, Verily, verily, I say unto you, I am the **door** of the sheep. John 10:7

ELECT OF GOD: Behold my servant, whom I uphold; **mine elect**, in whom my soul delighteth; I have put my spirit upon him: he shall bring forth judgment to the Gentiles. Isaiah 42:1

EVERLASTING FATHER: For unto us a child is born, unto us a son is given: and the government shall be upon his shoulder: and his name shall be called Wonderful, Counsellor, The Mighty God, The **Everlasting Father**, The Prince of Peace. Isaiah 9:6

FAITHFUL WITNESS: And from Jesus Christ, who is the **faithful witness**, and the first begotten of the dead, and the prince of the kings of the earth. Unto him that loved us, and washed us from our sins in his own blood. Revelation 1:5

FIRST AND LAST: And when I saw him, I fell at his feet as dead. And he laid his right hand upon me, saying unto me, Fear not; I am the **first and the last**. Revelation 1:17

FIRST BEGOTTEN: And from Jesus Christ, who is the faithful witness, and the **first begotten** of the dead, and the prince of the kings of the earth. Unto him that loved us, and washed us from our sins in his own blood. Revelation 1:5

FORERUNNER: Whither the **forerunner** is for us entered, even Jesus, made an high priest forever after the order of Melchisedec. Hebrews 6:20

GLORY OF THE LORD: And the **glory of the Lord** shall be revealed, and all flesh shall see it together: for the mouth of the Lord hath spoken it. Isaiah 40:5

GOD: The voice of him that crieth in the wilderness, Prepare ye the way of the Lord, make straight in the desert a highway for our **God**. Isaiah 40:3

GOD BLESSED: Whose are the fathers, and of whom as concerning the flesh Christ came, who is over all, **God blessed** forever. Amen. Romans 9:5

GOOD SHEPHERD: I am the **good shepherd**: the **good shepherd** giveth his life for the sheep. John 10:11

GOVERNOR: And thou Bethlehem, in the land of Juda, art not the least among the princes of Juda: for out of thee shall come a **Governor**, that shall rule my people Israel. Matthew 2:6

GREAT HIGH PRIEST: Seeing then that we have a **great high priest**, that is passed into the heavens, Jesus the Son of God, let us hold fast our profession. Hebrews 4:14

HEAD OF THE CHURCH: And hath put all things under his feet, and gave him to be the **head over all things to the church**. Ephesians 1:22

HEIR OF ALL THINGS: Hath in these last days spoken unto us by his Son, whom he hath appointed **heir of all things**, by whom also he made the worlds. Hebrews 1:2

HOLY CHILD: For of a truth against thy **holy child** Jesus, whom thou hast anointed, both Herod, and Pontius Pilate, with the Gentiles, and the people of Israel, were gathered together. Acts 4:27

HOLY ONE: But ye denied the **Holy One** and the Just, and desired a murderer to be granted unto you. Acts 3:14

HOLY ONE OF GOD: Saying, Let us alone; what have we to do with thee, thou Jesus of Nazareth? Art thou come to destroy us? I know thee who thou art, the **Holy One of God**. Mark 1:24

HOLY ONE OF ISRAEL: Fear not, thou worm Jacob, and ye men of Israel; I will help thee, saith the Lord, and thy redeemer, the **Holy One of Israel**. Isaiah 41:14

HORN OF SALVATION: And hath raised up an **horn of salvation** for us in the house of his servant David. Luke 1:69

I AM: Jesus said unto them, Verily, verily, I say unto you, Before Abraham was, **I am**. John 8:58

IMAGE OF GOD: In whom the god of this world hath blinded the minds of them which believe not, lest the light of the glorious gospel of Christ, who is the **image of God**, should shine unto them. 2 Corinthians 4:4

IMMANUEL: Therefore the Lord himself shall give you a sign; Behold, a virgin shall conceive, and bear a son, and shall call his name **Immanuel**. Isaiah 7:14

JEHOVAH: Trust ye in the Lord for ever: for in the Lord **Jehovah** is everlasting strength. Isaiah 26:4

JESUS: And she shall bring forth a son, and thou shalt call his name **Jesus** for he shall save his people from their sins. Matthew 1:21

JESUS OF NAZARETH: And the multitude said, This is **Jesus** the prophet **of Nazareth** of Galilee. Matthew 21:11

JUDGE OF ISRAEL: Now gather thyself in troops, O daughter of troops: he hath laid siege against us: they shall smite the **judge of Israel** with a rod upon the cheek. Micah 5:1

THE JUST ONE: Which of the prophets have not your fathers persecuted? And they have slain them which showed before of the coming of the **Just One**; of whom ye have been now the betrayers and murderers. Acts 7: 52

KING: Rejoice greatly, O daughter of Zion; shout, O daughter of Jerusalem: behold, thy **King** cometh unto thee: he is just, and having salvation; lowly, and riding upon an ass, and upon a colt the foal of an ass. Zechariah 9:9

KING OF THE AGES: Now unto the **King eternal**, immortal, invisible, the only wise God, be honour and glory for ever and ever. Amen. 1 Timothy 1:17

KING OF THE JEWS: Saying, Where is he that is born **King of the Jews**? For we have seen his star in the east, and are come to worship him. Matthew 2:2

KING OF KINGS: Which in his times he shall show, who is the blessed and only Potentate, the **King of kings**, and Lord of lords. 1 Timothy 6:15

KING OF SAINTS: And they sing the song of Moses the servant of God, and the song of the Lamb, saying, Great and marvelous are thy works, Lord God Almighty; just and true are thy ways, thou **King of saints**. Revelation 15:3

LAWGIVER: For the Lord is our judge, the Lord is our **lawgiver**, the Lord is our king; he will save us. Isaiah 33:22

LAMB: And all that dwell upon the earth shall worship him, whose names are not written in the book of life of the **Lamb** slain from the foundation of the world. Revelation 13:8

LAMB OF GOD: The next day John seeth Jesus coming unto him, and saith, Behold the **Lamb of God**, which taketh away the sin of the world. John 1:29

LEADER AND COMMANDER: Behold, I have given him for a witness to the people, a **leader and commander** to the people. Isaiah 55:4

THE LIFE: Jesus saith unto him, I am the way, the truth, and **the life**: no man cometh unto the Father, but by me. John 14:6

LIGHT OF THE WORLD: Then spake Jesus again unto them, saying, I am the **light of the world**: he that followeth me shall not walk in darkness, but shall have the light of life. John 8:12

LION OF THE TRIBE OF JUDAH: And one of the elders saith unto me, Weep not: behold, the **Lion of the tribe of Juda**, the Root of David, hath prevailed to open the book, and to loose the seven seals thereof. Revelation 5:5

LORD OF ALL: The word which God sent unto the children of Israel, preaching peace by Jesus Christ: (he is **Lord of all**). Acts 10:36

LORD OF GLORY: Which none of the princes of this world knew: for had they known it, they would not have crucified the **Lord of glory**. 1 Corinthians 2:8

LORD OF LORDS: Which in his times he shall show, who is the blessed and only Potentate, the King of kings, and **Lord of lords**. 1 Timothy 6:15

LORD OF OUR RIGHTEOUSNESS: In this days Judah shall be saved, and Israel shall dwell safely: and this is his name whereby he shall be called, The **Lord our Righteousness**. Jeremiah 23:6

MAN OF SORROWS: He is despised and rejected of men; a **man of sorrows**, and acquainted with grief: and we hid as it were our faces from him; he was despised, and we esteemed him not. Isaiah 53:3

MEDIATOR: For there is one God, and one **mediator** between God and men, the man Christ Jesus. 1 Timothy 2:5

MESSENGER OF THE COVENANT: Behold, I will send my messenger, and he shall prepare the way before me: and the Lord, whom ye seek, shall suddenly come to his temple, even the **messenger of the covenant**, whom ye delight in: behold, he shall come, saith the Lord of hosts. Malachi 3:1

MESSIAH: Know therefore and understand, that from the going forth of the commandment to restore and to build Jerusalem unto the **Messiah** the Prince shall be seven weeks, and threescore and two weeks: the street shall be built again, and the wall, even in troublous times. Daniel 9:26 He first findeth his own brother Simon, and saith unto him, We have found the **Messiah**, which is, being interpreted, the Christ. John 1:41

MIGHTY GOD: For unto us a child is born, unto us a son is given: and the government shall be upon his shoulder: and his name shall be called Wonderful, Counsellor, The **Mighty God**, The Everlasting Father, The Prince of Peace. Isaiah 9:6

MIGHTY ONE: Thou shalt also suck the milk of the Gentiles, and shalt suck the breast of kings: and thou shalt know that I the Lord am thy Saviour and thy Redeemer, the **mighty One** of Jacob. Isaiah 60:16

MORNING STAR: I Jesus have sent mine angel to testify unto you these things in the churches. I am the root and the offspring of David, and the bright and **morning star**. Revelation 22:16

NAZARENE: And he came and dwelt in a city called **Nazareth**: that it might be fulfilled which was spoken by the prophets, He shall be called a **Nazarene**. Matthew 2:23

ONLY BEGOTTEN SON: No man hath seen God at any time; the **only**

begotten Son, which is in the bosom of the Father, he hath declared him. John 1:18

OUR PASSOVER: Purge out therefore the old leaven, that ye may be a new lump, as ye are unleavened. For even Christ **our passover** is sacrificed for us. 1 Corinthians 5:7

PRINCE OF LIFE: And killed the **Prince of life**, whom God hath raised from the dead; whereof we are witnesses. Acts 3:15

PRINCE OF KINGS: And from Jesus Christ, who is the faithful witness, and the first begotten of the dead, and the **prince of the kings** of the earth. Unto him that loved us, and washed us from our sins in his own blood. Revelation 1:5

PRINCE OF PEACE: For unto us a child is born, unto us a son is given: and the government shall be upon his shoulder: and his name shall be called Wonderful, Counsellor, The Mighty God, The Everlasting Father, The **Prince of Peace**. Isaiah 9:6

PROPHET: And he said unto them, What things? And they said unto him, Concerning Jesus of Nazareth, which was a **prophet** mighty in deed and word before God and all the people. For Moses truly said unto the fathers, A **prophet** shall the Lord your God raise up unto you of your brethren, like unto me; him shall ye hear in all things whatsoever he shall say unto you. Acts 3:22; Luke 24:19

REDEEMER: For I know that my **redeemer** liveth, and that he shall stand at the latter day upon the earth. Job 19:25

RESURRECTION AND LIFE: Jesus said unto her, I am the **resurrection and the life**: he that believeth in me, though he were dead, yet shall he live. John 11:25

ROCK: And did all drink the same spiritual drink: for they drank of that spiritual **Rock** that followed them: and that **Rock** was Christ.1 Corinthians 10:4

ROOT OF DAVID: I Jesus have sent mine angel to testify unto you these things in the churches. I am the **root** and the offspring **of David**, and the bright and morning star. Revelation 22:16

ROSE OF SHARON: I am the **rose of Sharon**, and the lily of the valleys. Solomon 2:1

SAVIOUR: For unto you is born this day in the city of David a **Saviour**, which is Christ the Lord. Luke 2:1

SEED OF WOMAN: And I will put enmity between thee and the woman, and between thy seed and **her seed**; it shall bruise thy head, and thou shalt bruise his heel. Genesis 3:15

SHEPHERD AND BISHOP OF SOULS: For ye were as sheep going astray; but are now returned unto the **Shepherd and Bishop of your souls**. 1 Peter 2:25

SHILOH: The scepter shall not depart from Judah, nor a lawgiver from between his feet, until **Shiloh** come; and unto him shall the gathering of the people be. Genesis 49:10

SON OF THE BLESSED: But he held his peace, and answered nothing. Again the high priest asked him, and said unto him, Art thou the Christ, the **Son of the Blessed**? Mark 14:61

SON OF DAVID: The book of the generation of Jesus Christ, the **son of David**, the son of Abraham. Matthew 1:1

SON OF GOD: And was there until the death of Herod: that it might be fulfilled which was spoken of the Lord by prophet, saying, Out of Egypt have I called **my son**. Matthew 2:15

SON OF THE HIGHEST: He shall be great, and shall be called the **Son of the Highest**: and the Lord God shall give unto him the throne of his father David. Luke 1:32

SUN OF RIGHTEOUSNESS: But unto you that fear my name shall the **Sun of Righteousness** arise with healing in his wings; and ye shall go forth, and grow up as calves of the stall. Malachi 4:2

TRUE LIGHT: That was the **true Light**, which lighteth every man that cometh into the world. John 1:9

TRUE VINE: I am the **true vine**, and my Father is the husbandman. John 15:1

TRUTH: And the Word was made flesh, and dwelt among us, (and we beheld his glory, the glory as of the only begotten of the Father,) full of grace and **truth**. John 1:14

WITNESS: Behold, I have given him for a **witness** to the people, a leader and commander to the people. Isaiah 55:4

WORD: In the beginning was the **Word**, and the **Word** was with God, and the **Word** was God. John 1:1

WORD OF GOD: And he was clothed with a vesture dipped in blood: and his name is called The **Word of God**. Revelation 19:13

Afflictions Upon Man

Afflictions Upon Man

*But let none of you suffer as a murderer, or as a thief, or
as an evildoer, or as a busybody in other men's matters.*

1 Peter 4:15

Bless them which persecute you: bless, and curse not.

Romans 12:14

The mere definition of affliction denotes a matter of distress, misery, or
grief. A symbolic word more commonly misunderstood is the word,
curses. Man causes many forms of afflictions upon himself, loved ones,
friends, and strangers; individually, or as a society. The world events attest
to this destruction. The cultural atmosphere has digressed into an ungodly
state, and we are constantly under attack on a personal level as well as a
national one. Whether we call it an affliction or a curse, someone has to
initiate and inflict it.

There is a cause and effect ratio to everything in life, for it is an aspect
of the balancing system. Curses have a negative affect and impact our
lives, and we should be armored in God's Word to counter the attack.
*Finally, my brethren, be strong in the Lord, and in the power of his might.
Put on the whole armor of God, that ye may be able to stand against the
wiles of the devil. For we wrestle not against flesh and blood, but against*

principalities, against powers, against the rulers of the darkness of this world, against spiritual wickedness in high places. Wherefore take unto you the whole armor of God that ye may be able to withstand in the evil day, and having done all, to stand. Ephesians 6:10-13 Though God is telling us how to be prepared for spiritual warfare, His instructions also apply in the natural, or physical world. God gives us the arsenal to use in any battlefield. An invaluable strategy of being prepared is understanding your opponent.

These attacks come in the spoken word and can lay a heavy assault on the recipient. We have an innate ability to bring forth afflictions by not guarding our tongue. It is human nature to be influenced by the words told to us, over us, or about us. Often we accept derogatory comments as the truth, because they are spoken by people we know and care about which we believe warrants their comments. Unless we are polished with knowledge and understand how curses wreak havoc in our life, they go unchecked. The statements are never countered and nullified, destroying the curse before it takes root. *Let no corrupt communication proceed out of your mouth, but that which is good to the use of edifying, that it may minister grace unto the hearers.* Ephesians 4:29

When we think of a curse, the first thought may be the use of profanity, harsh verbiage, or something far more demonic. There is the individual who belts out comments whether slated in humor, or a deliberate act, to purposefully cause emotional injury to the recipient. This can be the most dangerous because often the person has grown accustomed to the assault and declines to retaliate, thus, breaking the curse. They become immune to the offense, especially if it occurs often, but the damage remains.

In reality, it sticks with them and does emotional, psychological, and eventually physiological harm. This is tampering with the spirit and soul of the person, a definite sin. Just because someone is unprepared to fight back, or block the curse, it is spiritually unlawful to place harm on another whether orally, or physically.

We should not let our guard down in warfare. What appears on the surface to be a battle among ourselves, never underestimate that the underlying current is of a spiritual nature. If you believe a curse has a stronghold on your life, or those you love, rebuke the words spoken. Curses do affect our lives whether we believe it, or not.

> *But I say unto you, Love your enemies, bless them that curse you do good to them that hate you, and pray for them which despitefully use you, and persecute you.*

Matthew 5:44

MAN - When a person speaks unfavorably, or negatively over someone whom they have a responsibility or authoritative jurisdiction, the individual can place a curse when using negative comments. For example, a parent to a child, or child to an elderly parent, employer to an employee, and so forth. A parent can easily bring a curse upon their children with the very words they speak over, to, and about them with such comments as, "He's always sick.", or "She isn't my brightest child." Confrontations with family, friends, and colleagues can release accusations whereby the words spoken may have negative connotation, or implications. There is power, be it for good or harm, in the spoken language.

> *For God commanded, saying, Honour thy father and mother: and, He that curseth father or mother, let him die the death.*

Matthew 15:4

SELF-INFLICTED - What are we saying about ourselves? If we are speaking negatively about our body, or state of being, then we are placing a curse on our life. For example, "I'm just not smart enough.", or "I guess

I was meant to be a fat person, I can't seem to lose the weight." Such statements hold us in bondage to the very words we speak which can be a reason for not succeeding in our endeavors. Making derogatory comments opposes the Kingdom. As a child of the Father, our body is a temple. We belong to God and in speaking ill-favorably of ourselves, it is an assault to Him.

> *What? know ye not that your body is the temple of the Holy Ghost which is in you, which ye have of God, and ye are not your own?*

1 Corinthians 6:19

SOWING AND REAPING - What we do is what we get, figuratively and literally. Doing bad things reaps hardship in our future, and equally so, doing good deeds according to God's Word will supply benefits and blessings hundredfold. What we do in this lifetime does make a difference now and forever.

> *And he that reapeth receiveth wages, and gathereth fruit unto life eternal: that both he that soweth and he that reapeth may rejoice together.*

John 4:36

PROPHETS - Refrain from speaking unkindly of the individuals who are in truth to the Spirit of Truth because in doing so we are speaking against the trinity of God: the Father, the Son, and the Holy Ghost. It becomes blasphemy against the Kingdom of Heaven and is against Christ's chosen people for His ministry.

He suffered no man to do them wrong: yea, he reproved kings for their sakes, Saying; Touch not mine anointed, and do my prophets no harm.

Psalm 105:14-15

THE ACCUSED - Being around someone who is cursed can bring that curse upon ourselves; however, let's qualify this statement. This is not referring to a curse rubbing off on us if we get to close to someone who is afflicted, but rather if we are not strong in our knowledge of Kingdom principles and hold firm to deflect the enemy, we can have their curse applied to us and not be aware of what is transpiring. This is easily performed in our communications when we accept derogatory words spoken about someone, and jump right in and start believing and conversing over the matter and take on the same mindset, spreading the negative.

Follow peace with all men, and holiness, without which no man shall see the Lord: Looking diligently lest any man fail of the grace of God; lest any root of bitterness springing up troubled you, and thereby many be defiled.

Hebrews 12:14-15

INHERITANCE - Curses that carry down through generations in a family and are unbeknown to the members. We curse ourselves and others by making such statements as, "My grandmother had it, my mother has it, and I guess I was next in line to get it." Another generational curse is spreading negativity with such words as, "He isn't going to amount to anything." Statements such as these are destroying families.

*To open their eyes, and to turn them from darkness to light,
and from the power of Satan unto God, that they may receive
forgiveness of sins, and inheritance among them which are
sanctified by the faith that is in me.*

Acts 26:18

UNFORGIVING - When we choose to live in bitterness without forgiveness towards someone, it makes us an accuser. It is a command of God that we forgive those who trespass against us, for whatever the reason. If we cannot forgive others, our Father will not forgive us. Forgiveness is mandatory in the Kingdom of Heaven.

*Then came Peter to him, and said, Lord, how oft shall my
brother sin against me, and I forgive him? till seven times?
Jesus saith unto him, I say not unto thee, until seven times:
but, until seventy times seven.*

Matthew 18:21-22

THE LAW - When the laws of the Kingdom are broken, it makes us vulnerable for Satan to gain entrance into our life. Satan's only inroad is when we are unfaithful to God's Word. We must repent and get back into the grace of God.

For I delight in the law of God after the inward man.

Romans 7:22

*And knowest his will, and approvest the things that are more
excellent, being instructed out of the law.*

Romans 2:18

I thank God through Jesus Christ our Lord. So then with the mind I myself serve the law of God; but with the flesh the law of sin.

Romans 7:25

For the law of the Spirit of life in Christ Jesus hath made me free from the law of sin and death.

Romans 8:2

DEMONIC - As faithful children of God under the hedge of protection within the Kingdom, Satan cannot reach us. It is through our thoughts that he deceives, so we must guard our mind; rebuke and repent anything that is not in truth to the Father's Word. The mind is the only means by which we can falter and come under attack of the enemy. If we do, Satan uses his deceitful wiles against us for the sole purpose of destruction, for the finality of death.

> *The thief cometh not, but for to steal, and to kill, and to destroy: I am come that they might have life, and that they might have it more abundantly.*

John 10:10

And there shall be no more curse: but the throne of God and of the Lamb shall be in it; and his servants shall serve him.

Revelation 22:3

The Unmistakable Mistake

The Unmistakable Mistake

Trust in the Lord with all thine heart; and lean not unto thine own understanding.

Proverbs 3:5

The **number one mistake** believers make is not trusting God. We think we do, but the reality of our life tells a different story. The presence of God can be witnessed in the lives of those who seek Him in truth and trust. God is a viable force, an Almighty power that is unshakable and all encompassing. His power will always shine through wherever there is His truth.

The **number one prayer** we call upon our heavenly Father is for healing. Everyone on this planet will have need of God's healing power. Presently, it may be for ourselves, our children, our parents, a family member, or a friend to be healed of a disease, illness, or ailment whether physical or emotional. We are imperfect human beings living in an imperfect world; therefore, we require God's supernatural power.

The **number one reason** for not receiving answered prayers is lack of God's Word. The truth will set you free. Wisdom, knowledge, and understanding in the truth of God's Word will free us from bondage. Many are not hearing from God because of insufficient or inaccurate information of Him and His Kingdom.

As Christians, we think we are accurate in our belief; however, when we put our faith to the test it doesn't get it done. Why is that? The answer is we are misinformed. If we adhere to a belief that is not precise to God's Word, the Holy Spirit who is the Spirit of Truth and is within us is restricted to responding to our pleas. The Holy Spirit responds only to the absolute truth in God's Word. After all, the Holy Spirit is God, and God will not go against the laws He established. If our truth is not His truth, we deal with the consequences which is unanswered prayers.

An analogy is likened to our physical body. We must have air, water, and food to survive. We can put good nutritional food in our body, or we can give it junk food. Whether it be fruits and vegetables, or cakes and pies, it is all considered food and the body accepts it as such. However, the body knows instinctively on a cellular level what it requires to maintain optimum health and knows when it is receiving it; likewise, it will falter in health if it doesn't get the expectant nutrients.

In the spirit realm, our spirit requires a diet of God's Word. If we are feeding it a false gospel, even a half-truth, it cannot respond with the anticipated results we desire. As junk food is to the physical, misguided information is junk food to the spirit. Our spirit becomes weakened for lack of the truth (nutrition) found in the Word rather than growing strong and maturing, whereby prayers are answered and miracles witnessed.

It is human nature that when we pray and there is no immediate answer forthcoming, we become disheartened and disillusioned as disparity and disappointment settles into our soul. Our emotions and thoughts run awry and finally we feel destitute. We ask the unmistakable question, why? Why didn't God answer my prayer? First, we have to understand the issue isn't with the Father, but within ourselves with our inability to tap into His perfection for our imperfection. The problem is not, nor will it ever be, with God.

Is this God's will, His plan or purpose that when we seek Him, He doesn't respond? Absolutely not! God knew each of us before we were ever conceived in our mother's womb, and He has a plan for our life; one of prosperity, health, and prominent wellbeing. If we can humble ourselves to accept the fault, then the question becomes how do we spiritually mend ourselves that we may be aligned with God and receive that which He has already given? The answer may seem as complex as it is simple.

Each person is individually responsible for a relationship with our heavenly Father. God makes it very personal and intimate and defines this when He taught us how to approach Him. First, He says when we seek Him to do so in private and all that we pray to Him in secret will He openly reveal to us. Second, we must pray in the right manner, not in repetitions but with a humbled heart, for He already knows what we have need of. The prayer is for our benefit, not God's. Third, we must be in truth to His Word for the Holy Spirit, our intercessor, to present our plea before the Father in His Kingdom. We are to study God's Word allowing the Holy Spirit to discern the truth. Secondhand information can be tainted with false interpretations. Fourth is to hold to the belief that what we have asked for has already been supplied by God before we ever had the need to request it. And fifth, stay strong in God's Word and patiently wait for the circumstance to change to the miraculous. As we remain resolute for the healing to manifest, we give thanksgiving to the Lord and glorify His name.

One major obstacle is when we do not see immediate results, we falter and question God. We should never question the competence of the Almighty King. There is a time lapse between the spirit realm and the physical realm. The mortal body has to undergo a process of healing and this takes time before it is manifested and witnessed in the natural. If it were an instantaneous manifestation, it would be considered a miracle.

However, a healing that is not an instant recognition is one in which a process is occurring. This is where we hold constant in unwavering faith, until the unseen becomes the seen. Remember the case in point with Daniel praying and waiting three weeks for his answer from God. (Daniel 10:1-13) God neither withheld nor delayed in His response. The angel explained he had an opposition that prevented his immediate arrival.

Angels are forthcoming for our situation, but we must not lose hope or belief, and trust that they will arrive because God sends them on the provision of the Holy Spirit. *For he shall give his angels charge over thee, to keep thee in all thy ways.* Psalm 91:11 What our heavenly Father promises, He provides, but we must seek Him in absolute truth and trust.

God vs Lucifer:

Tale of Two Kings

God vs Lucifer: Tale of Two Kings

How art thou fallen from heaven, O Lucifer, son of the morning!
How art thou cut down to the ground, which didst weaken the
nations! For thou hast said in thine heart, I will ascend into
heaven, I will exalt my throne above the stars of God: I will sit
also upon the mount of the congregation, in the sides of the
north: I will ascend above the heights of the clouds; I will be
like the most High.

Isaiah 14:12-14

Presently and theoretically, there are two gods which have an influence over the Christian life. We know them as Almighty God, and Lucifer who for a short duration has liberties to rule this planet having stolen the right from Adam. God is sovereign over all His creation, and Lucifer is desirous to be the king over everything God created. He has had nearly six thousand years (not knowing exactly how long Adam and Eve lived in the Garden of Eden before Satan showed up) to take the Kingdom of Earth which was given to Adam and became the ruler of this planet.

However, because God knew this would transpire and being a God of love, He gave every human being a free will. God is not coercing us into a relationship with Him, but allowing each person to use their free will to choose Him as our Almighty King and heavenly Father who promises an eternal life with Him. The first time we exercise our free will for the Father is to choose to be born-again through His Son, Jesus, and live a life in the authority of Christ and wisdom of the Holy Spirit. This is the most important decision we can ever make having been born into a corrupt world with an instinctive nature to sin. We literally must make a conscious effort to depart from the influences of this world and be joined in Christ for the Father.

Most Christians today believe in God, but carry on life governed by the physical attributes of this earthen world. We know of God, but don't truly live a life dedicated to Him in discipleship to His Kingdom. Only a small percentage of believers can claim to be living in the spirit of our Savior, diligently doing the works of the Father and fulfilling His plan. So how do we get off track? We have to understand our enemy and that he is always throwing negative circumstances to deflect our being focused on God. After all, his objective is to destroy our relationship with our heavenly Father. Our mind and heart must always be towards God, and never allow earthly influences to pull us away from His love and promises.

Satan can cleverly distract us through our senses, our carnality, and steer us in a direction of diluted belief, weakening our faithful stronghold. This can be done knowingly, or unbeknownst. It depends on how grounded we are in the Word of God, and how strong is our commitment in faith. Is our allegiance to Almighty God solely or to the god of this world, or have we misguidedly combined them? One's objective is to protect and provide while to other is to harm and destroy. Often, when we think we are honoring God but accept the ways of the world, we have voided God's power in our life. What we think is acceptable before God, our thoughts and actions may be otherwise according to His Kingdom principles. This is something we should take into account on a daily basis, never allowing entrance of the enemy to influence us away from God.

This leads to the most misunderstood, and yet, common question: Why does God allow bad things to occur? And, why doesn't He prevent them when we pray for His intervention? To answer these two questions we have to start at the beginning, God's beginning, with His plan for the creation of all. We know that God is a sovereign Father, and thus, we interpret this to mean that all things which happen are by His will, be it for good or for bad. Is this way of thinking accurate? This places all the responsibility on God, the Creator, and none on man. If this were true, then God need not give man a free will, for it would serve no purpose. Also, we would have no concern to pray and ask our heavenly Father anything, because He has already decided our fate beforehand. Though God is aware of the evil in the world, we have to remember He gave us the ability to choose. This is different from God having a planned destiny for each of His children.

God's plan for our lives would not include damage, destructive, and death. A Father of love, holiness, purity, perfection, mercy, grace, forgiveness, not forsaken, and who provides blessings, gifts, and promises is not One to dispense harm to His beloved children. Also, upon being born-again, we have two parts of the Trinity of God dwelling on the inside of us: Christ's Spirit entwined with our spirit, and the Holy Ghost. We then become the earthen vessels that God can use to accomplish His works on earth. Therefore, He would not place harm upon Himself, or His children as He has a purpose for us to fulfill His plan.

We fail to address the god of this earthen world, Satan. No one seems to see him as the villain destroying our lives. We only turn to God and blame Him, a distinctive trick of the devil. God came to earth in Christ to reclaim His children who were stolen from Him by Lucifer in the Garden of Eden. Our bondage of sickness, disparity, and disheartening events is not from a loving Father, but from a ruler who's goal is to keep us from a relationship with God. We need to redirect our attention on the love of God, and the goodness of His perfection, and know in our hearts that His love is always directed for our lives. In the midst of troubles, we fail to see God's love, mercy, and grace, because we want someone to blame and He becomes the best candidate based on His sovereignty. We completely misunderstand the meaning of sovereignty in this supreme context.

God so loves us that He gave man a part of Himself in His Trinity with the ability to have authority and a channel of communication with Him as He sits on the throne within His Kingdom. What do we do with such awesome ability? We discard it. How foolish can we be and still expect from our heavenly Father? We get to talk to the Almighty King, and He talks to us! Only to be physically in His presence is more awesome than this.

As believers in Christ, we have been given His authority to call upon heavenly powers, but Lucifer is right there attempting to steal it from you. He doesn't want us to have these fabulous treasures and apply them in our daily life because it voids His destruction. Access to God's power is the key point that Satan doesn't want us to know about, for it nullifies his ability to destroy our life.

The mere question, "Why doesn't God stop the bad things?" shows a lack of knowledge of His Kingdom principles. God has provided the means to stop bad things in our lives; however, we have to do it. The more accurate question should be: "What do I need to learn and apply in my life that I may call heavenly powers to earth?" The god of this world is always on the prowl seeking to enter into someone's life or family to destroy them. If we are uneducated to prevent this, then he will take hold and run havoc.

A few keynotes for remembrance:

1) When God created everything and claimed it finished, there would never be anything to be added, subtracted, or changed throughout all

the generations. If this was not so, then God would not be a perfect God, and would have made mistakes along the way and needed to make alterations and corrections as they appeared.

2) God knew each of us before we were conceived. He knew we would be born into a wrongful environment, a corrupt world, one with a ruler that is out to destroy our lives. He has a plan (destiny) for each of us, but gave us a free will that we may choose Him as our King. So depending on who we are living for, God or ourselves, determines what we get in this life.

3) If our choice is to choose God, then we must put Him first in our life above all else. We must listen to His voice, and follow His Kingdom principles (laws) that have been established to protect and provide. When we trust solely in Him, we receive His blessings, and therefore, may ask anything of Him, and He will answer. It gives God great pleasure to give to His children.

4) When we believe in Him, but don't trust in His Word, or we want to combine God with the ways of the world, He says: "No, I didn't establish my Kingdom to mix with the tainted and corrupt things of the earth." His holiness will not be destroyed by the evil of this fallen world.

5) By God's very nature of love and perfection, He can only give perfect gifts. *Every good gift and every perfect gift is from above, and cometh down from the Father of lights, with whom is no variableness, neither shadow of turning.* James 1:17 Satan wants us to believe that God gives imperfect gifts and causes destructive things to happen, so that we blame Him which creates a disconnect in our relationship with our heavenly Father. Satan is deceiving us when we believe that God is allowing negative circumstances as a test of our faithfulness. We are made righteous in Christ.

6) The problem to any circumstance we struggle with isn't because God is not answering, but rather we aren't asking in true faith. Our belief is tainted with unbelief, doubt, and mistrust. If we doubt God's ability, or question whether He will respond, then we just voided His blessings and power. This is what Satan does through our thoughts and emotions. He steals us away from God just as he did in the Garden of Eden, and like Eve we become a willing victim.

7) There is only one way to receive answered prayers from God and that is to believe it as though you already have it because in reality you do. Have the virtue of patience and witness God's provisions manifest in your life, for surely it will. God promises it!

Take note of the events surrounding your life and reevaluate your circumstances and you will find the answer is within yourself. God is not withholding His Kingdom treasures or supernatural power, nor is He causing negative circumstances to occur in your life. We are responsible for placing ourselves in bondage and becoming a hostage to carnality.

A Heart for Health

A Heart for Health

Peace I leave with you, my peace I give unto you: not as the world giveth, give I unto you. Let not your heart be troubled, neither let it be afraid.

John 14:27

Our human nature inclines towards fear when we find ourselves the recipient of bad news such as a negative health report. Fear fills our heart and mind and if we aren't careful, it will consume us, literally. We so quickly forget the very good news given to us by our Savior, Jesus. In times of turmoil, we are to bring to the forefront of our conscious the everlasting truth of the promises given by God and fulfilled in Christ at Calvary.

As believers, we must always seek God's truth and healing is no exception. A heart for God will always render a healed body. This is true on a spiritual, physical, and emotional plane. Why? Because God provided it for us through His Son. Search your heart and accept His truth, so that you may receive the good health He has promised and provided.

This good news has been for two thousand years since Christ, for He gave us this wonderful and valuable gift. As Jesus healed many during His time on earth, He didn't return to the Kingdom without securing the availability for man to continue to receive healing. *And ye shall serve the Lord your God, and he shall bless thy bread, and thy water; and I will take sickness away from the midst of thee.* Exodus 23:25 As God proclaimed His Word to the Israelites, today it remains a truth fulfilled in Christ for all who believe. Thus, the continuous good news is that healing is ours for the asking; a gift available at any time. God's truth must be in your heart in order for you to receive your healing.

Realize that your healing is but a fervent prayer away and receive what your heavenly Father has already given to you. Know the role of the Holy Spirit in your life because all that comes from God is through the third person of the Trinity. You need the Holy Spirit to receive God's infinite power in your daily circumstances. God has made Himself available to all His children through the Holy Spirit; therefore, allow the Holy Spirit to intercede through Christ's authority to obtain the power of God in your situation.

We must tend to our heart that we hold God's Word and elevate His truth as the essence of what we believe; putting God first, always. We should make certain, without doubt (unbelief), that we are following the principles that He set forth. In acquiring a healing from God, the heart must be addressed first, meaning what condition is your relationship with your heavenly Father? Your relationship and understanding of His <u>word</u>, His <u>truth</u>, His <u>promises</u>, and what He has <u>provided</u> is vital to your ability to receive healing whether it be physical or emotional. Even though healing is a freely given gift, we must know how to obtain it. Once you have a firm knowledge of God's Word, and know without doubt that our heavenly Father wants you to be well, healthy, and have prosperity in life, then the next step is to receive your healing; the healing that has been provided by Christ. *Beloved, I wish above all things that thou mayest prosper and be in <u>health</u>, even as thy soul prospereth.* 3 John 1:2 Christ's blood shed for you is not just for salvation, but for everything you require in this lifetime. Putting your heart right with the Lord and having an intimate relationship with Him enables you to *believe*, *accept*, and *receive*.

Now that your heart is for God and your relationship intact; set your mind to the task of praying with trust and belief. Believe you have your healing even when there is no immediate physical evidence. The healing is always first in the spirit realm because God is Spirit and then manifested into the natural, or physical realm. Once you firmly believe you are healed by the blood of Christ, and it is God's will that you be healed, then hold steadfast to your healing as a reality even though your senses may tell you otherwise. Do not listen to the carnal, but believe you are healed by the power of the Lord. Some believers will invariably question the validity of a healing even though in the depth of their heart they desire for it to be true. This is because they cannot see it as being this simple.

With your heart right with God, the mind is accepting and believing waiting for the manifestation, then the body goes to work on a cellular level to reprogram itself; to repair the trillions of cells that make up each bodily system. When you do this, the reborn spirit person you are in Christ, and with the power of the Holy Spirit who lives in your heart, will command these cells in your body to go to work at repairing, replenishing, rejuvenating, and renewing your physical body. As you hold this truth in your heart and mind that you are healed, the body accepts in the spirit because you are in sync with the principles of the Kingdom of Heaven and can receive God's provided promises. Simply put: you believe, trust, and hold the faith. You are receiving your healing each day as you experience the effects putting you on a pathway of good health.

Remember, the body was designed to live forever. It is the sin of Adam and Eve that destroyed the eternal spirit life of man and placed sickness, disease, and death as the outcome. However in Christ, we are bought with a ransom that He paid, so that we may be reunited in spirit with our heavenly Father, rebirthing our spirit person for an eternal life. Reborn in Christ for a spiritual life, it begins the moment you accept God as your Almighty King. Therefore, a life reborn in the spirit is one that is connected to God through the Holy Spirit; and thus, may receive the treasures in Heaven and healing is one of those gifts.

Healing in the spirit realm is instantaneous but in the natural (carnal) realm, the body requires time to reveal good health from physical deterioration and damage. This is why it is so imperative to understand the difference between the spirit and the natural and how each is separate but functions in unison. Often, we only see the physical and forget that we are spiritual beings in Christ. Should we witness an immediate result from a prayer for healing, for ourselves or someone else, it would be considered a miracle; the very hand of God giving the transformation. A healing always begins in the spirit and then identified in the natural.

It is very simple, but we tend to complicate matters.We really don't believe it could be this easy and that God would heal our body especially when we see no evidence of a quick fix. We fail to understand some important principles regarding healing. For many Christians, we feel the need to do something, to take charge thinking our way will get quicker results. It is human nature to want instant gratification. Waiting is a hard thing for many, and yet, the Scriptures tell us patience is a virtue. We need to step outside of our own abilities, for they will always bring us short, and trust that God has already taken care of the matter.

Another concern in receiving a healing is to obey God's instructions to put our faith in His power and not in the wisdom of man. We often do the opposite. *That your faith should not stand in the wisdom of men, but in the power of God.* 1 Corinthians 2:6 The first thing we do is accept the knowledge of man rather than turning to the Creator of all, our Almighty King, who gave us life and designed this magnificent body. We forget to look at circumstances through the eyes of the spirit person we are and instead tend to focus on the natural which is guided by our senses. In listening to man's interpretation of our physical conditions and not the Master Physician, the original designer who holds the schematic to our physical existence, its like going to a generic, or secondhand layperson rather than the professional. We put our confidence in the reports of another person and then pray for God to bless their efforts. This is not how God operates His Kingdom. God requires us to choose Him over everyone else. We may go to a physician and obtain a report to learn exactly what our ailment may be, but then we should be taking this information and turning it over to God, and ask Him on His promises to fix it, and He will because He already provided it through His Son. Healing is a gift waiting for you to claim. This is very hard for many to accept, but God requires that He be first, always in every aspect of our life. Perhaps, there will be a time when a doctor's expertise is required, but the emphasis is to put your faith solely in God.

When we listen to the advice of another person, take to heart what they tell us, and their words become the gospel for our health and life, we often can set ourselves up to lose if this individual isn't attuned to God's promises of health and wellness. We accept reports and comments of a "cure" without hesitation. Why? Because it is tangible and easy to believe, whereby having faith in someone or something we cannot validate with our senses is difficult for some. In the attempt at having faith, believers will choose to combine God and man, accepting man's words of wisdom and then pray for the power of God to intervene. This is opposite to what God instructs us, for He explicitly tells us to NOT put our faith in the wisdom of men, but in His power. We have chosen man first and then we go to God. We expect God to change and do as we pray. The result is we don't receive our healing and are left wondering why. In reality, we didn't trust Him.

God has equipped the earth with the natural substances to help man maintain a healthy lifestyle. Therefore, God has supplemented our planet with all the requirements for man's participation in maintaining good health and/or to assist the healing of the body. We find His "medicines" in the vegetation such as herbs, plants, vegetables, fruits, berries, nuts, and seeds. Nutrients found in these foods such as vitamins, minerals, trace minerals, amino acids, enzymes, proteins, complex carbohydrates and fats are exactly what each cell in the human body requires to keep it functioning healthy.

Once we give the body what it requires, instinctively it takes charge and utilizes these nutrient-dense foods to maintain optimum health. The physical body is always regenerating either to wellness or towards illness. Our cells are constantly in a state of replicating either healthy cells, or damaged cells. Damaged cells lead to a breakdown of the body which eventually renders disease; therefore, we do have a responsibility to maintaing a healthy body. Another reason for maintaining optimum health is that our body is the temple of the Holy Spirit.

In summary, have an intimate relationship with your heavenly Father by putting Him first in your life, always. Know His truths, promises and what He has provided through the blood sacrifice of His Son, Jesus. Accept and believe His truths to be the guidepost of your life in any situation, and without fail, pray and give thanksgiving for what you have already been given in Heaven (spirit) and wait patiently knowing it will soon manifest into your life (natural). Your healing and good health is but a heartbeat of a prayer away. Set your heart for God and receive all that He has for you. We are born into a world of sin and unless we choose God and His gift of healing, we are bound for a life of disease by the very nature of what happened six thousand years ago in a garden.

The Sabbath and Sanctuary

The Sabbath and Sanctuary

Ye shall keep my Sabbath and reverence my sanctuary:
I am the Lord.

Leviticus 26:2

Today there still remains a division among Christians regarding the keeping of a Sabbath day. Many, traditionally, believe the Sabbath is on Sunday; and therefore, various churches hold worship on this day. Some say Saturday, the seventh day of the week, is a day of rest as God rested on the seventh day from His work. The final sector believes that with the new covenant in Christ, we can choose any day to honor God whichever is most convenient with our individual lifestyles. Consequently, Christians are scattered under various religious doctrines regarding a time set aside to honor the Lord. The obvious question becomes, who is correct?

We need to begin at the core of these beliefs. Sunday worship began in the era of the Roman Empire with Pope Constantine changing the day from Saturday to Sunday; from the Jewish day of worship to a Gentile day of worship, and Catholicism becoming the valid religion since 313 AD. In 1054 AD was the beginning of denominations; however, they all remain under the same umbrella of the Catholic teachings which continues in churches today. Therefore, the attendance on Sunday and beliefs taught today originated from the Catholic. A pope set the standard and generation later we continue to follow teachings instituted by man.

When we look specifically at honoring the Sabbath, there are two general studies on the subject with teachings following one or the other. We find within the lessons two prominent theological teachers of their time: Herbert W. Armstrong (1892-1986) who founded the Worldwide Church of God and later the Ambassador College; and Kenneth E. Hagin (1917-2003) who pioneered the Word of Faith movement based on Pentecostal Christianity and later founded the Rhema Bible Training College. Amongst these two Bible scholars, we have garnered our interpretation of the Sabbath along with other doctrines, and thus, a division as to the accuracy.

Herbert Armstrong's foundation of belief and teachings is based on the Seventh Day Adventist Church who believe in observing Saturday as the Sabbath to the Lord. This falls under the Old Testament carnal laws of Moses given to the Jewish population as we see reflected in our study of the Old Testament. However, Kenneth Hagin followed the studies of the Pentecostal doctrine based on the New Testament taking the belief of a new and better covenant through Christ and our Sabbath is any day of the week; individuals can choose the day most convenient with their lifestyle to set aside to honor God. His teaching was not regarding a designated timeframe, but that Christ is in us and our worshipping Him is not relevant to a specific day.

These are two opposing beliefs with both rigorous studies sought vigorously throughout the following generations and taught under various religious doctrines. Its easy to depict these interpretations when listening to preachers and know who stands on what foundation, but the question remains, is either one correct? Are we required by God to give honor on the seventh day of the week, Saturday, or with the New Testament in Christ, any day is a good time to stop and give God praise and glory? To answer this question, we have to understand God's purpose for the Sabbath and look at the people God gave the Sabbath to, the Jews. In doing so, we can gain insight of what and why God set forth a seventh day in His creation: a Sabbath day, a Sabbath month, and a Sabbath year.

It is imperative to study the Scriptures in their original language, Hebrew, for accurate interpretation of God's Word; though there were three languages, Hebrew, Aramaic, and Greek. The Israelites spoke Hebrew and the Torah is written in Hebrew, their common dialect. Now that we know who God created the Sabbath for, we must understand for what purpose was it given to them; and finally, are the Gentiles responsible to follow the Jewish law?

There are one hundred and forty-seven references to the Sabbath in the Bible with ninety-two in the Old Testament and fifty-five in the New Testament. It is the fourth of the Ten Commandments God gave to Moses to instruct the Israelites. It was not given to all people, both Jews and Gentiles, but only to the Jews. We know that instead of accepting God and worshipping Him as their Lord, they took on the traditions of the surrounding Gentile nations and followed their lifestyles making their own gods to praise. Even so, this did not alter God's plan for His chosen people, for God knew this would be their behavior.

In the beginning, the first mention in the Bible of a day that is set apart from the others is at God's creation. *Thus the heavens and the earth were finished, and all the host of them. And on the seventh day God ended his work which he had made; and he rested on the seventh day from all his work which he had made. And God **blessed** the seventh day, and **sanctified** it: because that in it he had rested from all his work which God created and made.* Genesis 2:1-3 In understanding that God created in six days and His work was complete by the seventh, and we know that each day represents one thousand years, then we can see that each day of creation is a thousand years of man's life on earth. *But, beloved, be not ignorant of* *this one thing, that one day with the Lord is a thousand years, and a thousand years as one day.* 2 Peter 3:8 We have four thousand years of man as shown in the Old Testament and two thousand years after Christ in the New Testament. We are the generation living in the last days of the sixth day of creation, or the six thousand years of man's life in the flesh. There is one day remaining to be fulfilled, the seventh.

The seventh day of creation is the final one thousand years, for a total of seven days or seven thousand years of man's life before the faithful believers enter into heaven. The last one thousand years, the seventh day, is the Kingdom of Peace (Millennium) and belongs to Christ when He will return for the saints (His bride) and reign as our King on earth during this period. The seventh day of creation was sanctified for Christ.

So how does the Sabbath apply to man's life during these generations before Christ returns to earth? Though the seventh day is blessed and sanctified for Christ, it is during these six thousand years that God commands His people, the Jews, to honor this day. Just as they were instructed to acknowledge the feast days as "a shadow of things to come" which was honoring Christ before He came to earth the first time, the Jews were to observe the Sabbath also as "a shadow of things to come," the true Sabbath in Christ, when He returns a second time and reigns in the Kingdom of Peace. Then and now, Jews continue to celebrate the first three feasts; Passover, Unleavened Bread, and First Fruits which is Christ's death, burial, and resurrection. They celebrated these days before Jesus lived in the flesh, died, and returned to the Kingdom. Also, then and now, they celebrate the last three feasts before Christ's second coming; Trumpets, Atonement, and Tabernacles. Jews celebrate the Sabbath knowing the time will come and Yeshua will reign in His holy temple, Jerusalem.

Knowing why God created a seventh day, why He sanctified it, why it is set apart, who He made it for (Christ), who was to honor it (Jews), and why it was important to do so reveals God's purpose, His plan from beginning to end. It revolves around the second person of the Trinity of God, Christ. It was planned for Christ in the beginning and ends with Christ in His Kingdom of Peace. This is essential to understanding the Sabbath, the Sanctuary, and who is to honor God's appointed day. Everything concerning man's life for God comes to us through Jesus. When Christ said He would give us rest, it is because He is the Sabbath; our rest is in Him. *Come unto me, all ye that labour and are heavy laden, and I will give you rest.* Matthew 11:28

In the scripture, *Ye shall keep my Sabbath and reverence my sanctuary: I am the Lord* (Leviticus 26:2) is commanding that man honors both God's Sabbath and His Sanctuary. What does sabbath and sanctuary mean? Sabbath means **rest** or to **cease** and sanctuary means **holy place,** and who is God speaking to? This is directed to His chosen people, the Israelites, or Jewish population. God has given instructions that the Jewish people, whom He removed from bondage in Egypt, should know that He is their God and that He requires they worship Him as their Lord. However, we learn throughout biblical history this isn't what happened.

When God rested on the seventh day, it wasn't meant as a literal rest because He was tired, nor intended that man should rest from laboring six days because man would be fatigued. God ceased from His *work* because it was complete, finished like an artist who has made the final stroke of the brush across the canvas. He blessed this day (placed His seal) that all His creation was perfect. Nothing would ever need to be changed, added, or removed. What God established at the foundation of creation would be forever.

God blessed the seventh day of His creation, sanctified it for the second person of the Trinity, Christ. A holy one thousand years. So when Jesus declares: *And he said unto them, The Sabbath was made for man, and not man for the Sabbath. Therefore, the Son of man is Lord also of the*

Sabbath. Mark 2:27-28 He is telling the Pharisees that He is in charge of this day, though they didn't understand what He was saying. Christ was God in the flesh, and He knew the Sabbath day belonged to Him because He created it, for His purpose.

God established many Sabbaths, for there is a Sabbath day (last day of the week), a month (first day of the seventh month), a year (the last year of a seven year cycle), as well as a Jubilee year (seven times seven years equals forty-nine years) which is the following fiftieth year. Why did God design a Sabbath that would include the seventh day of the week, seventh month, and seventh year? We know God's number is seven and signifies holiness and perfection because God is holy and perfect. This specific day is meant to be a returning to God. Therefore, God's time (week, month, and year) has been set aside to be a sanctuary unto Himself until the time of the *true* Sanctuary (Kingdom of Peace) and the *eternal* Sabbath in Christ. Until this one thousand year period begins, faithful believers, Jews and Gentiles, are to acknowledge the seventh day of creation as the Lord's Sanctuary, and we do this by ceasing from our own thoughts, removing ourselves from carnality, and concentrate on our King during this time that God has set aside for man to do so; a time of repentance. A Sabbath day is for the individual believers, but a Sabbath year is God dealing with nations. Our Sabbath is in Christ and His Sanctuary is the holy seventh day.

What does God expect during these Sabbath periods? Is there more to the Sabbath than first thought? Those who consider honoring a Sabbath day tend to view it literally and seek only to rest, or cease from working because Sabbath means rest or cease, but it isn't what God has in His plan. During these sanctioned periods, God requires two things of man: first is to honor Him as our Lord and King; and second, to show our faithfulness by relinquishing all materialism to God which exemplifies we have no other gods in our life. Meaning, during these Sabbaths man is to declare that all the materialism, wealth, and accomplishments belong to God. Such as gold, silver, land, animals, etcetera; and today, that equates to any materialism, money, careers, and achievements that we guard closely. We relinquish them to our Almighty King through prayer. It is a time of acknowledgment that God is first in our life.

With an understanding of the Sabbath and God's purpose for creating the Sabbath, when was it officially given to man? It was given to His chosen people, the Israelites, when He took them out of Egypt. It was at Mount Sinai that God spoke to the populous defining the statutes, ordinances, and commandments that would govern them. It was the covenant God made with Moses for Israel. There is no mention of a Sabbath observance by Adam, or any of the generations prior to Moses. However, we learn of the faithful, obedient relationship observed by the individuals set aside by God. There were twenty-six generations before Moses which are: Adam, Seth, Enosh, Kenan, Mahalaleel, Jared, Enoch, Methuselah, Lamech, Noah, Shem, Arphaxad, Shelah, Eber, Peleg, Reu, Serug, Nahor, Terah, Abraham, Isaac, Jacob, Levi, Kohath, Amram, and Moses.

Though these generations did not follow a Sabbath ritual, they did live under the laws of God's Kingdom. An example of this is noted in Genesis with Abraham. *Because that Abraham obeyed my voice, and kept my charge, my commandments, my statutes, and my laws.* Genesis 26:5 God had a special covenant with Abraham, and he was faithful to God; however, there isn't any reference in the Bible that Abraham specifically honored a Sabbath day though he did obey the laws of the Kingdom. Abraham was faithful to his Almighty King, God. Likewise, there is no evidence that Adam, while in the Garden of Eden, honored a specific day as a Sabbath unto the Lord. Though he was a flesh body, he lived a spirit life and every day was a day of acknowledgment to God as they communed daily. With the initiation of the Sabbath through the Commandments by Moses, it was a measurement of sin under the law. A day meant for repentance.

The Sabbath was first introduced as the Fourth Commandment in the Ten Commandments. And in Leviticus 26:2, *Ye shall keep my Sabbath and reverence my sanctuary: I am the Lord* means that on the Sabbath day, month, or year, they were to glorify God by ceasing from their own *will* and *way*. God allowed the people to have six days, six months, six years, and forty-nine years to "do their own thing", to make a living, to acquire possessions, to become monetarily rich in gold and silver; to have materialism but on this one day of the week, month, seventh year, and fiftieth Jubilee year it was to be given to God, figuratively. In doing so, it was telling God that He was first, honor and glory was given to Him, and that all they possessed belonged to Him. In doing this, they would be blessed and prosper; however, if they didn't, it meant judgment. God added or subtracted on the Sabbath depending on their faithfulness and repentance to Him as their King.

Moving forward to the physical life of Christ, we discover when the Sabbath is mentioned, it is Jesus' declaration of ownership of the Sabbath. Remember, God came to earth born of the flesh in Christ and has all rights of ownership to everything and everyone. Jesus defended the Sabbath, declaring: *And he said unto them, The Sabbath was made for man, and not man for the Sabbath. Therefore, the Son of man is Lord also of the Sabbath.* Mark 2:27-28, He had full right to make such statements challenging the Pharisees. Often, Jesus was placed in a position to defend actions taken on the Sabbath. *And it came to pass on the second Sabbath after the first, that he went through the corn fields; and his disciples plucked the ears of corn, and did eat, rubbing them in their hands. And certain of the Pharisees said unto them, Why do ye that which is not lawful to do on the Sabbath day? And he said unto them, That the Son of man is Lord also of the Sabbath.* Luke 6:1-5 Jesus took rightful possession of the Sabbath understanding that this day belonged to Him from the day of creation. He did not bend to the Pharisees' judgment and condemnation for what they perceived to be an obvious disrespect of the law. He taught, healed, performed miracles, and allowed His disciples to do things on the

Sabbath that the Pharisees considered unlawful.

On the first day of each seventh month, as with the seventh year, or after seven consecutive years, the Jewish population were to have a celebration to God. *Speak to the children of Israel, saying, In the seven month, in the first day of the month, shall ye have a Sabbath, a memorial of blowing the trumpets, an holy convocation.* Leviticus 23:24 They worked in their fields and vineyards but on the seventh year of the Sabbath, they were to do no work and opened their fields and vineyards to the people and to strangers to take of the fruit and vegetables of the land. They were to share all they had within their household and in doing so it was a declaration to God. If they did this, God would bless them on the last day of the seventh year (Elul 29/Hebrew calendar) by removing all debt and blessing them with more crops and animals in the upcoming six years until the next seventh Sabbath year. This was the cycle throughout generations since Moses and as seven cycles passed until the Jubilee year, the fiftieth year, which is significant in receiving the blessings of forgiveness among the people, debts removed, slaves were released, and family members returned home. In each seventh day or seventh year, the Sabbath, the purpose was a repentance and returning to God.

When we look at the number seven and the Sabbath together, we see a pattern that depicts God's perfection in man's relationship to Him. This is why Sabbath means rest, or ceasing (man ceases from his own efforts, wants, and desires) and remembers God. He removes himself from his own will and way and focuses on his Lord. This is done on a personal level with man following a Sabbath day; and collectively, as a nation observant of the seventh month and year.

The next question would be are the Gentiles included in honoring a Sabbath? If it has always been about the Jewish population, are the Gentiles exempt from a Sabbath observance? As Gentiles, can we choose to honor, or not honor a Sabbath? If the Gentiles were to be considered exempt from obeying a Sabbath, then it would seem that God doesn't care about the Gentiles, that His focus remains only to the Jewish people. However, we know this isn't true because of Christ dying for all mankind, that would be Jews and Gentiles alike. Upon our free will to choose Christ, and in doing so, we become "grafted in" or "adopted" by God as one of His children. In our adoption into His "family" through the blood of Christ, we get the same blessings and/or judgment as our brothers and sisters, the Jews.

Thus, it would seem that once adopted into the family of God, we are required to be observant of God's commands as well, for we are now one of His children. So in observance of the seventh day of the week, we are to give God all that we have achieved, accomplished, acquired, attained, and acclaimed in all facets regarding materialism; monetarily, and otherwise. We give all to Him showing He is first in our life and we honor Him as our King (we do this in prayer). Each seventh day when we do this, God will give His blessings upon our life.

Therefore, the seventh day of the week, the first day of the seventh month, the seventh year of a seven year cycle, and the fiftieth year of a forty-ninth year cycle, we are to remember the Sabbath and the Sanctuary that God has set aside for man. *Ye shall keep my Sabbath and reverence my sanctuary: I am the Lord.* Leviticus 26:2 We cease from our own will, from attaining, from the focus on ourselves, and put the attention on God. God allows us six days, six months and six years to do our own thing, but one day out of a week, one day (first) of the seventh month, and a full year (seventh), we remember our King and not allow the materialism and monetary gain attained from the world to become our god. The Sabbath day within a week is a personal time between God and each faithful believer; however, the Sabbath of a year concerns nations as a whole repenting and acknowledging God as King.

If we observe the Sabbath as the Jewish custom, we would do no labor which includes bathing, washing our hair, shaving, etcetera as this is considered labor. We would use no electrical appliances (stove, television, radios, computers, telephones, cell phones, etcetera), and we would not drive a motorized vehicle (car, truck, go-carts, and so forth). We would not cook (stove, microwaves, crockpots, etcetera) as electricity cannot be used. In other words, we disconnect from the elements of the world.

However, with a new covenant given to man through Christ and having two persons, Christ and the Holy Spirit of the Trinity of God living on the inside of each born-again believer, this does change man's relationship with God. God has made it personal, one-on-one with Him, unlike His relationship with the Israelites. Before Christ, God dealt with the Jews as a nation, a group of people, but after Christ, He deals with man individually having given each person the free will to choose Him and make Him our Lord and King. Thus, our responsibility is to remember God, to acknowledge Him, to relinquish our possessions to Him (in prayer, a repentance), and give God honor and praise as our King. We put God first. Therefore, the absence of carnality doesn't become a factor because materialism is not our God; meaning to abstain from using electricity, cooking, bathing, or driving doesn't affect our relationship with God because we have made Him first above all these things. To cease from use is not the point when we understand His purpose for the Sabbath and His Sanctuary. Our cessation is for remembrance and giving praise, honor, and glory to our Lord. What God wants and requires of His children is that we not forget He is our King and allow no one and nothing to be before Him. This is the first commandment.

God allows man to conquer, achieve, and acquire those things necessary to maintain a physical life, for He does want us to prosper but the time comes, God's appointed time, when we honor our Lord. It requires understanding the purpose God established the Sabbath and His Sanctuary. To know God's ultimate plan, we need to look at the bigger picture. Then we can better fulfill our responsibilities of obedience to His

Sabbath and Sanctuary once we acknowledge who He created it for, and why He desires we honor it.

We can better understand because in man being *conscious* of the Sabbath, he will be *considerate* of God. If it were not so, man would never give thought, praise, and glory to His Almighty King. God made it personal when He gave His Son so that man could return to Him. Now, we are to make it personal with our heavenly Father by remembering Him specifically at His appointed time. Both Jew and Gentile should honor the Sanctuary (day/place) for the Sabbath (rest) is in Christ. *Buried with him in baptism, wherein also ye are risen with him through faith of the operation of God, who hath raised him from the dead. And you, being dead in your sins and the uncircumcision of your flesh, hath he quickened together with him, having forgiven you all trespasses; Blotting out the handwriting of ordinances that was against us, which was contrary to us, and took it out of the way, nailing it to his cross: And having spoiled principalities and powers, he made a shew of them openly, triumphing over them in it. Let no man therefore judge you in meat, or in drink, or in respect of any holy day, or of the new moon, or of the sabbath days: things to come; but the body is Christ.* Colossians 2:12-17

In summary, it is a complete returning to God, acknowledging He is our Lord until the one thousand years when we will be in the Sanctuary with our King, and we will have a perpetual Sabbath in Christ. Today, in this lifetime, our Sabbath is in Christ and we honor His Sanctuary which is the seventh day of creation *before* entering into Christ's Kingdom. We honor our King, the "shadow of things to come", before Christ's second coming. The Jews continue to celebrate the second coming of Yeshua on the seventh day, and the Gentiles who are adopted into the family of God (faithful believers) are to do the same.

We are children of the Almighty King. *For we which have believed do enter into rest, as he said, As I have sworn in my wrath, if they shall enter into my rest: although the works were finished from the foundation of the world. For he spake in a certain place of the seventh day on this wise, And God did rest the seventh day from all his works. And in this place again, If they shall enter into my rest. For if Jesus had given them rest, then would he not afterward have spoken of another day. There remaineth therefore a rest to the people of God. For he that is entered into his rest, he also hath ceased from his own works, as God did from his. Let us labour therefore to enter into that rest, lest any man fall after the same example of unbelief.* Hebrews 4:3-11 As faithful believers in Christ, we are to rest or cease from our works meaning our will and way of thinking and enter into a communion with God that we seek Him. Our trust is in God and not in ourselves.

When Christ returns and we are with Him, and He is at the throne of His temple, Jerusalem, then it becomes a reality, and we are no longer honoring a shadow of things to come.

Era of Miracles

God's Gift of Miracles

God also bearing them witness, both with signs and wonders, and with divers miracles, and gifts of the Holy Ghost, according to his own will?

Hebrews 2:4

He therefore that ministereth to you the Spirit, and worketh miracles among you, doeth he it by the works of the law, or by the hearing of faith?

Galatians 3:5

In some translations of the Bible the word miracle is used; and yet, the terms *wonder, mighty work* or *sign* is also referenced for the same purpose to draw awareness to God's presence and power being manifested in the situation.

A miracle is an event in the external world brought about by God operating without the use of means capable of being discerned by the senses and designed to authenticate His divinity. It is an occurrence that cannot be defined by nature, nor man to show the intervention of a power

243

that is not limited by the laws either of matter or the mind; a power interrupting the fixed laws which govern their movements, a supernatural power.

A miracle is an instantaneous act of God. It occurs in a nanosecond as God has placed His hand on the matter. This is different to the Holy Spirit providing the power. Though the Holy Spirit is God, His power flows to us from His Kingdom in a different methodology. We should not confuse the two in our expectations. Having knowledge of the functionality of each enables us to understand the importance of how to pray to receive.

We learn in the Bible of the many occasions when God and Christ performed miracles, each for their divine purpose. Today, some believe miracles ceased when Jesus died, and yet, we can witness God's miracles around us everyday if we only take the time to see them. In our hope for a miracle for our personal need, we become disillusioned when one doesn't appear. God, literally, has to stop time in that nanosecond and go against the principles of the Kingdom that He established to perform a miracle. Will He do it? Of course, and has on numerous occasions; however, He established within His Kingdom the ability for man to receive His power on an ongoing basis through the second person of the Trinity. On the authority given in the name of Jesus Christ, and with the Holy Spirit, we are entitled to bring forth heavenly powers into our circumstance. God set forth the laws that are driven by faithfulness to His Word which allows us to receive power for all our requirements.

The Bible shows 123 references to Miracles

God performed   - 86
Christ performed - 37

Category of Biblical Miracles

Nature
Supply
Healing
Power

Miracles Exemplified for these Purposes

Creative actions
Acts of destruction
Wonders
Miracles concerning food/water
Judgments
Control over nature
Curing disease and disability
Healing and casting out of demons
Power over death
Supernatural knowledge

God's Timetable for Miracles

- Time of creation and flood
- Time period of Moses
- Time period of Elijah and Elisha, establishing of prophets
- Time period of Christ
- Time of disciples given the Holy Spirit to proclaim the gospel

Miracles Performed by God

Because all those men which have seen my glory, and my miracles, which I did in Egypt and in the wilderness, and have tempted me now these ten times, and have not hearkened to my voice.
Numbers 14:22

The great temptations which thine eyes have seen, the signs, and those great miracles: Yet the Lord hath not given you an heart to perceive, and eyes to see, and ears to hear, unto this day.
Deuteronomy 29:3

And his miracles, and his acts, which he did in the midst of Egypt unto Pharaoh the king of Egypt, and unto all his land.
Deuteronomy 11:3

EIGHTY-SIX MIRACLES PERFORMED BY GOD

1. Creation of the World - Genesis 1:1
2. The Great Flood - Genesis 7:8
3. The Confusion of Languages - Genesis 11:1-9
4. The Fire on Abraham's Sacrifice - Genesis 15:17
5. The Conception of Isaac - Genesis 17:17; 18:12; 21:2
6. The Destruction of Sodom - Genesis 19
7. Lot's Wife turned into a Pillar of Salt - Genesis 19:26
8. The Closing of the Wombs of Abimelech's Household - Genesis 20: 17-18
9. The Opening of Hagar's Eyes - Genesis 21:19
10. The Conception of Jacob and Esau - Genesis 25:21
11. The Opening of Rachel's Womb - Genesis 30:22
12. The Flaming Bush - Exodus 3:2
13. The Transformation of Moses's Rod into a Serpent - Exodus 4:3-4, 30; 7:10-12
14. Moses' Leprosy - Exodus 4:6-7, 30
15. The Plagues in Egypt - Numbers 16:46-50
16. The Pillar of Cloud and Fire - Exodus 13:21-22; 14:19-20
17. Passage through the Red Sea - Exodus 14:22
18. The Destruction of Pharaoh and His Army - Exodus 14:23-30
19. Sweetening the Waters of Marah - Exodus 15:25
20. Manna - Exodus 16:13
21. Quails - Exodus 16:13
22. The Defeat of Amalek - Exodus 17:9-13
23. The Transfiguration of the Face of Moses - Exodus 34:29-35
24. Water from the Rock - Exodus 17:5-7
25. Thunder and Lightning on Mount Sinai - Exodus 19:16-20; 24:10, 15-17; Deuteronomy 4:33
26. Miriam's Leprosy - Numbers 12:10-15
27. Judgment by Fire - Numbers 11:1-3
28. The Destruction of Korah - Numbers 16:31-35; Deuteronomy 11:6-7

29. The Plague - Numbers 16:46-50
30. Aaron's Rod Buds - Numbers 17:1-9
31. Water from the Rock in Kadesh - Numbers 20:8-11
32. The Scourge of the Serpents - Numbers 21:6-9
33. The Destruction of Nadeb and Abide - Leviticus 10:1-2
34. Balaam's Donkey Speaks - Numbers 22:23-30
35. The Preservation of Moses - Deuteronomy 34:7
36. The Jordan River Divided - Joshua 3:14-17; 4:16-18
37. The Fall of Jericho - Joshua 6:20
38. The Midianites Destroyed - Judges 7:16-22
39. Hailstones on the Confederate Kings - Joshua 10:11
40. The Sun and the Moon Stand Still - Joshua 10:12-14
41. Dew on Gideon's Fleece - Judges 6:37-40
42. Samson's Strength - Judges 14:6; 16:3, 29-30
43. Samson Supplied with Water - Judges 15:19
44. The Falling of the God Dagon - 1 Samuel 5:1-4
45. Nursing Cows return the Ark of the Covenant (leaving their calves) - 1 Samuel 6:7-14
46. The Plague of Hemorrhoids on the Philistines - 1 Samuel 5:9-12; 6:1-18
47. The Destruction of the People of Bethshemesh - 1 Samuel 6:19-20
48. Thunder - 1 Samuel 12:16-18
49. The Death of Uzzah - 2 Samuel 6:1-8
50. The Plague of Israel - 1 Chronicles 21:14-26
51. Fire on the Sacrifices of Aaron - Leviticus 9:24
52. Of Gideon - Judges 6:21
53. Of Manoah - Judges 13:19-20
54. Of Solomon - 2 Chronicles 7:1
55. Of Elijah - 1 Kings 18:38
56. Jeroboam's Hand Withered - 1 Kings 13:3-6
57. The Appearance of Blood - 2 Kings 3:20-22
58. The Panic of the Syrians - 2 Kings 7:6-7
59. Elijah is Fed by Ravens - 1 Kings 17:6

60. Elijah fed by an Angel - 1 Kings 19:1-8
61. Increases the Widow's Meal and Oil - 1 Kings 17:9-16; Luke 4:26
62. Raises the Widow's Son - 1 Kings 17:17-24
63. Brings Fire Down upon Ahaziah's Army - 2 Kings 18:41-45
64. Divides the Jordan River - 2 Kings 2:8
65. Elijah Transported to the Heavens - 2 Kings 2:11
66. Elisha Divides the Jordan River - 2 Kings 2:14
67. Sweetens the Waters of Jericho - 2 Kings 2:19-20
68. Increased a Widow's Supply of Oil - 2 Kings 4:1-7
69. Raises the Shunammite Woman's Child - 2 Kings 4:18-37
70. Renders the Poisoned Stew Harmless - 2 Kings 4:38-41
71. Feeds One Hundred Men - 2 Kings 4:42-44
72. Cures Naaman - 2 Kings 5:1-19
73. Strikes Down Gehazi with Leprosy - 2 Kings 5:26-27
74. Causes the Axe to Float - 2 Kings 6:6
75. Reveals the Counsel of the King of Syria - 2 Kings 6:12
76. Causes the Eyes of His Servant to be Opened - 2 Kings 6:17
77. Strikes the Army of the King of Syria with Blindness - 2 Kings 6:18
78. The Dead Man was Restored to Life - 2 Kings 13:21
79. The Destruction of Sennacherib's Army - 2 Kings 19:35; Isaiah 37:36
80. Return of the Shadow on the Sun Dial - 2 Kings 20:9-11
81. Hezekiah's Cure - Isaiah 38:21
82. The Deliverance of Shadrach, Meshach, and Abednego - Daniel 3:23-27
83. Of Daniel - Daniel 6:22
84. The Sea was Calmed when Jonah was Thrown into It - John 1:15
85. Jonah in the Belly of the Great Fish - Jonah 1:17; 2:10
86. Jonah's Gourd - Jonah 4:6-7

Miracles Performed by Christ

And truly Jesus did many other signs in the presence of His disciples, which are not written in this book; but these are written that you may believe that Jesus is the Christ, the Son of God, and that believing you may have life in His name.
John 20:30-31

And immediately he rose, took up his bed, and went forth before them all; insomuch that they were all amazed, and glorified God, saying, We never saw it on this fashion.
Mark 2:12

And he went up unto them into the ship; and the wind ceased and they were sore amazed in themselves beyond measure, and wondered. For they considered not the miracle of the loaves: for their heart was hardened.
Mark 6:51-52

And were beyond measure astonished, saying He hath done all things well: he maketh both the deaf to hear, and the dumb to speak.
Mark 7:37

THIRTY-SEVEN MIRACLES PERFORMED BY JESUS

1. Marriage at Cana, Wine to Water - John 2:1-11
2. Exorcism at the Synagogue in Capernaum - Mark 1:21-28;Luke 4:31-37
3. Miraculous Draught of Fishes - Luke 5:1-11
4. Young Man from Nain - Luke 7:11-17
5. Cleansing a Leper - Matthew 8:1-4; Mark 1:40-45; Luke 5:12-16
6. The Centurion's Servant - Matthew 8:5-13; Luke 7:1-10; John 4:46-54
7. Healing the Mother of Peter's Wife - Matthew 8:14-17; Mark 1:29-34;
   Luke 4:38-41
8. Exorcising at Sunset - Matthew 8:16-17; Mark 1:32-34; Luke 4:40-41
9. Calming the Storm - Matthew 8:23-27; Mark 4:35-41; Luke 8:22-25
10. Gergesenes Demonic - Matthew 8:28-34; Mark 5:1-20; Luke 8:26-39
11. Paralytic at Capernaum - Matthew 9:1-8; Mark 2:1-12; Luke 5:17-26
12. Daughter of Jails - Matthew 9:18-26; Mark 5:21-43; Luke 8:40-56
13. The Bleeding Woman - Matthew 9:20-22; Mark 5:24-34; Luke 8:43-48
14. Two Blind Men at Galilee - Matthew 9:27-31
15. Exorcising a Mute - Matthew 9:32-34
16. Paralytic at Bethesda - John 5:1-18
17. Man with Withered Hand - Matthew 12:9-13; Mark 3:1-6; Luke 6:6-11
18. Exorcising the Blind, Mute Man - Matthew 12:22-28; Mark 3:20-30;
    Luke 11:14-23
19. An Infirm Woman - Luke 13:10-17
20. Feeding the Five Thousand - Matthew 14:13-21; Mark 6:31-34;
    Luke 9:10-17; John 6:5-15
21. Walking on Water - Matthew 14:22-33; Mark 6:45-52; John 6:16-21
22. Healing in Generate - Matthew 14:34-36; Mark 6:53-56
23. Canaanite Woman's Daughter - Matthew 15:21-28; Mark 7:24-30
24. Deaf Mute of Decapolis - Mark 7:31-37
25. Feeding the Four Thousand - Matthew 15:32-39; Mark 8:1-9
26. Blind Man of Bethsaida - Mark 8:22-26
27. Transfiguration of Jesus Matthew 17:1-13; Mark 9:2-13; Luke 9:28-36

28. Boy Possessed by a Demon - Matthew 17:14-21; Mark 9:14-29; Luke 9:37-49
29. Coin in the Fish's Mouth - Matthew 17:24-27
30. Man with Dropsy - Luke 14:1-6
31. Cleansing Ten Lepers - Luke 17:11-19
32. The Blind at Birth - John 9:1-12
33. Blind near Jericho - Matthew 20:29-34; Mark 10:46-52;Luke 18:35-43
34. Raising of Lazarus - John 11:1-44
35. Cursing the Fig Tree - Matthew 21:18-22; Mark 11:12-14
36. Healing the Ear of a Servant - Luke 22:49-51
37. Catch of One hundred Fifty-Three Fish - John 21:1-24

Seven Feasts of the Lord

Seven Feasts of the Lord

There are seven feasts God instructed the Israelites at Mount Sinai to observe and each has everything to do with the coming of the Messiah; His first and second appearance on earth. The Jews have always understood this and prepared accordingly in worship of these holy days.

In the season of Spring, Christ is born, died, resurrected, and gave man the Holy Spirit in His place. The first three feasts: Passover, Unleavened Bread, and First Fruits fall in March and April. The fourth, Pentecost, occurs in late May or early June.

In the Old Testament, Christ was always the main focus of the Jews for they honored Yeshua as a "shadow of things to come" and celebrated each feast on the holy days as observed on the Hebrew calendar.

FEAST DURING THE SPRING (Book of Leviticus)

1) Passover - Christ's Death (Pesach) Nisan 14-15

2) Unleavened Bread - Christ is Buried (Chag Hamotzi) Nisan 15-22

3) First Fruits - Christ's Resurrection (Yom Habikkurim) Nisan 16-17

4) Pentecost - Holy Spirit; Church Age Begins (Shavuot) Sivan 6-7

In the fall season, September and October, the last three feasts are celebrated: Trumpets, Atonement, and Tabernacles. Christ will return for the second time to earth as the Bridegroom to claim His bride, the faithful saints, so that we may be with our King forever. We are the generation living in the last feast days; the end of the sixth day of creation, or the six thousand years of man on earth in the flesh. Soon we will be with Christ in the Kingdom of Peace.

FEAST DURING THE FALL (Book of Leviticus)

5) Trumpets - Announces the Return of Christ (Yom Teruah) Tishri 1

6) Atonement - Christ Returns to Earth (Yom Kippur) Tishri 10

7) Tabernacles - Saints are with Christ (Sukkot) Tishri 15-22

The *Feast of Trumpets* is the beginning of the tribulation period, but not to fear for God protects His faithful saints.

The *Feast of Atonement* is a special holy day, a repentance of sins, and complete forgiveness.

The *Feast of Tabernacles* is Christ's second coming; returning for His bride, and harvesting of the saints.

Since the first appearance of Christ reflected in the New Testament, the Jews and Gentiles (born-again believers) continue today to honor Christ as the "shadow of things to come." Unlike the Israelites, we have Christ and the Holy Ghost dwelling on the inside of each born-again person. We all await the return of our Messiah.

God's Timeline

from

Creation to Christ

God's Timeline from Creation to Christ

But, beloved, be not ignorant of this one thing, that one day is with the Lord as a thousand years, and a thousand years as one day.

2 Peter 3:8

In God's creation of seven days, He fashioned the heavens, the earth, the animal kingdom, and man in six days, and the seventh day was made a holy day. When we take the Scriptures and apply the *one day with the Lord is as a thousand years*, we see that each day represents a one thousand year period of time. That would put man on earth for nearly six thousand years, and we are the generation living in the last days of the sixth day.

On the seventh day, God finished His works and appointed this day to Christ. We can understand why this is so because the seventh day is the seventh Covenant of God which is the Kingdom of Peace. This is the one thousand year reign of Christ with the saints and there is peace on the earth (Satan is locked away). After the one thousand years, Satan will be released for a short period for the final spiritual battle with God and then the earth will be destroyed with fire, made anew, and the New Jerusalem, our final home, will come down from the Kingdom of Heaven.

Timeline of seven days of God's Creation:

Creation	=	Time of the Father (2,000 years)
Abraham	=	Time of the Jews (2,000 years)
Christ	=	Time of Christ (2,000 years/Pentecost/Church Age)
Christ	=	Time of Christ (1,000 years/Kingdom of Peace)

Old Testament	New Testament	Kingdom of Peace
4,000 years	2,000 years	1,000 years

7 days/7,000 years of Creation

Measurement of time:

Lunar (Jewish calendar)	354 2/3 days
Solar (Man's calendar)	365 1/4 days
Prophetic (God's calendar)	360 - days

God's timeline shows that we are the final generation living in the last days of creation and will experience the return of Christ. Scripture teaches that we will not know the day or the hour of the Lord's return; however, it doesn't say we will not know the year. *But of that day and hour knoweth no man, no, not the angels of heaven, but my Father only. Watch therefore: for ye know not what hour your Lord doeth come.* Matthew 24:36,42 Though we are not made aware of the specifics, in following God's prophetic timeline, we can closely calculate the year of Christ's return.

There are no surprises with God. He always gives us signs and warnings of preeminent events. The second coming of Christ is no different, for it is detailed in the Scriptures. God wants us to be prepared and ready when our Lord returns.

In the Book of Daniel, we learn the timeline Daniel prophesied (Daniel 9:24-27) when Israel became a nation on May 14,1948. The Jewish People's Council met at the Tel Aviv Museum and announced the state of Israel. The declaration reads: "This right is the natural right of the Jewish people to be masters of their own fate, like all other nations, in their own sovereign State." In 2018, it will be seventy years as Daniel prophesied. The Lord declared He would be with His people seventy years from the time they became a nation.

When the sixth day/six thousand years ends, it would appear that the next one thousand years begins the seventh day, seventh Covenant, set at the foundation of creation which means the saints are with Christ. However, before we enter into the Kingdom of Peace to be with the Lord, we have seven years of troubled times or the tribulation period as we read in the Book of Revelation. Interestingly, the tribulation period is set for seven years, running from one Sabbath year to the next Sabbath (seventh) year.

In following God's timeline within the Scriptures and the prophecies given throughout the Bible, it can be calculated that we are ending a Sabbath year on September 13, 2015 (Elul 29/Hebrew calendar) and moving into the final years of the sixth day of creation. We need to be prepared for the coming of our King.

God's Mathematics

It is fascinating to study how God has a mathematical equation to His creation. A timetable that the sun, moon, and stars are set, one in which the earth and planetary systems are strategically placed. God uses the sun and moon to set forth daylight and darkness which establishes a pattern for a calendar that we can measure time. Though man's Gregorian calendar is based on the sun, God uses the moon (lunar) and stars.

We can see His formula for time.

1) When God created daylight and darkness, this division gave us a mathematical measurement we later associated with a calendar and a clock. He tells us of seven days, and we base our calendar on a seven day cycle.

2) Each day of creation is one thousand years; seven days equals seven thousand years.

3) God said His Spirit will only be with man for one hundred twenty years. *And the Lord said, My spirit shall not always strive with man, for that he also is flesh; yet his days shall be an hundred and twenty years.* Genesis 6:3 God is setting the timeframe for one hundred twenty years that He is with man (flesh) which equates to one hundred twenty

generations and a generation is fifty years. If one generation in the life of man is fifty years, and God says there will be one hundred twenty generations then do the math: 120 X 50 = 6,000 years. Where are we today in God's timeline? We are at the end of the one hundred twenty years, or the one hundred twenty generations, or the one hundred twenty Jubilees (Jewish Sabbath year), or the end of the sixth creation day, or the end of the six thousand years. It's all the same time period from God's different mathematical prospectives which all lead to the return of our Savior. It also gives us multiple verifications.

4) There are one hundred twenty Jubilee years, and we are nearing the last year. In this final Jubilee year, Israel will rebuild their temple for the return of Yeshua. A Jubilee (considered a mega Sabbath) is celebrated by the Jews every fifty years; thus, with the upcoming Jubilee celebration beginning September 2015 to September 2016, it is prophesied to be the last one (Leviticus 25:10-21). It is considered a Sabbath or Shemitah year of celebration (jubilee) for no work is done, sins are forgiven, family members return home, slaves are released to establish their own homes, and all debts are cleared. It is a time of full forgiveness, repentance, and celebration which continues to be honored today in the Jewish populous. It is the first time in modern history that Jews are flocking back home to Israel.

We can see the various ways God declares to man His prophetic timeline. In His Word, God reveals all things with only one exception which is the day of Christ's return. Everything else has been given to man to know, but it requires our earnest desire and diligence to seek knowledge within the Scriptures. God keeps no secrets from His children, but wants us to have wisdom. He purposefully selected individuals throughout the Old Testament era to prophesy of the events that would affect man's life, so we would have an understanding of what is to occur. We are not to be unaware, for God always instructs and warns His children.

Portrait of Man's Life

Portrait of Man's Life

So God created man in his own image, in the image of God created he him; male and female created he them.

Genesis 1:27

Our linage in the Kingdom of Heaven begins with God's creation of Adam, made of the earth, and man born of the seed of Adam onto the earth. The second Adam, Christ, redeems man from his sinful nature and gives us a new birth in spirit which returns us to the Spirit Kingdom. In God's portrait of the cycle of man's life, we come full circle.

Man is made in God's image
Man is made for God's pleasure
Man is made to be God's children
Man is made to be God's temple on earth
Man is made with a plan for his life

God gives man the gift of Christ
God gives man the gift of the Holy Spirit
God gives man the gifts of mercy, grace, faith; heavenly treasures
God gives man a free will to return to the Kingdom of Heaven
God gives man salvation, eternal life

We are the beloved children of God; unconditionally loved, forgiven our prodigal betrayal and sinful disobedience, and returned to the Kingdom of Heaven, spiritually, that we may one day be with Christ in our eternal homeland, the New Jerusalem. This is a portrait of the Father's *everlasting love* for His children.

Praise to God, Most High, Amen!

Kingdom of Heaven

Kingdom of Heaven

Throne of the Almighty King

God

Two Heavens for Man

HEAVEN ON EARTH	NEW JERUSALEM
Garden of Eden	Kingdom of Peace
King - Adam	King - Christ
1st Adam	2nd Adam
Carnal - Sin	Spirit - Saint

Cycle of Man's Life

Man 1st birth of Adam's seed	Man 2nd birth of Christ's Spirit
Man born of flesh	Man born of spirit

Cycle of Man's Life, continued...

Born with sin nature	Reborn spirit, cleansed of sin
Laws of Moses	Principles of the Kingdom
Ten Commandments	Fruits of the Spirit
Laws Written in Stone	Laws Written in Man's Heart
Man's Unbelief	Man's Belief
Wrath of God	Grace of God
Punishment	Blessings
Death	Eternal Life

Part V

Companion
Study Guide

Lessons of Love

The Father's Divine Love for You

For God is not unrighteous to forget your work and labour of love which ye have showed toward his name, in that ye have ministered to the saints, and do minister.

Hebrews 6:10

Biblical Love

There are 547 references in the Bible to God's Love

Old Testament - 284 times
New Testament - 263 times

There are four types of love referenced in the Bible

Agape - a selfless, sacrificial, unconditional love, the highest love

Storge - a family love; the bond of mothers, fathers, sisters, and brothers

Philia - a close friendship or brotherly love, one for another

Eros - a physical, sensual love between a husband and wife

Jesus commanded to His disciples regarding Love

A new commandment I give to you, that you love one another; as I have loved you, that you also love one another.
John 13:34

By this all will know that you are My disciples, if you have love for one another.
John 13:35

This is My commandment, that you love one another as I have loved you.
John 15:12

These things I command you, that you love one another.
John 15:17

Trinity of God is for Man

According as he hath chosen us in him before the foundation of the world, that we should be holy and without blame before him in love.
Ephesians 4:1

We can experience the expressed love of God through the Trinity.

God gives **LOVE**

He that loveth not knoweth not God; for God is Love.
1 John 4:8

1 - God is Love
2 - God's Love is for His Children
3 - God's Love is Enduring, Everlasting, Eternal

Christ gives **FREEDOM**

For all have sinned, and come short of the glory of God;
being justified freely by his grace through the redemption
that is in Christ Jesus.
Romans 3:32-34

1 - Christ frees us from sin, bondage, curses, disease
2 - Christ frees us from carnal law
3 - Christ frees us from the second death

Holy Spirit gives **POWER**

And whatsoever ye shall ask in my name, that will I do,
that the Father may be glorified in the Son. If ye shall
ask any thing in my name, I will do it.
John 14:13-14

1 - Holy Spirit gives us wisdom, knowledge, and understanding
2 - Holy Spirit gives us Kingdom gifts
3 - Holy Spirit gives us supernatural power

Gifts from the Trinity

For to one is given by the Spirit the word of wisdom; to another the word of knowledge by the same Spirit; To another faith by the same Spirit; to another the gifts of healing by the same Spirit; To another the working of miracles; to another prophecy; to another discerning of spirits; to another divers kinds of tongues; to another interpretation of tongues.
1 Corinthians 12:8-10

God Loves You

If we love one another, God dwelleth in us, and his love is perfected in us.
John 4:12

1 - God *teaches* us how to Love
2 - Christ *allows* us to live in Love
3 - Holy Spirit *provides* because of Love

4 - God *gives* good gifts

5 - Christ *grants* His authority to acquire gifts

6 - Holy Spirit *provides* the manifestation of gifts

God Gives Love

And we have known and believed the love that God hath to us. God is love; and he that dwelleth in love dwelleth in God, and God in him.
1 John 4:16

Our heavenly Father is *Love,* and because of His *Love*, we are made spirit beings in His image from His Spirit in *Love*.

God is the Almighty, Most High, Alpha and Omega, the beginning and the end, the same yesterday, today, and tomorrow; never changing, Creator of the heavens and earth, and all thereof. He is King of kings and Lord of lords. God is love, this is His nature. *Before the mountains were brought forth, or ever thou hadst formed the earth and the world, even from everlasting to everlasting, thou art God.* Psalm 90:2 God has always been.

His love is an agape love unconditional without boundaries, manipulations, or stipulations for it has no dimension. There is no measure of depth, width, or height, nor limitations. Such a love greatly surpasses our carnal ability to comprehend as our human instinct places conditions on this emotion.

There is nothing in existence that God did not create and before the heavens and earth, before Adam, and before we were in the womb yet born of flesh, we were with God. *According as he hath chosen us in him before the foundation of the world, that we should be holy and without blame before him in love; having predestinated us unto the adoption of children by Jesus Christ to himself, according to the good pleasure of his will.* Ephesians 1:4-5 Because we come from God and He is Spirit, we are spirit of His Spirit.

How would you answer these questions?

1) God's love is pure and perfect
   What has been the greatest expression of God's love in your life?

   > *For God so loved the world that he gave his only begotten Son, that whosoever believeth in him should not perish, but have everlasting life.*
   > John 3:16

_____

_____

2) God's greatest commandment is to love Him and love one another
   Is God first in your life above your spouse, children, family, and

friends?

> *And thou shalt love the Lord thy God with all thy heart, and with all thy soul, and with all thy mind, and with all thy strength: this is the first commandment. And the second is like, namely this, Thou shalt love thy neighbour as thyself. There is none other commandment greater than these.*
> Mark 12:30-31

---

3) A love worth dying for
How strong is your love reflected in your relationships?

> *Greater love hath no man than this, that a man lay down his life for his friends.*
> John 15:13

---

4) A life governed by love
Is all that you say and do a commitment of kindness and compassion?

But I say unto you, Love your enemies, bless them that curse you, do good to them that hate you, and pray for them which despitefully use you, and persecute you.
Matthew 5:44

_____

_____

5) God's love cannot be earned
   What do you believe you should do to express your love for God?

   The blessing of the Lord, it maketh rich, and he addeth no sorrow with it.
   Proverbs 10:22

_____

_____

6) Begin each day with a prayer of thanksgiving
   Do you communicate daily with your heavenly Father?

   God is a Spirit: and they that worship him must worship him in spirit and in truth.
   John 4:24

_____

_____

7) Know God's love is plentiful and forever

How often do you rely on God, trusting Him explicitly?

> *The Lord is good, a strong hold in the day of trouble; and he*
> *knoweth them that trust in him.*
> Nahum 1:7

_____

_____

8) Trust in God's love for you

Do you believe God answers your prayers?

> *For all things are for your sakes, that the abundant grace*
> *might through the thanksgiving of many rebound to the glory*
> *of God.*
> 2 Corinthians 4:15

_____

_____

Christ gives Freedom

For unto us a child is born, unto us a son is given: and the government shall be upon his shoulder: and his name shall be called Wonderful, Counsellor, The Mighty God, The Everlasting Father, The Prince of Peace.

Isaiah 9:6

Jesus is God manifested as the Son of God. He is the second of the Trinity of the Father, the Son, and the Holy Ghost. Christ is the Living Word, the Son of God, the Lamb of God, the Good Shepherd, the Counselor, Light of the World, and the Prince of Peace. Jesus is Lord and Savior, Messiah, El Shaddai, Yeshua, King of kings and Lord of lords; Almighty, our mediator to the Father and our Redeemer from sin. *For there is one God, and one mediator between God and men, the man Christ Jesus.* 1 Timothy 2:5

Everything God created He spoke into existence, and as He spoke, Jesus was the Living Word fashioning the foundation of all creation. *And to make all men see what is the fellowship of the mystery, which from the beginning of the world hath been hid in God, who created all things by Jesus Christ.* Ephesians 3:9 And, *All things were created by Him and for Him. For by him were all things created, that are in heaven, and that are in earth, visible and invisible, whether they be thrones, or dominions, or principalities, or powers: all things were created by him, and for him: And he is before all things, and by him all things consist.* Colossians 1:16-17

When it was necessary for Christ to come down to earth to save man, the Living Word became flesh. *Which were born, not of blood, nor of the will of the flesh, nor of the will of man, but of God. And the Word was made flesh, and dwelt among us, and we beheld his glory, the glory as of the only begotten of the Father, full of grace and truth.* John 1:13-14 In accepting the relationship between the Father and the Son, we can see a picture that tells a story that has always been about man from the very beginning. *For through him we both have access by one Spirit unto the Father.* Ephesians 2:18

Sin separated man from God; however, Jesus reconciled man fulfilling the Father's plan that we be reunited with Him. *For he hath made him to be sin for us, who knew no sin; that we might be made the righteousness of God in him.* 2 Corinthians 5:21 Jesus' main purpose wasn't to take away man's sins which occurs when we repent. Christ's objective was to reestablish man's relationship with the Father. The spiritual connection God had with His children, Adam and Eve, was severed in the Garden of Eden. Christ came to rectify and reconcile man to his heavenly Father. Jesus brings man full circle to the garden before sin.

How would you answer these questions?

1) Accepting Christ as the Son of God
   Do you have Christ as your Savior?

   > *And, having made peace through the blood of his cross, by him to reconcile all things unto himself; by him, I say, whether they be things in earth, or things in heaven.*
   > Colossians 1:20

   _____

   _____

2) In Christ you are given a rebirth
   Are you living a new life in Christ?

   > *Therefore if any man be in Christ, he is a new creature: old things are passed away; behold, all things are become new.*
   > 2 Corinthians 5:17

   > *And that ye put on the new man, which after God is created in righteousness and true holiness.*
   > Ephesians 4:24

_____

_____

3) Understanding what Jesus did
   Do you believe you are forgiven?

> *Hereby know we that we dwell in him, and he in us, because he*
> *hath given us of his Spirit.*
> 1 John 4:13

> *But now being made free from sin, and become servants to God,*
> *ye have your fruit unto holiness, and the end everlasting life.*
> Romans 6:22

_____

_____

4) A daily walk with Christ
   How has Christ changed your life?

> *But of him are ye in Christ Jesus, who of God is made unto us*
> *wisdom, and righteousness, and sanctification, and redemption:*
> *That, according as it is written, He that glorieth, let him glory in*
> *the Lord.*

1 Corinthians 1:30-31

_____

_____

5) A relational commitment in Christ
   How do you live for Christ?

   And all things are of God, who hath reconciled us to himself by
   Jesus Christ, and hath given to us the ministry of reconciliation;
   To wit, that God was in Christ, reconciling the world unto himself,
   not imputing their trespasses unto them; and hath committed unto
   us the word of reconciliation.
   2 Corinthians 5:18-19

_____

_____

6) Trust in the Lord with all your might
   What do you trust Christ for the most?

   Jesus said unto him, If thou canst believe, all things are
   possible to him that believeth.
   Mark 9:23

7) Salvation is for every believer
   Do you believe you are saved through Jesus?

> *I am the way, the truth and the life: no man cometh unto*
> *the Father, but by me.*
> John 14:6

8) Coming face to face with Jesus
   What would you say to Christ?

> *Beloved, I wish above all things that thou mayest prosper*
> *and be in health, even as they soul prospereth.*
> 3 John 1:2

The Holy Spirit gives Power

Now we have not received, not the spirit of the world, but the spirit which is God; that we might know the things that are freely given to us of God.

1 Corinthians 2:12

The Holy Spirit is the third in the Trinity and is sent on the authority of Christ that each born-again person may have an intimate communion with the Father. He is our tutor, intercessor, and advocate before the Lord. We are virtually helpless to receive anything from the Kingdom without the Holy Spirit, for heavenly gifts and power come through the Spirit of Truth who is God. Jesus teaches: *And I will pray the Father, and he shall give you another Comforter, that he may abide with you for ever; Even the Spirit of truth; whom the world cannot receive, because it seeth him not, neither knoweth him: but ye know him; for he dwelleth with you, and shall be in you.* John 14:16-17 This is why Jesus told His disciples He must go, but would send a Comforter knowing the need man would have for the Holy Ghost. *Who hath also sealed us, and given the earnest of the Spirit in our hearts.* 2 Corinthians 1:22 What Jesus spoke to His disciples remains effectual today. As Jesus is our Savior and mediator, the Holy Spirit is our intercessor and advocate within the Kingdom of Heaven. We can understand the trinity of God as Christ, and as the Holy Spirit, for His Kingdom purpose in reuniting man for a relationship with Himself as it once was with Adam.

The Holy Spirit knows what is in our heart and mind so when we pray, He submits our prayerful petitions to be in accordance with the precepts of the Kingdom. Because God knows our desires before we ask, our prayers should be sincere with an expected resolution. *And he that searcheth the hearts knoweth what is the mind of the Spirit, because he maketh intercession for the saints according to the will of God.* Romans 8:27

To personally receive the Holy Spirit, we must first be reborn into the spirit person we were created, and we already know to do so with a repentance prayer. Christ comes into our life and God sends the Comforter. Think about what must transpire when we ask to be received, spiritually, into the Kingdom. It is an awesome occurrence and so joyous that surely angels must sing because another child has returned to the Father. *Likewise, I say unto you, there is joy in the presence of the angels of God over one sinner that repenteth.* Luke 15:10

How would you answer these questions?

1) Baptism of the Holy Spirit
   Have you received the baptism of the Holy Ghost?

I indeed have baptized you with water: but he shall baptize you with the Holy Ghost.
Mark 1:8

Who hath also sealed us, and given the earnest of the Spirit in our hearts.
2 Corinthians 1:22

---

2) Understanding God's plan for the Holy Spirit
Do you allow the Holy Spirit to teach you all things of God's Kingdom?

And he said unto them, Unto you it is given to know the mystery of the kingdom of God: but unto them that are without, all these things are done in parables: That seeing they may see, and not perceive; and hearing they may hear, and not understand; lest at any time they should be converted, and their sins should be forgiven them.
Mark 4:11-12

---

3) Listening to the Holy Spirit

Can you hear the Holy Spirit speaking to you?

> *And he that searcheth the hearts knoweth what is the mind*
> *of the Spirit, because he maketh intercession for the saints*
> *according to the will of God.*
> Romans 8:27

_____

_____

4) The Holy Spirit will guide your life

Do you accept the guidance of the Holy Spirit?

> *If ye then, being evil, know how to give good gifts unto your*
> *children: how much more shall your heavenly Father give the*
> *Holy Spirit to them that ask him?*
> Luke 11:13

_____

_____

5) Living by the Fruits of the Spirit

Is your daily life equipped with fruitful manifestations?

Every good gift and every perfect gift is from above, and
cometh down from the Father of lights, with whom is no
variableness, neither shadow of turning.
James 1:17

---

6) Gifts of the Holy Spirit
What gifts have you requested from the Holy Spirit?

But the manifestation of the Spirit is given to every man to
profit withal. For to one is given by the Spirit the word of
wisdom; to another the word of knowledge by the same
Spirit; To another faith by the same Spirit; to another the
gifts of healing by the same Spirit; To another the working
of miracles; to another prophecy; to another discerning of
spirits; to another divers kinds of tongues; to another the
interpretation of tongues: But all these worketh that one
and the selfsame Spirit, dividing to every man severally as
he will.
1 Corinthians 7:11

---

7) Operating in the gifts of the Holy Spirit
   When and how do you apply your gifts?

> *He have not chosen me, but I have chosen you, and ordained you, that ye should go and bring forth fruit, and that your fruit should remain: that whatsoever ye shall ask of the Father in my name, he may give it you.*
> John 15:16

---

8) Receiving the empowerment of the Holy Spirit
   Are you exercising supernatural power through the Holy Spirit?

> *And whatsoever ye shall ask in my name, that will I do, that the Father may be glorified in the Son. If ye shall ask any thing in my name, I will do it.*
> John 14:13-14

> *If ye abide in me, and my words abide in you, ye shall ask what ye will, and it shall be done unto you.*
> John 15:7

Gifts of Love
Fruit of the Spirit

There are gifts from the holy trinity of God, the Father; Christ, the Son; and the Holy Ghost. The gifts of God are all encompassing and divided among Christ and the Holy Spirit. God's gifts are administrative in the function of His Kingdom. Christ's gifts are for the continuation of His ministry, and the Holy Spirit gifts provide supernatural power.

Now there are diversities of gifts, but the same Spirit. And there are differences of administrations, but the same Lord. And there are diversities of operations, but it is the same God which worketh all in all.
1 Corinthians 12:4-6

But the fruits of the Spirit is love, joy, peace, longsuffering, gentleness, goodness, faith, meekness, temperance; against such there is no law.
Galatians 5:22

Gifts of God - **ADMINISTRATION**

Apostles	Healing
Prophets	Helps
Teachers	Governments
Miracles	Diversities of Tongues

Gifts of Christ - **MINISTRY**

Apostles	Pastors
Prophets	Teachers
Evangelists	

Gifts of the Holy Spirit - **POWER**

Knowledge	Prophecy
Faith	Discerning of Spirits
Healing	Speaking in Tongues
Miracles	Interpretation of Tongues
Wisdom	

How would you answer these questions?

1) God gives His children gifts and talents
   Do you know what your gifts are?

> *Now concerning spiritual gifts brethren, I would not have you ignorant.*
> 1 Corinthians 12:1

_____

_____

2) Ask and you shall receive
   What gifts have you asked for?

> *For every one that asketh receiveth; and he that seeketh findeth; and to him that knocketh it shall be opened.*
> Luke 11:10

_____

_____

3) God knows which gifts are best for us

What gifts have you received?

But the manifestation of the Spirit is given to every man to profit withal.
1 Corinthians 12:7

_____

_____

4) Name your speciality
   What gifts would you like to have?

Having then gifts differing according to the grace that is given to us.
Romans 12:6

_____

_____

5) Gifts are directed by the Holy Spirit
   How would you like to use your gifts?

Now ye are the body of Christ, and members in particular.
1 Corinthians 12:27

_____

_____

6) Maturity to receive what we ask for

Have you asked for a special gift but didn't receive it?

> *But covet earnestly the best gifts: and yet show I unto you a*
> *more excellent way.*
> Corinthians 12:31

_____

_____

7) Applying your gifts

Have you learned how to use your gifts?

> *For the perfecting of the saints, for the work of the ministry,*
> *for the edifying of the body of Christ.*
> Ephesians 4:12

_____

_____

8) Steward in the Kingdom

What has been the greatest satisfaction you have experienced in using a gift?

Now there are diversities of gifts, but the same Spirit.
1 Corinthians 12:4

_____

_____

Notes:

LOVE + ONE = YOU!

*For thou hast possessed my reins: thou hast covered me in
my mother's womb. I will praise thee; for I am fearfully and
wonderfully made: marvelous are thy works; and that my
soul knoweth right well. My substance was not hid from thee,
when I was made in secret, and curiously wrought in the lowest
parts of the earth. Thine eyes did see my substance, yet being
unperfect; and in thy book all my members were written, which
in continuance were fashioned, when as yet here was none of
them. How precious also are thy thoughts unto me, O God!
How great is the sum of them!*

Psalm 139:13-17

1 - God *teaches* us how to Love

God is love, and we learn how to love Him and one another through
the example given in His Son. Though His love is pure and perfect, an
agape love, that surpasses our carnal ability to comprehend, it exemplifies
how we are to express ourselves in love. Everything God created He made

for man with love; therefore, we shouldn't forget how precious and endearing our Father's love remains for His children. Love is the fundamental foundation to all His creation.

2 - Christ *allows* us to live in Love

God came to earth, in Christ, to save man because of His *everlasting love* for His children. It is through the teachings of Jesus during His short time on earth that we learn of our heavenly Father, and all that He has within His Kingdom was established for man. His promises and gifts are to help us in our daily life on earth. Christ allows us to call upon His authority in the Kingdom to acquire what we need. Our needs were set forth in God's plan at the foundation of His creation.

3 - The Holy Spirit *provides* because of Love

God manifests Himself as the Holy Spirit that we may have a communion with Him. It is the Holy Spirit who teaches all things of our Father, gives heavenly treasures and gifts, and protects and provides for us. Our prayers are answered through the Holy Spirit. It is the Holy Ghost who has supernatural power to accomplished whatever we call upon our heavenly Father for.

The Challenge

Everything God created was an *act of love*, everything Christ did was an *act of love*, everything the Holy Spirit gives is an *act of love*, and everything we do must be *done in love*.

We must never forget that we are children of the Almighty King, joint-heirs in Christ in the Kingdom of Heaven. We are greater than the angels and so preciously loved by our Father. As we love our children, God loves us so much more. He has given generously in blessings, promises, gifts, and power to each of His children that we may live happy, healthy, and prosperous lives, today. This is the reason that He presents Himself in the Trinity because each has a specific purpose in our life.

We fail to understand and accept our rightful place as a child of the King; however, once we grasp and accept how much we are truly loved, it will change us and how we conduct our life. Love is the most powerful of emotions and conquers everything we may face. Christ taught it often to His disciples, and love continues to be taught in His Word.

Love will turn your life around, for it repairs the soul, provides forgiveness, and generates hope. Truth is discovered in love, healing is manifested in love, miracles are witnessed because of God's love. We are responsible for understanding and exemplifying love. Take charge of your life today, and let it begin with an acceptance and appreciation of God's love for you.

How would you answer these questions?

1) What is the greatest thing you have ever done to help someone else?

_____

_____

2) How did it make you feel at the time?

_____

_____

3) What would you like to do to be a good steward in God's Kingdom?

_____

_____

4) How would you accomplish it?

_____

_____

5) Would you do it alone, or seek others to become involved?

_____

_____

6) What has kept you from doing it?

_____

_____

7) What would motivate you to do it today?

_____

_____

8) Would you be willing to do it without reservations?

_____

_____

Notes:

God's Principles for Healing and Miracles

The Father's Gift to You

My words are life unto those that find them, and health to all your flesh.

Proverbs 4:22

Healing the Spirit, Soul, and Body

How God anointed Jesus of Nazareth with the Holy Ghost and with power: who went about doing good, and healing all that were oppressed of the devil; for God was with him.

Acts 10:38

There are two components to healing the body of any emotional and/or physical health crisis which exemplifies the correlation between our spirit and our flesh. Just as we see God in the trinity of the Father, the Son and the Holy Ghost, knowing He is all three, so must we view ourselves as the trinity of man with a spirit, soul, and body. To have victory in healing, we have to address the trinity as one; thus to heal the flesh, we have to also consider the spirit and soul.

We cannot separate one from the other and expect a full recovery; however, when we accept all three component of man's existence, the spirit, the soul, and the body, then we can align ourselves and receive healing through God's trinity with authority in the Son, and the channel (pathway) through the Holy Spirit. It becomes imperative to understand the trinity of the Father and man to receive our miracle or healing.

The two-part healing consideration of the body (flesh):

Spiritual and Physical

1st ~ Heal the Body - Spiritually

    Eliminate: strife, sins, and curses
    Result: purification and balance in your spirit and soul
    Source: Holy Spirit

2nd ~ Heal the Body - Physically

    Eliminate: toxins, chemicals, and drugs
    Results: cleanse and remove harm from your body
    Source: God's medicine, nature; vegetation from the earth

Protocol for Healing

God's principles within His Kingdom are succinctly planned and provided for man. When we follow His instructions, we gain victory.

I. Clear your mind
    Release false beliefs

II. Repent of unbelief and sin
     Listen only to God's voice

III. Rebuke curses
      Release all curses placed in your life, known and unknown

IV. Pray for the Father's forgiveness
     Pray for forgiveness of anything that isn't His truth

V. Accept your healing
    Believe through the blood of Christ you are healed

VI.   Understand healing is spiritual and natural (flesh)
Learn that healing is first in the spirit realm, then in the carnal

VII.   Purify your body
Detoxification to remove harmful substances

VIII.   Help heal the body with God's natural medicine
Promote your body's healing with good nutrition

IX.   Pray continuously
Give thanksgiving, praise, and glory to God for your healing

X.   Love your heavenly Father, your Almighty King!

God's Kingdom Principles are Simple

Who his own self bare our sins in his own body on the tree, that we, being dead to sins, should live unto righteousness: by whose stripes ye were healed.

1 Peter 2:24

My son, attend to my words; incline thine ear unto my sayings. Let them not depart from thine eyes; keep them in the midst of thine heart. For they are life unto those that find them, and health to all your flesh.

Proverbs 4:20-22

Likewise the Spirit also helpeth our infirmities: for we know not what we should pray for as we ought: but the Spirit itself maketh intercession for us with groanings which cannot be uttered.

Romans 8:26

God wants you well and provided it through His Son, Jesus. We know that everything Christ suffered and died was in God's plan and purpose for our benefit. God provided for our healing, but we are remiss in under standing how to acquire it.

It is important to understand how God created the human body. Our physical body was designed to live forever; however, sin changed this fact. Because it was fashioned for longevity, the systems within our flesh have not changed. The trillions of cells that make the composition of our existence work harmoniously renewing, replenishing, and repairing on an ongoing basis. Sin didn't change how the body functions by design. Each system from Cardiovascular, Digestive, Endocrine, Immune, Integumentary, Lymphatic, Muscular, Nervous, Reproductive, Respiratory, Skeletal, and Urinary all work diligently to keep us in optimum health.

It is our choices that change the dynamics of how our body works. Simply put, bad things in renders bad things out. We truly do reap what we sow, both figuratively and literally, in life circumstances and in health and wellbeing. Cells are constantly duplicating themselves, and replicate into wellness or disease as we witness the evidence within ourselves. We are responsible for the welfare of our body, God's temple, and because we live in an unhealthy environment both spiritually and physically, it becomes imperative to take charge of our life.

God's plan is that we live in good health, but man doesn't accept His plan, and this becomes the reason many believers are not receiving their healing. We have shifted our faith and trust into man's knowledge rather than seeking and trusting in what our heavenly Father instructs, or at the least, we attempt to combine God's Word with man's wisdom. This will void Kingdom power.

Principle #1 - God made you *perfect*.

God is perfect and He made man in His image from His perfection. Born into a world of sin with a sinful nature, we have to be born-again in spirit to escape the imperfections and unhealthiness of this fallen world.

So God created man in his own image, in the image of God created he him; male and female created he them.

Genesis 1:27

Principle #2 - God made your body to *replenish*, *renew*, and *repair*.

Within our body our cells are continuously replicating every nanosecond, and how they duplicate themselves is what establishes our health and wellbeing. God provided in the earth all the components necessary for maintaining life. We cannot survive without food, water, and oxygen while our general health requires the fruits, vegetables, herbs, etcetera from the earth. The nutrients from these resources such as protein, minerals, trace minerals, fats, carbohydrates, enzymes, and so forth become the tools the body uses for rebuilding and repairing. God has provided all the mechanisms our body requires to replenish, renew, and repair.

Our health is a spiritual journey of belief in all that Christ has given us in freedom from disease and sickness, but also it is important to note that our soul, our thought process, must align in belief for our healing because it will determine the state of our ability to receive.

Beloved, I wish above all things that thou mayst prosper and be in good health, even as thy soul prosperity.

3 John 1:2

Principle #3 - God wants you *well*.

    As a born-again child of the Father, we have Christ and the Holy Spirit living on the inside of us; therefore, we have the supernatural power within us to call upon the authority in Christ and receive through the Holy Spirit our healing (and anything else we desire of God) from the Kingdom of Heaven. It is our Father's great pleasure to give to His children, to see us whole and healthy, prospering in our earthen life, and living for the glory of His Kingdom.

> *I will take sickness away from the midst of thee.*
> *...the number of thy days I will fulfill.*

Exodus 23:25-26

Why are so many believers not healed?

God anointed Jesus of Nazareth with the Holy Spirit and with power, who went about doing good and healing all who were oppressed by the devil, for God was with Him.

Acts 10:38

And Jesus went all about Galilee, teaching in their synagogues, and preaching the gospel of the kingdom, and healing all manner of sickness and all manner of disease among the people.

Matthew 4:23

Is God holding out, or are we missing an important element in acquiring healing power from the Kingdom? First, we know God is not withholding His power, for He gives it freely through the Holy Spirit. Therefore, the answer must lie within us. Having knowledge and understanding of God's principles is crucial to receiving. We have not learned how to receive and apply what our heavenly Father has established for us.

In Christ, we are children of the Almighty King, and joint-heirs to the Father's Kingdom; and yet, we do not live with this understanding of who we are and what we have been given through God's Son. We hear the

Scriptures, and read the verses, but we do not accept them in our heart and allow them to resonate in true belief. Why? Because we do not see ourselves as worthy. We have been fed a lie for so long, that we accept the false before we gravitate and hold tightly to the truth, God's Word. Many have been deceived with false doctrines such as everything falls on God because He is a sovereign God, and He is the one who decides who will be healthy, sick, or die. Others put all the responsibility on God with a misguided idea of maybe He will heal, and maybe He won't, it's a matter of waiting to see what God will do. This is plain deception and will prevent healing. We must believe what He has told us in His Word. This is not a question of God's sovereignty.

Everyone who is a child of the Father should be receiving answered prayers and healing because it is God's desire, and He established it at the foundation of creation. If you are not, it isn't because God hasn't put it in His master plan for your life, but rather you are not understanding how to obtain it. He has freely provided, but we must know how to receive healing. The issue lies with us and not with God. Our misconceptions and lack of the truth severs us from what God has provided and given through the blood of Christ.

We must understand how the principles within God's Kingdom work. When we pray, believe, and trust God for our healing, we then exercise patience and hold steadfast for it to manifest from the spiritual realm into the natural. Healing is not an instant realization for the flesh has to undergo a transitional period of restoration. Should it be instantaneous, it would be a miracle by the very hand of God as opposed to working through the Holy Spirit. Have a stronghold in God's truth.

Hindrances for Healing and Identification

For I will restore health unto thee, and I will heal thee of thy wounds, saith the Lord.

Jeremiah 30:17

Hindrances can be emotional, physical, or spiritual that cause a state of *dis-ease* which over the course of time breaks down our bodies innate ability to replenish and repair; thus, the body succumbs to disease. It has been medically proven that guilt causes emotional digression, fear causes stress which becomes the forefront for many diseases, shame causes insecurity, and worshipping idols, statues, or symbols destroys our relationship with our heavenly Father.

There are two perspectives to consider; God's and man's. First, we must understand what God has established; and second, not fall into worldly traps that prohibit our success in attaining our healing. It is human nature to confront more than one from the following list, but the key is to not remain in emotional bondage because when we do it changes our thoughts and emotions; and thus, our actions and beliefs. We all will suffer unhappiness, sorrow, disappointment, emotional pain, and so forth, but we should remember we are renewed in Christ and children of the Almighty King. We are responsible for removing the blocks that keep us from God.

Kingdom Blocks

1 - Not Understanding God's Nature
2 - Not Understanding God's Kingdom Principles (Laws)
3 - Lack of Knowledge
4 - Lack of Application

Personal Blocks

1 - Unforgiving
2 - Strife
3 - Curses
4 - Fear
5 - Pride
6 - Guilt
7 - Shame
8 - Grief
9 - Idolatry

10 - Hopelessness
11 - Thanklessness
12 - Lack of Patience
13 - Lack of Faith
14 - Lack of Love
15 - Double-minded
16 - Ignorance
17 - Judgmental
18 - Unbelief

Identification of Personal Blocks

There are many things that can block the power of God from entering into our life. It only takes one to obstruct the pathway. We should take a serious look at each of the following and determine if any apply as the reason for not receiving a healing.

1) Unforgiving

> *For if ye* **forgive** *men their trespasses, your heavenly Father will also* **forgive** *you: But if ye* **forgive** *not men their trespasses, neither will your Father* **forgive** *your trespasses.*
> Mark 6:14-15

Holding grudges blocks love. If we do not forgive those who have done injustices towards us, how then can we expect God to forgive us. God tells us in His Word and is very explicit in His command: *Beloved, let us love one another: for love is of God; and every one that loveth is born of God, and knoweth God.* 1 John 4:7 It cannot be explained any more succinctly than this. God requires that we have brotherly love for each other and when we face objection, then we forgive the person their wrongdoing and walk away. *Verily I say unto you, Inasmuch as ye have done it unto one of the least of these my brethren, ye have done it unto me.* Matthew 25:40 Pray for forgiveness of anything you are harboring in your heart against another, so that you release any bondage that has entrapped you within.

2) Strife

*Hatred stirreth up **strifes**: but love covereth all sins.*
Proverbs 10:12

Strife is a complex matter. It encompasses so many things in our life from how we feel about ourselves, to our relationships with our loved ones, to how we interact with others. It can be born of an emotional or spiritual nature and when not recognized, can be very destructive in hearing from God and receiving healing power. *A wrathful man stirreth up strife: but he that is slow to anger appeaseth strife.* Proverbs 15:18 Anger, contention, upheaval, meddling, and so forth bring strife and discontent among family and friends which causes disharmony. *It is an honor for a man to cease from strife: but every fool will be meddling.* Proverbs 20:3

3) Curses

*Bless them which persecute you: bless, and **curse** not.*
Romans 12:14

By the very words we speak, we can curse ourselves and others. Negative words whether spoken in humor or seriousness, places bondage on the person spoken to or about. God instructs us to guard our tongue for there is power in our words, just as there is power in God's Word. Curses are real and do affect our life and our health. Man causes many forms of afflictions upon himself, loved ones, friends, and strangers; individually, or as a society. *But I say unto you, Love your enemies, bless them that curse you, do good to them that hate you, and pray for them which despitefully use you, and persecute you.* Matthew 5:44 Be armored in God's Word and pray that any curses, known or not, be removed from your life and the lives of your loved ones. *Pleasant words are as an honeycomb, sweet to the soul, and health to the bones.* Proverbs 16:24 It is only a prayer away to receive freedom from a curse.

4) Fear

> *For God hath not given us the spirit of **fear**, but of power, and of love, and of a sound mind.*
> 1 Timothy 1:7

If we are in fear then we cannot be in faith, for fear voids faith. Fear is a negative emotion and is not of God. Fear is an emotional response that renders uncertainty and confusion. *For ye have not received the spirit of bondage again to fear; but ye have received the Spirit of adoption, whereby we cry, Abba, Father.* Romans 8:15 Fear draws us away from God's promises and holds us captive to the emotion which affects our decisions. When fear arises, it should be immediately replaced with faith. We must hold strong and allow our faith to command over fear, and trust in the Father's Word. *Therefore being justified by faith we have peace with God through our Lord Jesus Christ: By whom also we have access by faith into this grace wherein we stand, and rejoice in hope of the glory of God.* Romans 5:1-2

5) Pride

> *For all that is in the world, the lust of the flesh, and the lust of the eyes, and the **pride** of life, is not of the Father, but is of the world.*
> 1 John 2:16

Pride is an interesting subject because it's often misconstrued as confidence. What we consider to be confidence in ourselves can in actuality be pride, so how do we distinguish the difference? *The wicked, through the pride of his countenance, will not seek after God: God is not in all his thoughts.* Psalm 10:4 God doesn't accept pridefulness. Typically, a prideful person will seldom change their mind, nor accept they could be incorrect, and believe they know best. However, a confident individual will ponder and accept evaluation and make the necessary changes accordingly without losing their confidence. *A man's pride shall bring him low; but honor shall uphold the humble in spirit.* Proverbs 29:23 Often, we don't see this element within ourselves, but it's a major stumbling block to receiving from God.

6) Guilt

> *Deliver me from blood **guiltiness**, O God of my salvation: and my tongue shall sing aloud of thy righteousness.*
> Psalm 51:14

We can all find reason to feel guilty about something we have said or done in our lifetime; however, it is what we do with guilt that determines if we remain in bondage to our thoughts and feelings. When guilty of a word or act, asking forgiveness and letting go is the healthy thing to do. *Accuse not a servant unto his master, lest he curse thee, and though be found guilty.* Proverbs 30:10 Don't hold onto guilt because it will surely strip you from living in righteousness as you are meant to do in Christ.

7) Shame

> *O my god, I trust in thee: let me not be **ashamed**, let not mine enemies triumph over me.* Psalm 25:2

Shame comes from an outside source usually because of something someone has said or done to us that destroys our self-worth, self-esteem, and self-confidence making us feel unworthy. There can also be occasions when we bring shame upon ourselves by our own actions. This is a dangerous mindset because its roots are destructive and emotionally paralyzing. *For the scripture saith, Whosoever believeth on him shall not be ashamed.* Roman 10:11 In Christ, before our heavenly Father, we are cleansed and made righteous by His blood whereby there is no shame. As with sin, shame is washed away by the blood of Jesus. *According to my earnest expectation and my hope, that in nothing I shall be ashamed, but that with all boldness, as always, so now also Christ shall be magnified in my body, whether it be by life, or by my death.* Philippians 1:20 If there is shame within your soul, remember you are free from sin and shame. You are always worthy in the eyes of the Lord.

8) Grief

*Surely he hath borne our **griefs**, and carried our sorrows:*
yet we did esteem him stricken, smitten of God, and afflicted.
Isaiah 53:4

Everyone experiences grief and perhaps the most commonly know is the loss of a loved one; grief due to death is difficult. There is also grief from the termination of a relationship or friendship, or from accidents that leave someone physically challenged. There are many things that can cause grief but it's not a state of mind to remain in. Grief can quickly take our happiness, peace, and joy away leaving us feeling hopeless and helpless. *But if any have caused grief, he hath not grieved me, but in part: that I may not overcharge you all. Sufficient to such a man is this punishment, which was inflicted of many. So that contrariwise ye ought rather to forgive him, and comfort him, lest perhaps such a one should be swallowed up with overmuch sorrow. Wherefore I beseech you that ye would confirm your love toward him.* 2 Corinthians 2:5-8 Don't allow grief to consume you, break free that your life may be of joy and peace in Christ.

9) Idolatry

*Wherefore, my dearly beloved, flee from **idolatry**.*
1 Corinthians 10:14

Idolatry is a clever and dangerous element when our attention is focused on persons or things making them important in our lives. It is critical to be very astute in this area and not allow possessions or interests to predominate our thoughts and desires. *Mortify therefore your members which are upon the earth; fornication, uncleanness, inordinate affection, evil concupiscence, and covetousness, which is idolatry.* Colossians 3:5 Fascinations can easily turn into obsessions and take us in a direction whereby we are more mindful of our desires rather than astute to God. *Now the works of the flesh are manifest, which are these; Adultery, fornication, uncleanness, lasciviousness, idolatry, witchcraft, hatred, emulations, wrath, strife, seditions, heresies, envying, murders, drunkenness, revelings, and such like: of the which I tell you before, and I have also told you in time past, that they which do such things shall not inherit the kingdom of God.* Galatians 5:19-21

10) Hopelessness

*For we are saved by **hope**: but **hope** that is seen is not **hope**: for what man seeth, why doth he yet **hope** for? But if we **hope** for that we see not, then do we with patience wait for it.*
Romans 8:24-25

Our foundation of faith is based on hope. Hope brings the unseen, the things of God, into existence through our continual faith as we pray and stand in hope for what we seek to manifest into our lives. It is hope we cleave to as we hold firm in faith and patiently await the heavenly outcome. *Hope deferred makes the heart sick: but when the desire cometh, it is a tree of life.* Proverbs 13:12 Hope is a critical element in faith defined as the substance of having faith. *The hope of the righteous shall be gladness: but the expectation of the wicked shall perish.* Proverbs 10:28 Never give up hope in God's ability to supply for your needs. Remember, hope is just as important as faith because it is a component of faith. *Therefore did my heart rejoice, and my tongue was glad; moreover also my flesh shall rest in hope.* Acts 2:26 Cleave to hope in faith and you shall receive the blessings our heavenly Father has promised.

11) Thanklessness

> *Enter into his gates with **thanksgiving**, and into his courts with praise: be **thankful** unto him, and bless his name.*
> Colossians 3:15

In all of life, give praise, honor, glory, and thanksgiving to the Lord for His mercy and grace, and His blessings and promises, for they are bountiful. *Being enriched in every thing to all bountifulness, which causeth through us thanksgiving to God.* 2 Corinthians 9:11 We often forget to thank our heavenly Father for all the wonderful things He has done through His Son. We must not become ungrateful; therefore, if we are limited in our thanksgiving we can easily slip into thoughtlessness. *For the administration of this service not only supplieth the want of the saints, but is abundant also by many thanksgivings unto God.* 2 Corinthians 9:11-12 We thank each other upon receiving gifts, much more should we remember to thank God for His mighty gifts.

12) Lack of Patience

*And besides this, giving all diligence, add to your faith virtue;
and to virtue knowledge; And to knowledge temperance; and to
temperance **patience**; and to **patience** godliness; And to godliness
brotherly kindness; and to brotherly kindness charity.*
2 Peter 1:5-7

Patience is truly a virtue and commendable before the Lord. In our deliverance from personal troubled times, a rough passage in our daily life, we are to have patience as God's resolution manifest. During this hardship, our patience as shown in our unrelenting and steadfast faith is accountable as virtue to God. Patience is a direct reflection of our maintaining faith in our moment of crisis and holding to His Word. *According as his divine power hath given unto us all things that pertain unto life and godliness, through the knowledge of him that hath called us to glory and virtue.* 2 Peter 1:3 Living in a fallen world, an imperfect environment, is going to breed mishaps and offensive situations; however, in our faith we have hope, and with hope, we gain patience, and through patience we acquire virtue. All work towards the attaining of the supernatural power of the Holy Spirit by the authority given in Christ. *My brethren, count it all joy when ye fall into divers temptations; Knowing this, that the trying of your faith worketh patience. But let patience have her perfect work, that ye may be perfect and entire, wanting nothing.* James 1:2-4

13) Lack of Faith

*Therefore being justified by **faith** we have peace with God
through our Lord Jesus Christ: By whom also we have access*

*by **faith** into this grace wherein we stand, and rejoice in hope of the glory of God.* Romans 5:1-5

Without faith we are lost to anything of the Kingdom of Heaven. All treasures of blessings, gifts, and promises are void to our life when we do not have faith. Jesus said only a small amount of true faith will open the Kingdom doors to receive. However, along with faith, we stay in hope of the anticipation of the answers to our prayers. We wait for the unseen to become the seen, the supernatural power from heaven to be witnessed in the natural. *For I say, through the grace given unto me, to every man that is among you, not to think of himself more highly than he ought to think; but to think soberly, according as God hath dealt to every man the measure of faith.* Romans 12:3 Faith is our stronghold to all answered prayers, the key to the Kingdom of Heaven.

14) Lack of Love

*And we have known and believed in the **love** that God hath for us. God is **love**; and he that dwelleth in **love** dwelleth in God, and God in him.*
1 John 4:16

Love is a word that is spoken frequently but often without meaning. It easily becomes second nature to apply the word love in our signature statements, but do we truly mean it when we say it? Love begins with loving God and understanding the very nature of His love. From His agape love, we learn to love ourselves and accept ourselves worthy to be loved, so that we may be equipped to love another. Love surpasses all things, and makes all things complete as God teaches us in His perfect love for His children. *And thou shalt love the Lord thy God with all thy heart, and with all thy soul, and with all thy mind, and with all thy strength: this is the first commandment. And the second is like, namely this, Thou shalt love thy neighbor as thyself. There is none other commandment greater than these.* Mark 12:30-31 Love is the beginning and the end to all things of God; and likewise, is the beginning to our faith, our hope, our patience, our forgiveness, and so forth. It all begins with love. We must have a heart of love to conquer hatred, anger, disillusionment, disappointment, discouragement, and the list goes on.

15) Double-minded

*A **double minded** man is unstable in all his ways.*
James 1:8

Having two sets of standards to suit the occasion is not worthy of any attention and does not make for accountability in our relationship with our heavenly Father, nor with those we are close to. It makes us unreliable and untrustworthy. *Draw nigh to God, and he will draw nigh to you. Cleanse your hands, ye sinners; and purify your hearts, ye double minded.* James 4:8 Hold to one standard, one belief, one trusting nature in all matters, and be sure that it is in the Lord.

16) Ignorance

*For they being **ignorant** of God's righteousness, and going about to establish their own righteousness, have not submitted themselves unto the righteousness of God.*
Romans 10:3

As a child of the Father, ignorance of His Word will never be an acceptable excuse. Becoming born-again to the spiritual being we are in Christ, we then accept our journey into learning how to live our new spirit life as we remain in the natural. We cannot claim "I didn't know" and have expectations of God. Maybe our children can use that excuse with us from time to time when they haven't been obedient, but it doesn't work that way as children of God. *But if any man be ignorant, let him be ignorant.* 1 Corinthians 14:38 If your choice is to not know God's Word, then remain without knowledge, but don't expect Kingdom privileges.

17) Judgmental

> **Judge** *not, that ye be not* **judged**. *For with what* **judgment** *ye* **judge**, *ye shall be* **judged** *and with what measure ye mete, it shall be measured to you again.*
> Matthew 7:2

God is very explicit in His Word. If we choose to judge others based on our opinion, then what we hold them in unfavorableness will be placed on us, and God will measure equal judgment onto us. We all have opinions, and it is easy to find fault with another simply by reason of not agreeing, but it is a dangerous mindset to speak accusations of disapproval in judgment. *Judge not, and ye shall not be judged condemn not, and ye shall not be condemned: forgive, and ye shall be forgiven. Give, and it shall be given unto you; good measure, pressed down, and shaken together, and running over, shall men give into your bosom. For with the same measure that ye mete withal it shall be measured to you again.* Luke 6:37-38 Therefore, *Let a man so account of us, as of the ministers of Christ, and stewards of the mysteries of God. Moreover it is required in stewards, that a man be found faithful. But with me it is a very small thing that I should be judged of you, or of man's judgment: yea, I judge not mine own self. For I know nothing by myself; yet am I not hereby justified: but he that judge me is the Lord.* 1 Corinthians 4:1-4 God is the only One who passes judgment. We will stand before Christ on the Judgment Day and be held accountable for our earthen behavior. Because of our carnal tendencies, we often slip in this arena; however, when we find ourselves voicing our opinion in judgment of another, we should take notice and withdraw our statement of accusation. *For what have I to do to judge them also that are without? Do not ye judge them that are within? But them that are without God judgeth. Therefore put away from among yourselves that wicked person.* 1 Corinthians 5:12-13 God calls us wicked who judges another. In John 8:15-16, *Ye judge after the flesh, I judge no man. And yet if I judge, my judgment is true: for I am not alone, but I and the Father that sent me.* There is only One who may pass judgment. There is a difference between disapproval and placing judgment on another person.

18) Unbelief

*And he did not many mighty works there because of their **unbelief**.*
Matthew 13:58

There I say unto you, What things soever ye desire, when ye pray, believe that ye receive them, and ye shall have them.
Mark 11:24

Without belief, we are in unbelief. It begins with believing in the Lord and relying on His Word; being faithful, obedient, and trusting in hope for the manifestation of His blessings, and knowing it will be forthcoming. We may think ourselves faithful, but doubt can be just as prevalent as our belief, and it can wash away our belief in an instant. *Jesus said unto him, if thou canst believe, all things are possible to him that believeth. And straightway the father of the child cried out, and said with tears, Lord, I believe; help thou mine unbelief.* Mark 9:23-24 When we doubt to seeing the supernatural power of God exemplified in the natural, we have voided our prayer of faith. This is the major reason many do not receive from God. Though they believe their faith to be strong, there can be questionable doubt, unbelief.

Just as we learn in the Bible of the miracles and healing by God as reflected in the Old Testament and by Jesus in the New Testament, they are still prevalent today in our lifetime. However, as God and His Son performed the miracles and healing in past generations, we are responsible through faith and belief to acquire them in our generation. Know how to receive the supernatural power in the Kingdom to heal yourself and others. Christ has given to each faithful believer His authority within the Kingdom of Heaven, and through the Holy Spirit, to receive that which we ask. Do not allow unbelief to block God's supernatural power from flowing continuously in your life.

Unbelief prevents us from having a relationship with our heavenly Father. Of all the obstacles that can block our communication and commitment to God, unbelief trumps all others.

Steps to Reclaim Health

That your faith should not stand in the wisdom of men, but in the power of God.

1 Corinthians 2:5

The supernatural power of healing is for each of the Father's children and has been established at the foundation of His creation through the Living Word. In Christ, we may claim our healing through His blood shed at Calvary and by the Holy Spirit receive it.

Prepare - believe you are healed
Accept - your healing has two components; spirit and natural
Remove - yourself from bondage
Pray - concentrate on healing scriptures
Hold - in faith
Patience - for manifestation
Claim - the healing

Realign your relationship with God

1) Pray for forgiveness of sins, repent
2) Pray for release from bondage, curses, captivity
3) Remove strife
4) Remove idolatry
5) Remove unbelief
6) Pray for your healing with authority
7) Meditate on healing scriptures daily
8) Accept that you are healed, know the truth in Christ
9) Accept that God made your body to renew, replenish, and repair
10) Know your healing is in the spirit realm and then the natural
11) Have patience with unwavering faith as your healing manifests
12) Accept the physical body's transformation of the healing process

Claim the Victory

God has proclaimed our healing and Christ has provided it. As His children, we may receive what our heavenly Father has given through mercy, grace, and faith. We must understand that God provides for His children, but we need to believe in His Word and be willing to accept His most precious gifts.

Ask yourself these questions to identify your specific (or someone else) ailment. Once you focus on what your healing is for, then pray with the knowledge and understanding that you have been given the gift of healing by your faith. What you are doing is claiming your rightful ownership of the healing gift as a child of the Almighty King. It is the Father's gift to you made possible through the blood of His Son, and God desires for you to have it. Take possession with victory in your health!

1) **Who** - is the healing for (you or a loved one)?

_____

2) **What** - is the *dis-ease* (name the illness)?

_____

3) **When** - did the *dis-ease* occur (timeframe it has been in your body)?

_____

4) **Where** - in the body (organ affected)?

_____

5) **Why** - you have it (how did it occur)?

_____

Notes:

Part VI

The Trinity Scriptures

King James Bible

Part I ~ Trinity of God, Scriptures

Romans 8:38-39 For I am persuaded, that neither death, nor life, nor angels, nor principalities, nor powers, nor things present, nor things to come; Nor height, nor depth, nor any other creature, shall be able to separate us from the love of God, which is in Christ Jesus our Lord.

1 Peter 4:11 If any man speak, let him speak as the oracles of God; if any man minister, let him do it as of the ability which God giveth: that God in all things may be glorified through Jesus Christ, to whom be praise and dominion for ever and ever. Amen.

Genesis 2:2-4 And on the seventh day God ended his work which he had made; and he rested on the seventh day from all his work which he had made. And God blessed the seventh day, and sanctified it: because that in it he had rested from all his work which God created and made. These are the generations of the heavens and of the earth when they were created, in the day that the Lord God made the earth and the heavens.

Psalm 12:6 The words of the Lord are pure words: as silver tried in a furnace of earth, purified seven times.

Acts 6:3 Wherefore, brethren, look ye out among you seven men of honest report, full of the Holy Ghost and wisdom, whom we may appoint over this business.

Genesis 7:2-3 Of every clean beast thou shalt take to thee by sevens, the male and his female: and of beasts that are not clean by two, the male and his female. Of fowls also of the air by sevens, the male and the female; to keep seed alive upon the face of all the earth.

Genesis 7:4 For yet seven days, and I will cause it to rain upon the earth for forty days and forty nights; and every living substance that I have made will I destroy from off the face of the earth.

Genesis 41:29-31 Behold, there come seven years of great plenty throughout all the land of Egypt: And there shall arise after them seven years of famine; and all the plenty shall be forgotten in the land of Egypt; and the famine shall consume the land; And the plenty shall not be known in the land by reason of that famine following, for it shall be very grievous.

Luke 23:33 And when they were come to the place, which is called Calvary, there they crucified him, and the malefactors, one on the right hand, and the other on the left.

Luke 23:39-43 And one of the malefactors which were hanged railed on him, saying, If thou be Christ, save thyself and us. But the other answering rebuked him, saying, Dost not thou fear God, seeing thou art in the same condemnation? And we indeed justly; for we receive the due reward of our deeds: but this man hath done nothing amiss. And he said unto Jesus, Lord, remember me when thou comest into thy kingdom. And Jesus said unto him, Verily I say unto thee, To day shalt thou be with me in paradise.

Matthew 12:39-40 But he answered and said unto them, An evil and adulterous generation seeketh after a sign; and there shall no sign be given to it, but the sign of the prophet Jonas: For as Jonas was three days and three nights in the whale's belly; so shall the Son of man be three days and three nights in the heart of the earth.

Revelation 1:18 I am he that liveth, and was dead; and, behold, I am alive for evermore, Amen; and have the keys of hell and of death.

James 3:17 But the wisdom that is from above is first pure, then peaceable, gentle, and easy to be entreated, full of mercy and good fruits, without partiality, and without hypocrisy.

1 John 2:27 But the anointing which ye have received of him abideth in you, and ye need not that any man teach you: but as the same anointing teacheth you of all things, and is truth, and is no lie, and even as it hath taught you, ye shall abide in him.

1 Corinthians 2:5 That your faith should not stand in the wisdom of men, but in the power of God.

James 5:16 The effectual fervent prayer of a righteous man availeth much.

John 8:32 And ye shall know the truth, and the truth shall make you free.

Matthew 6:6 But thou, when thou prayest, enter into thy closet, and when thou hast shut thy door, pray to thy Father which is in secret; and thy Father which seeth in secret shall reward thee openly.

Matthew 17:20 And Jesus said unto them, Because of your unbelief: for verily I say unto you, If ye have faith as a grain of mustard seed, ye shall say unto this mountain, Remove hence to yonder place; and it shall remove; and nothing shall be impossible unto you.

Colossians 3:17 And whatsoever ye do in word or deed, do all in the name of the Lord Jesus, giving thanks to God and the Father, by him.

Genesis 1:27 So God created man in his own image, in the image of God created he him; male and female created he them.

Ephesians 1:4-5 According as he hath chosen us in him before the foundation of the world, that we should be holy and without blame before him in love; having predestinated us unto the adoption of children by Jesus Christ to himself, according to the good pleasure of his will.

Genesis 2:7 And the Lord God formed man of the dust of the ground, and breathed into his nostrils the breath of life; and man became a living soul.

Genesis 5:1-2 This is the book of the generations of Adam. In the day that God created man, in the likeness of God made he him. Male and female created he them; and blessed them, and called their name Adam, in the day when they were created.

Genesis 2:8 And the Lord God planted a garden eastward in Eden; and there he put the man whom he had formed.

Genesis 2:19-20 And out of the ground the Lord God formed every beast of the field, and every fowl of the air; and brought them to Adam to see what he would call them: and whatsoever Adam called every living creature, that was the name thereof. And Adam gave names to all cattle, and to the fowl of the air, and to every beast of the field; but for Adam there was not found an help meet for him.

Genesis 2:23 And Adam said, This is now bone of my bones, and flesh of my flesh: she shall be called Woman, because she was taken out of Man.

Genesis 3:20 And Adam called his wife's name Eve; because she was the mother of all living.

Romans 5:17-19 For if by one man's offence death reigned by one; much more they which receive abundance of grace and of the gift of righteousness shall reign in life by one, Jesus Christ. Therefore as by the offence of one judgment came upon all men to condemnation; even so by the righteousness of one the free gift came upon all men unto justification of life. For as by one man's disobedience many were made sinners, so by the obedience of one shall many be made righteous.

Genesis 3:22 And the Lord God said, Behold, the man is become as one of us, to know good and evil: and now, lest he put forth his hand, and take also also of the tree of life, and eat, and live for ever.

Genesis 3:16-17 Unto the woman he said, I will greatly multiply thy sorrow and thy conception; in sorrow thou shalt bring forth children; and thy desire shall be to thy husband, and he shall rule over thee. And unto Adam he said, Because thou hast hearkened unto the voice of thy wife, and hast eaten of the tree, of which I commanded thee, saying, Thou shalt not eat of it: cursed is the ground for thy sake; in sorrow shalt thou eat of it all the days of thy life.

Genesis 4:1 And Adam knew Eve his wife; and she conceived, and bare Cain, and said, I have gotten a man from the Lord.

1 Corinthians 15:22 For as in Adam all die, even so in Christ shall all be made alive.

2 Corinthians 5:21 For he hath made him to be sin for us, who knew no sin; that we might be made the righteousness of God in him.

1 John 4:8 He that loveth not knoweth not God; for God is love.

Isaiah 45:18 For thus saith the Lord that created the heavens; God himself that formed the earth and made it; he hath established it, he created it not in vain, he formed it to be inhabited: I am the Lord; and there is none else.

Psalm 90:2 Before the mountains were brought forth, or ever thou hadst formed the earth and the world, even from everlasting to everlasting, thou art God.

2 Corinthians 4:15 For all things are for your sakes, that the abundant grace might through the thanksgiving of many redound to the glory of God.

1 John 4:16 And we have known and believed the love that God hath to us. God is love; an he that dwelleth in love dwelleth in God, and God in him.

John 4:24 God is a Spirit: and they that worship him must worship him in spirit and in truth.

John 3:16 For God so loved the world that he gave his only begotten Son, that whosoever believeth in him should no t perish, but have everlasting life.

Mark 12:30-31 And thou shalt love the Lord thy God with all thy heart, and with all thy soul, and with all thy mind, and with all thy strength: this is the first commandment. And the second is like, namely this, Thou shalt love thy neighbour as thyself. There is none other commandment greater than these.

2 Timothy 1:9 Who hath saved us, and called us with an holy calling, not according to our works, but according to his own purpose and grace, which was given us in Christ Jesus before the world began.

Matthew 12:31 Wherefore I say unto you, All manner of sin and blasphemy shall be forgiven unto men: but the blasphemy against the Holy Ghost shall not be forgiven unto men.

James 1:26 If any man among you seem to be religious, and bridleth not his tongue, but deceiveth his own heart, this man's religion is vain.

1 Peter 3:10 For he that will love life, and see good days, let him refrain his tongue from evil, and his lips that they speak no guile.

Proverbs 18:21 Death and life are in the power of the tongue: and they that love it shall eat the fruit thereof.

Romans 2:11 For there is no respect of persons with God.

1 Corinthians 4:1 Let a man so account of us, as of the ministers of Christ, and stewards of the mysteries of God.

Luke 8:10 And he said, Unto you it is given to know the mysteries of the kingdom of God: but to others in parables; that seeing they might not see, and hearing they might not understand.

Colossians 3:17 And whatsoever ye do in word or deed, do all in the name of the Lord Jesus, giving thanks to God and the Father by him.

Proverbs 10:22 The blessing of the Lord, it maketh rich, and he addeth no sorrow with it.

Matthew 5:44 But I say unto you, Love your enemies, bless them that curse you, do good to them that hate you, and pray for them which despitefully use you, and persecute you.

3 John 1:2 Beloved, I wish above all things that thou mayest prosper and be in health, even as thy soul prospereth.

Deuteronomy 30:19-20 I call heaven and earth to record this day against you, that I have set before you life and death, blessing and cursing: therefore choose life, that both thou and thy seed may live: That thou mayest love the Lord thy God, and that thou mayest obey his voice, and that thou mayest cleave unto him: for he is thy life, and the length of thy days: that thou mayest dwell in the land which the Lord sware unto thy fathers, to Abraham, to Isaac, and to Jacob, to give them.

Proverbs 8:22-32 The Lord possessed me in the beginning of his way, before his works of old. I was set up from everlasting, from the beginning, or ever the earth was. When there were no depths, I was brought forth; when there were no fountains abounding with water. Before the mountains were settled, before the hills was I brought forth: While as yet he had not made the earth, nor the fields, nor the highest part of the dust of the world. When he established the clouds above: when he strengthened the fountains of the deep: When he gave to the sea his decree, that the waters should not pass his commandment: when he appointed the foundations of the earth: Then I was by him, as one brought up with him: and I was daily his delight, rejoicing always before him; Rejoicing in the habitable part of his earth; and my delights were with the sons of men. Now therefore hearken unto me, O ye children: for blessed are they that keep my ways.

1 Timothy 2:5 For there is one God, and one mediator between God and men, the man Christ Jesus.

Ephesians 3:9 And to make all men see what is the fellowship of the mystery, which from the beginning of the world hath been hid in God, who created all things by Jesus Christ.

Colossians 1:16-17 For by him were all things created, that are in heaven, and that are in earth, visible and invisible, whether they be thrones, or dominions, or principalities, or powers: all things were created by him, and for him: And he is before all things, and by him all things consist.

Isaiah 9:6 For unto us a child is born, unto us a son is given: and the government shall be upon his shoulder: and his name shall be called Wonderful, Counsellor, The mighty God, The everlasting Father, The Prince of Peace.

John 1:13-14 Which were born, not of blood, nor of the will of the flesh, nor of the will of man, but of God. And the Word was made flesh, and dwelt among us, (and we beheld his glory, the glory as of the only begotten of the Father), full of grace and truth.

Ephesians 2:18 For through him we both have access by one Spirit unto the Father.

2 Corinthians 5:21 For he hath made him to be sin for us, who knew no sin; that we might be made the righteousness of God in him.

2 Corinthians 5:18-19 And all things are of God, who hath reconciled us to himself by Jesus Christ, and hath given to us the ministry of reconciliation; To wit, that God was in Christ, reconciling the world unto himself, not imputing their trespasses unto them; and hath committed unto us the word of reconciliation.

Colossians 1:20 And, having made peace through the blood of his cross, by him to reconcile all things unto himself; by him, I say, whether they be things in earth, or things in heaven.

2 Corinthians 5:17 Therefore if any man be in Christ, he is a new creature: old things are passed away; behold, all things are become new.

Ephesians 2:15-18 Having abolished in his flesh the enmity, even the law of commandments contained in ordinances; for to make in himself of twain one new man, so making peace; And that he might reconcile both unto God in one body by the cross, having slain the enmity thereby: And came and preached peace to you which were afar off, and to them that were nigh. For through him we both have access by one Spirit unto the Father.

Genesis 1:28 And God blessed them, and God said unto them, be fruitful, and multiply, and replenish the earth, and subdue it: and have dominion over the fish of the sea, and over the fowl of the air, and over every living thing that moveth upon the earth.

Matthew 7:15 Beware of false prophets, which come to you in sheep's clothing, but inwardly they are ravening wolves.

Genesis 1:1 In the beginning God created the heaven and the earth.

Genesis 1:26 And God said, Let us make man in our image, after our likeness: and let them have dominion over the fish of the sea, and over the fowl of the air, and over the cattle, and over all the earth, and over every creeping thing that creepeth upon the earth.

Hosea 4:6 My people are destroyed for lack of knowledge: because thou hast rejected knowledge, I will also reject thee, that thou shalt be no priest to me: seeing thou hast forgotten the law of thy God, I will also forget thy children.

Genesis 3:5 For God doth know that in the day ye eat thereof, then your eyes shall be opened, and ye shall be as gods, knowing good and evil.

Psalm 22:16 For dogs have compassed me: the assembly of the wicked have enclosed me: they pierced my hands and feet.

John 19:34 But one of the soldiers with a spear pierced his side, and forthwith came there out blood and water.

2 Corinthians 5:10 For we must all appear before the judgement seat of Christ; that every one may receive the things done in his body, according to that he hath done, whether it be good or bad.

John 17:11-14 And now I am no more in the world, but these are in the world, and I come to thee. Holy Father, keep through thine own name those whom thou hast given me, that they may be one, as we are. While I was with them in the world, I kept them in thy name: those that thou gavest me I have kept, and none of them is lost, but the son of perdition; that the scripture might be fulfilled. And now come I to thee; and these things I speak in the world, that they might have my joy fulfilled in themselves. I have given them thy word; and the world hath hate them, because they are not of the world, even as I am not.

Hebrews 8:10 For this is the covenant that I will make with the house of Israel after those days, saith the Lord; I will put my laws into their mind, and write them in their hearts: and I will be to them a God, and they shall be to be me a people.

James 3:6 And the tongue is a fire, a world of iniquity: so is the tongue among our members, that it defileth the whole body, and setteth on fire the course of nature; and it is set on fire of hell.

2 Timothy 1:14 That good thing which was committed unto thee keep by the Holy Ghost which dwelleth in us.

2 Corinthians 5:10 For we must all appear before the judgment seat of Christ; that every one may receive the things done in his body, according to that he hath done, whether it be good or bad.

2 Corinthians 5:17 Therefore if any man be in Christ, he is a new creature: old things are passed away; behold, all things are become new.

1 Corinthians 1:30-31 But of him are ye in Christ Jesus, who of God is made unto us wisdom, and righteousness, and sanctification, and redemption: That, according as it is written, He that glorieth, let him glory in the Lord.

Nehemiah 9:13-15 Thou camest down also upon Mount Sinai, and spakest with them from heaven, and gavest them right judgments, and true laws, good statutes and commandments: And madest known unto them thy holy sabbath, and commandedst them precepts, statutes, and laws, by the hand of Moses thy servant: And gavest them bread from heaven for their hunger, and broughtest forth water for them out of the rock for their thirst, and promisedst them that they should go in to possess the land which thou hadst sworn to give them.

Nehemiah 9:16-17 But they and our fathers dealt proudly, and hardened their necks, and hearkened not to thy commandments; And refused to obey, neither were mindful of thy wonders that thou didst among them; but hardened their necks, and in their rebellion appointed a captain to return to their bondage: but thou art a God ready to pardon, gracious and merciful, slow to anger, and of great kindness, and forsookest them not.

Nehemiah 9:18 Yea, when they had made them a molten calf, and said, this is thy God that brought thee up out of Egypt, and had wrought great provocations.

Colossians 2:17 Which are a shadow of things to come; but the body is of Christ.

2 Corinthians 4:16 For which cause we faint not; but though our outward man perish, yet the inward man is renewed day by day.

1 John 4:13 Hereby know we that we dwell in him, and he in us, because he hath given us of his Spirit.

1 Peter 1:19-21 But with the precious blood of Christ, as of a lamb without blemish and without spot: Who verily was foreordained before the foundation of the world, but was manifest in these last times for you, Who by him do believe in God, that raised him up from the dead, and gave him glory; that your faith and hope might be in God.

Luke 22:44 And being in an agony he prayed more earnestly: and his sweat was as it were great drops of blood falling down to the ground.

1 Peter 2:24 Who his own self bare our sins in his own body on the tree, that we, being dead to sins, should live unto righteousness: by whose stripes ye were healed.

Matthew 27:29 And when they had platted a crown of thorns, they put it upon his head, and a reed in his right hand: and they bowed the knee before him, and mocked him, saying, Hail, King of the Jews!

John 17:4 I have glorified thee on earth: I have finished the work which thou gavest me to do.

1 Peter 3:18 For Christ also hath once suffered for sins, the just for the unjust, that he might bring us to God, being put to death in the flesh, but quickened by the Spirit.

John 19:30 When Jesus therefore had received the vinegar, he said, It is finished: and he bowed his head, and gave up the ghost.

Ephesians 4:24 An that ye put on the new man, which after God is created in righteousness and true holiness.

Romans 6:22 But now being made free from sin, and become servants to God, ye have your fruit unto holiness, and the end everlasting life.

Mark 9:23 Jesus said unto him, If thou canst believe, all things are possible to him that believeth.

John 3:6 That which is born of the flesh is flesh; and that which is born of the Spirit is spirit.

John 14:6 I am the way, the truth and the life: no man cometh unto the Father, but by me.

Romans 8:26 Likewise the Spirit also helpeth our infirmities: for we know not what we should pray for as we ought: but the Spirit itself maketh intercession for us with groanings which cannot be uttered.

Mark 4:11-12 And he said unto them, Unto you it is given to know the mystery of the kingdom of God: but unto them that are without, all these things are done in parables: That seeing they may see, and not perceive; and hearing they may hear, and not understand; lest at any time they should be converted, and their sins should be forgiven them.

Matthew 13:13 Therefore speak I to them in parables: because they seeing see not; and hearing they hear not, neither do they understand.

2 Corinthians 1:22 Who hath also sealed us, and given the earnest of the Spirit in our hearts.

Romans 8:27 And he that searcheth the hearts knoweth what is the mind of the Spirit, because he maketh intercession for the saints according to the will of God.

John 14:16-17 And I will pray the Father, and he shall give you another Comforter, that he may abide with you for ever; Even the Spirit of truth; whom the world cannot receive, because it seeth him not, neither knoweth him: but ye know him; for he dwelleth with you, and shall be in you.

Luke 11:13 If ye then, being evil, know how to give good gifts unto your children: how much more shall your heavenly Father give the Holy Spirit to them that ask him?

Mark 1:8 I indeed have baptized you with water: but he shall baptize you with the Holy Ghost.

1 Corinthians 12:4-6 Now there are diversities of gifts, but the same Spirit. And there are differences of administrations, but the same Lord. And there are diversities of operations, but it is the same God which worketh all in all.

Ephesians 4:9-12 Now that he ascended, what is it but that he also descended first into the lower parts of the earth? He that descended is the same also that ascended up far above all heavens, that he might fill all things. And he gave some, evangelists; and some, pastors and teachers; For the perfecting of the saints, for the work of the ministry, for the edifying of the body of Christ.

1 Corinthians 12:7-11 But the manifestation of the Spirit is given to every man to profit withal. For to one is given by the Spirit the word of wisdom; to another the word of knowledge by the same Spirit; To another faith by the same Spirit; to another the gifts of healing by the same Spirit; To another the working of miracles; to another prophecy; to another discerning of spirits; to another divers kinds of tongues; to another the interpretation of tongues: But all these worketh that one and the selfsame

Spirit, dividing to every man severally as he will.

Romans 12:6-8 Having then gifts differing according to the grace that is given to us, whether prophecy, let us prophesy according to the proportion of faith; Or ministry, let us wait on our ministering: or he that teacheth, on teaching; Or he that exhorteth, on exhortation: he that giveth, let him do it with simplicity; he that ruleth, with diligence; he that showeth mercy, with cheerfulness.

James 1:17 Every good gift and every perfect gift is from above, and cometh down from the Father of lights, with whom is no variableness, neither shadow of turning.

John 14:13-14 And whatsoever ye shall ask in my name, that will I do, that the Father may be glorified in the Son. If ye shall ask any thing in my name, I will do it.

John 15:7 If ye abide in me, and my words abide in you, ye shall ask what ye will, and it shall be done unto you.

John 15:16 Ye have not chosen me, but I have chosen you, and ordained you, that ye should go and bring forth fruit, and that your fruit should remain: that whatsoever ye shall ask of the Father in my name, he may give it you.

Hebrews 10:22 Let us draw near with a true heart in full assurance of faith, having our hearts sprinkled from an evil conscience, and our bodies washed with pure water.

Hebrews 13:9 Be not carried about with divers and strange doctrines. For it is a good thing that the heart be established with grace; not with meats, which have not profited them that have been occupied therein.

Matthew 26:41 Watch and pray, that ye enter not into temptation: the spirit indeed is willing, but the flesh is weak.

John 15:26-27 But when the Comforter is come, whom I will send unto you from the Father, even the Spirit of truth, which proceedeth from the Father, he shall testify of me. And ye also shall bear witness, because ye have been with me from the beginning.

2 Corinthians 5:1-2 For we know that if our earthly house of this tabernacle were dissolved, we have a building of God, an house not made with hands, eternal in the heavens. For in this we groan, earnestly desiring to be clothed upon with our house which is from heaven.

1 Corinthians 12:27-31 Now ye are the body of Christ, and members in particular. And God hath set forth some in the church, first apostles, secondarily prophets, thirdly teachers, after that miracles, then gifts of healings, helps, governments, diversities of tongues. Are all apostles? are all prophets? are all teachers? are all workers of miracles? Have all the gifts of healing? do all speak with tongues? Do all interpret? But covet earnestly the best gifts: and yet show I unto you a more excellent way.

Hebrews 8:10 For this is the covenant that I will make with the house of Israel after those days, saith the Lord; I will put my laws into their mind, and write them in their hearts: and I will be to them a God, and they shall be to me a people.

1 Corinthians 3:16 Know ye not that ye are the temple of God, and that the Spirit of God dwelleth in you?

Luke 8:10 And he said, Unto you it is given to know the mysteries of the kingdom of God: but to others in parables; that seeing they might not see, and hearing they might not understand.

Luke 11:13 If ye then, being evil, know how to give good gifts unto your children: how much more shall your heavenly Father give the Holy Spirit to them that ask him?

John 4:23-24 But the hour cometh, and now is, when the true worshippers shall worship the Father in spirit and in truth: for the Father seeketh such to worship him. God is a Spirit: and they that worship him must worship him in spirit and in truth.

Philippians 2:2 Fulfill ye my joy, that ye be likeminded, having the same love, being of one accord, of one mind.

John 1:14 And the Word was made flesh, and dwelt among us (and we beheld his glory, the glory as of the only begotten of the Father), full of grace and truth.

Matthew 26:41 Watch and pray, that ye enter not into temptation: the spirit indeed is willing, but the flesh is weak.

1 Corinthians 2:12 Now we have received, not the spirit of the world, but the spirit which is God; that we might know the things that are freely given to us of God.

2 Corinthians 5:18 And all things are of God, who hath reconciled us to himself by Jesus Christ, and hath given to us the ministry of reconciliation.

James 5:16 Confess your faults one to another, and pray one for another, that ye may be healed. The effectual fervent prayer of a righteous man availeth much.

John 8:42 Jesus said unto them, If God were your Father, ye would love me: for I proceeded forth and came from God; neither came I of myself, but he sent me.

Matthew 21:22 And all things, whatsoever ye shall ask in prayer, believing, ye shall receive.

Mark 10:19-27 Thou knowest the commandments, Do not commit adultery, Do not kill, Do not steal, Do not bear false witness, Defraud not, Honour thy father and mother. And he answered and said unto him,

Master, all these have I observed from my youth. Then Jesus beholding him loved him, and said unto him, One thing thou lackest: go thy way, sell whatsoever thou hast, and give to the poor, and thou shalt have treasure in heaven: and come, take up the cross, and follow me. And he was sad at that saying, and went away grieved: for he had great possessions. And Jesus looked round about, and saith unto his disciples, How hardly shall they that have riches enter into the kingdom of God! And the disciples were astonished at his words. But Jesus answereth again, and saith unto them, Children, how hard is it for them that trust in riches to enter into the kingdom of God! It is easier for a camel to go through the eye of a needle, than for a rich man to enter into the kingdom of God. And they were astonished out of measure, saying among themselves, Who then can be saved? And Jesus looking upon them saith, With men it is impossible, but not with God: for with God all things are possible.

1 John 2:21-22 I have not written unto you because ye know not the truth, but because ye know it, and that no lie is of the truth. Who is a liar but he that denieth that Jesus is the Christ? He is antichrist, that denieth the Father and the Son.

1 John 2:23-29 Whosoever denieth the Son, the same hath not the Father: (but) he that acknowledgeth the Son hath the Father also. Let that therefore abide in you, which ye have heard from the beginning. If that which ye have heard from the beginning shall remain in you, ye also shall continue in the Son, and in the Father. And this is the promise that he hath promised us, even eternal life. These things have I written unto you concerning them that seduce you. But the anointing which ye have received of him abideth in you, and ye need not that any man teach you: but as the same anointing teacheth you of all things, and is truth, and is no lie, and even as it hath taught you, ye shall abide in him. And now, little children, abide in him; that, when he shall appear, we may have confidence, and not be ashamed before him at his coming. If ye know that he is righteous, ye know that every one that doeth righteousness is born of him.

Ephesians 6:24 Grace be with all them that love our Lord Jesus Christ in sincerity.

Philippians 1:9 And this I pray, that your love may abound yet more, and more in knowledge and in all judgment.

Matthew 3:16-17 And Jesus, when he was baptized, went up straightway out of the water: and, lo, the heavens were opened unto him, and he saw the Spirit of God descending like a dove, and lighting upon him. And lo a voice from heaven, saying, This is my beloved Son, in whom I am well pleased.

Matthew 5:17-20 Think not that I am come to destroy the law, or the prophets: I am not come to destroy, but to fulfill. For verily I say unto you, till heaven and earth pass, one jot or one tittle shall in no wise pass from the law, till all be fulfilled. Whosoever therefore shall break one of these least commandments, and shall teach men so, he shall be called the least in the kingdom of heaven: but whosoever shall do and teach them, the same shall be called great in the kingdom of heaven. For I say unto you, that except your righteousness shall exceed the righteousness of the scribes and Pharisees, ye shall in no case enter into the kingdom of heaven.

Matthew 5:36-38 Master, which is the great commandment in the law? Jesus said unto him, thou shalt love the Lord thy God with all thy heart, and with all thy soul, and with all thy mind. This is the first and great commandment.

John 8:42 Jesus said unto them, If God were your Father, ye would love me: for I proceeded forth and came from God; neither came I of myself, but he sent me.

John 14:21 He that hath my commandments, and kept them, he it is that loveth me: and he that loveth me shall be loved of my Father, and I will love him, and will manifest myself to him.

John 14:23 Jesus answered and said unto him, If a man love me, he will keep my words: and my Father will love him, and we will come unto him.

John 14:26-27 But the Comforter, which is the Holy Ghost, whom the Father will send in my name, he shall teach you all things, and bring all things to your remembrance, whatsoever I have said unto you. Peace I leave with you, my peace I give unto you: not as the world giveth, give I unto you. Let not your heart be troubled, neither let it be afraid.

Romans 8:28 And we know that all things work together for good to them that love God, to them who are the called according to his purpose.

1 Corinthians 2:9 But as it is written, eye hath not seen, nor ear heard, neither have entered into the heart of man, the things which God hath prepared for them that love him.

1 Corinthians 2:10-12 But God hath revealed them unto us by his Spirit: for the Spirit searcheth all things, yea, the deep things of God. For what man knoweth the things of a man, save the spirit of man which is in him? Even so the things of God knoweth no man, but the Spirit of God. Now we have received, not the spirit of the world, but the spirit which is of God; that we might know the things that are freely given to us of God.

2 Timothy 1:7-8 For God hath not given us the spirit of fear; but of power, and of love, and of a sound mind. Be not thou therefore ashamed of the testimony of our Lord, nor of me his prisoner: but be thou partaker of the afflictions of the gospel according to the power of God.

John 17:11-14 And now I am no more in the world, but these are in the world, and I come to thee. Holy Father, keep through thine own name those whom thou hast given me, that they may be one, as we are. While I was with them in the world, I kept them in thy name: those that thou gavest me I have kept, and none of them is lost, but the son of perdition; that the scripture might be fulfilled. And now come I to thee; and these things I speak in the world, that they might have my joy fulfilled in themselves. I have given them thy word; and the world hath hated them, because they are not of the world, even as I am not.

John 14:12-17 Verily, verily, I say unto you, He that believeth on me, the works that I do shall he do also; and greater works than these shall he do; because I go unto my Father. And whatsoever ye shall ask in my name, that will I do, that the Father may be glorified in the Son. If ye shall ask any thing in my name, I will do it. If ye love me, keep my commandments. And I will pray the Father, and he shall give you another Comforter, that he may abide with you for ever. Even the Spirit of truth; whom the world cannot receive, because it seeth him not, neither knoweth him: but ye know him; for he dwelleth with you, and shall be in you.

Matthew 4:23 And Jesus went about all Galilee, teaching in their synagogues, and preaching the gospel of the kingdom, and healing all manner of sickness and all manner of disease among the people.

Matthew 5:17-18 Think not that I am come to destroy the law, or the prophets: I am not come to destroy, but to fulfill. For verily I say unto you, till heaven and earth pass, one jot or one tittle shall in no wise pass from the law, till all be fulfilled.

Matthew 7:21 Not every one that saith unto me Lord, Lord, shall enter into the kingdom of heaven; but he that doeth the will of my Father which is in heaven.

Matthew 15:7-9 Ye hypocrites, well did Esaias prophesy of you, saying, This people draweth nigh unto me with their mouth, and honoureth me with their lips; but their heart is far from me. But in vain they do worship me, teaching for doctrines the commandments of men.

Matthew 28:19-20 Go ye therefore, and teach all nations, baptizing them in the name of the Father, and of the Son, and of the Holy Ghost: Teaching them to observe all things whatsoever I have commanded you: and, lo, I am with you always, even unto the end of the world.

Colossians 3:16-17 Let the word of Christ dwell in you richly in all wisdom; teaching and admonishing one another in psalms and hymns and spiritual songs, singing with grace in your hearts to the Lord. And whatsoever ye do in word or deed, do all in the name of the Lord Jesus, giving thanks to God and the Father by him.

Titus 2:12-13 Teaching us that, denying ungodliness and worldly lusts, we should live soberly, righteously, and godly, in this present world. Looking for that blessed hope, and the glorious appearing of the great God and our Savior Jesus Christ.

1 Corinthians 2:2-5 For I determined not to know any thing among you, save Jesus Christ, and him crucified. And I was with you in weakness, and in fear, and in much trembling. And my speech and my preaching was not with enticing words of man's wisdom, but in demonstration of the Spirit and of power. That your faith should not stand in the wisdom of men, but in the power of God.

1 Corinthians 2:16 For who hath known the mind of the Lord, that he may instruct him? But we have the mind of Christ.

1 Corinthians 4:10 We are fools for Christ's sake, but ye are wise in Christ we are weak, but ye are strong; ye are honourable, but we are despised.

1 Corinthians 8:6 But to us there is but one God, the Father, of whom are all things, and we in him; and one Lord Jesus Christ, by whom are all things, and we by him.

1 Corinthians 16:18 For they have refreshed my spirit and yours: therefore acknowledge ye them that are such.

2 Corinthians 10:5 Casting down imaginations, and ever high thing that exalteth itself against the knowledge of God, and bringing into captivity every thought to the obedience of Christ.

2 Corinthians 1:13-14 For we write none other things unto you, than what ye read or acknowledge; and I trust ye shall acknowledge even to the end. As also ye have acknowledged us in part, that we are your rejoicing, even as ye also are ours in the day of the Lord Jesus.

Deuteronomy 25:3 Forty stripes he may give, and not exceed: lest, if he should exceed, and beat him above these with many stripes, then thy brother should seem vile unto thee.

1 Timothy 1:7 For God has not given us the spirit of fear; but of power, and of love, and of a sound mind.

Romans 8:15 For ye have not received the spirit of bondage again to fear; but ye have received the Spirit of adoption, whereby we cry, Abba, Father.

Luke 15:10 Likewise, I say unto you, there is joy of the angels of God over one sinner that repenteth.

Part II ~ Trinity of Man, Scriptures

1 Corinthians 6:20 For ye are bought with a price: therefore glorify in your body, and in your spirit, which are God's.

Psalm 139:13-17 For thou hast possessed my reins: thou hast covered me in my mother's womb. I will praise thee; for I am fearfully and wonderfully made: marvelous are thy works; and that my soul knoweth right well. My substance was not hid from thee, when I was made in secret, and curiously wrought in the lowest parts of the earth. Thine eyes did see my substance, yet being unperfect; and in thy book all my members were written, which in continuance were fashioned, when as yet there was none of them. How precious also are thy thoughts unto me, O God! How great is the sum of them!

1 Corinthians 15:44 It is sown a natural body; it is raised a spiritual body. There is a natural body, and there is a spiritual body.

Romans 8:5 For they that are after the flesh do mind the things of the flesh; but they that are after the Spirit the things of the Spirit.

Galatians 5:17 For the flesh lusteth against the Spirit, and the Spirit against the flesh: and these are contrary the one to the other: so that ye cannot do the things that ye would.

Romans 13:14 But put ye on the Lord Jesus Christ, and make not provision for the flesh, to fulfill the lusts thereof.

John 3:6 That which is born of the flesh is flesh; and that which is born of the Spirit is spirit.

Matthew 6:24 No man can serve two masters: for either he will hate the one, and love the other; or else he will hold to the one, and despise the other. Ye cannot serve God and mammon.

1 John 2:15-16 Love not the world, neither the things that are in the world. If any man love the world, the love of the Father is not in him. For all that is in the world, the lust of the flesh, and the lust of the eyes, and the pride of life, is not of the Father, but is of the world.

Romans 8:1 There is therefore now no condemnation to them which are in Christ Jesus, who walk not after the flesh, but after the Spirit.

1 Peter 1:21 Who by him do believe in God, that raised him up from the dead, and gave him glory; that your faith and hope might be in God.

1 Corinthians 2:5 That your faith should not stand in the wisdom of men, but in the power of God.

1 Corinthians 3:18-19 Let no man deceive himself. If any man among you seemeth to be wise in this world, let him become a fool, that he may be wise. For the wisdom of this world is foolishness with God. For it is written, He taketh the wise in their own craftiness.

Romans12:2 And be not conformed to this world: but be ye transformed by the renewing of your mind, that ye may prove what is that good, and acceptable, and perfect, will of God.

Ephesians 6:12 For we wrestle not against flesh and blood, but against principalities, against powers, against the rulers of the darkness of this world, against spiritual wickedness in high places.

Romans1:18-19 For the wrath of God is revealed from heaven against all ungodliness and unrighteousness of men, who hold the truth in unrighteousness; Because that which may be known of God is manifest in them; for God hath showed it unto them.

Romans 8:28-32 And we know that all things work together for good to them that love God, to them who are the called according to his purpose. For whom he did foreknow, he also did predestinate to be conformed to the image of his Son, that he might be the firstborn among many brethren. Moreover whom he did predestinate, them he also called: and whom he called, them he also justified: and whom he justified then he also glorified. He that spared not his own Son, but delivered him up for us all, how shall he not with him also freely give us all things?

3 John 1:2 Beloved, I wish above all things that thou mayest prosper and be in health, even as thy soul prospereth.

Romans 8:7-8 Because the carnal mind is enmity against God: for it is not subject to the law of God, neither indeed can be. So then they that are in the flesh cannot please God.

Colossians 2:8 Beware lest any man spoil you through philosophy and vain deceit, after the tradition of men, after the rudiments of the world, and not after Christ.

2 Corinthians 9:8 And God is able to make all grace abound toward you; that ye, always having all sufficiency in all things, may abound to every good work.

Ephesians 4:23-24 And be renewed in the spirit of your mind: And that ye put on the new man, which after God is created in righteousness and true holiness.

1 Peter 2:9 But ye are a chosen generation, a royal priesthood, an holy nation, a peculiar people; that ye should show forth the praises of him who hath called you out of darkness into his marvelous light.

James 1:6 But let him ask in faith, nothing wavering. For he that wavereth is like a wave of the sea driven with the wind and tossed.

1 Corinthians 6:20 For ye are bought with a price: therefore glorify in your body, and in your spirit, which are God's.

1 Corinthians 1:30-31 But of him are ye in Christ Jesus, who of God is made unto us wisdom, and righteousness, and sanctification, and redemption; That, according as it is written, He that glorieth, let him glory in the Lord.

Romans 6:4 Therefore we are buried with him by baptism into death: that like as Christ was raised up from the dead by the glory of the Father, even so we also should walk in newness of life.

Romans 8:17 And if children, then heirs; heirs of God, and joint-heirs with Christ; if so be that we suffer with him, that we may be also glorified together.

Romans 1:5 By whom we have received grace and apostleship, for obedience to the faith among all nations, for his name.

Genesis 6:3 And the Lord said, My spirit shall not always strive with man, for that he also is flesh: yet his days shall be an hundred and twenty years.

Romans 5:9 Much more then, being now justified by his blood, we shall be saved from wrath through him.

Romans 7:6 But now we are delivered from the law, that being dead wherein we were held; that we should serve in newness of spirit, and not in the oldness of the letter.

1 Corinthians 15:45 And so it is written, The first man Adam, was made a living soul; the last Adam was made a quickening spirit.

Acts 9:15 But the Lord said unto him, Go thy way: for he is a chosen vessel unto me, to bear my name before the Gentiles, and kings, and the children of Israel.

1 Thessalonians 4:4 That every one of you should know how to possess his vessel in sanctification and honor.

1 Corinthians 3:16-17 Know ye not that ye are the temple of God, and that the spirit of God dwelt in you? If any man defile the temple of God, him shall God destroy; for the temple of God is holy, which temple ye are.

1 Corinthians 6:19 What? Know ye not that your body is the temple of the Holy Ghost which is in you, which ye have of God, and ye are not your own?

Romans 12:1 I beseech you therefore, brethren, by the mercies of God, that ye present your bodies a living sacrifice, holy, acceptable unto God, which is your reasonable service.

Romans 7:25 I thank God through Jesus Christ our Lord. So then with the mind I myself serve the law of God; but with the flesh the law of sin.

2 Timothy 2:21 If a man therefore purge himself from these, he shall be a vessel unto honor, sanctified, and meet for the master's use, and prepared unto every good work.

2 Corinthians 6:17 Wherefore come out from among them, and be ye separate, saith the Lord, and touch not the unclean things; and I will receive you.

Romans 7:18-20 For I know that in me (this is, in my flesh) dwelt no good thing: for to will is present with me; but how to perform that which is good I find not. For the good that I would I do not: but the evil which I would not, that I do. Now if I do that I would not, it is no more I that do it, but sin that dwelleth in me.

Romans 1:20-25 For the invisible things of him from the creation of the world are clearly seen, being understood by the things that are made, even his eternal power and Godhead; so that they are without excuse: Because that, when they knew God, they glorified him not as God, neither were thankful; but became vain in their imaginations, and their foolish heart was darkened. Professing themselves to be wise, they became fools, And changed the glory of the incorruptible God into an image made like to corruptible man, and to birds, and fourfooted beasts, and creeping things. Wherefore God also gave them up to uncleanness through the lusts of their own hearts, to dishonour their own bodies between themselves: Who changed the truth of God into a lie, and worshipped and served the creature more than the Creator, who is blessed for ever. Amen.

Matthew 6:25 Therefore I say unto you, Take no thought for your life, what ye shall eat, or what ye shall drink; nor yet for your body, what ye shall put on. Is not the life more than meat, and the body than raiment?

Genesis 2:7 And the Lord God formed man of the dust of the ground, and breathed into his nostrils the breath of life; and man became a living soul.

Romans 6:4 Therefore we are buried with him by baptism into death: that like as Christ was raised up from the dead by the glory of the Father, even so we also should walk in newness of life.

Psalm 118:8 It is better to trust in the Lord than to put confidence in man.

1 Thessalonians 5:23 And the very God of peace sanctify you wholly; and I pray God your whole spirit and soul and body be preserved blameless unto the coming of our Lord Jesus Christ.

Titus 2:12 Teaching us that, denying ungodliness and worldly lusts, we should live soberly, righteously, and godly, in this present world.

Deuteronomy 4:9 Only take heed to thyself, and keep thy soul diligently, lest thou forget the things which thine eyes have seen, and lest they depart from thy heart all the days of thy life: but teach them thy sons, and thy sons' sons.

Deuteronomy 10:12-13 And now, Israel, what doth the Lord thy God require of thee, but to fear the Lord thy God, to walk in all his ways, and to love him, and to serve the Lord thy God with all thy heart and with all thy soul, To keep the commandments of the Lord, and his statutes, which I command thee this day for thy good?

Romans 13:1 Let every soul be subject unto the higher powers. For there is no power but of God: the powers that be are ordained of God.

Matthew 6:24 No man can serve two masters: for either he will hate the one, and love the other; or else he will hold to the one, and despise the other. Ye cannot serve God and mammon.

Matthew 10:24 The disciple is not above his master, nor the servant above his lord.

2 Corinthians 3:18 But we all, with open face beholding as in a glass the glory of the Lord, are changed into the same image from glory to glory, even as by the Spirit of the Lord.

1 Corinthians 2:13 Which things also we speak, not in the words which man's wisdom teacheth, but which the Holy Ghost teacheth; comparing spiritual things with spiritual.

Romans 12:2 And be not conformed to this world: but be ye transformed by the renewing of your mind, that ye may prove what is that good, and acceptable, and perfect, will of God.

Galatians 5:25 If we live in the Spirit, let us also walk in the Spirit.

2 Corinthians 4:7 But we have this treasure in earthen vessels, that the excellency of the power may be of God, and not of us.

Romans 8:5 For they that are after the flesh do mind the things of the flesh; but they that are after the Spirit the things of the spirit.

1 Corinthians 15:45-47 The first man Adam was made a living soul; the last Adam was made a quickening spirit. Howbeit that was not first is spiritual, but that which is natural; and afterward that which is spiritual. The first man is of the earth and the second is the Lord for heaven.

John 4:24 God is a spirit and they that worship him must worship him in spirit and in truth.

1 Timothy 6:17 Charge them that are rich in this world, that they be not highminded, nor trust in uncertain riches, but in the living god, who giveth us richly all things to enjoy.

1 Corinthians 2:11 For what man knoweth the things of a man, save the spirit of man which is in him? Even so the things of God knoweth no man, but the spirit of God.

Romans 7:6 But now we are delivered from the law, that being dead wherein we were held; that we should serve in newness of spirit, and not in the oldness of the letter.

John 5:28-29 Marvel not at this: for the hour is coming, in the which all that are in the graves shall hear his voice, And shall come forth; they that have done good, unto the resurrection of life; and they that have done evil, unto the resurrection of damnation.

1 Corinthians 15:51-52 Behold, I show you a mystery; We shall not all sleep, but we shall all be changed, In a moment, in the twinkling of an eye, at the last trump: for the trumpet shall sound, and the dead shall be raised incorruptible, and we shall be changed.

John 4:6 That which is born of the flesh is flesh; and that which is born of the Spirit is spirit.

Isaiah 24:5 The earth also is defiled under the inhabitants thereof; because they have transgressed the laws, changed the ordinance, broken the everlasting covenant.

1 Corinthians 15:50 Now this I say, brethren, that flesh and blood cannot inherit the kingdom of God; neither doth corruption inherit incorruption.

2 Corinthians 10:12 For we dare not make ourselves of the number, or compare ourselves with some that commend themselves: but they measuring themselves by themselves, and comparing themselves among themselves, are not wise.

Romans 1:21 Because that, when they knew God, they glorified him not as God, neither where thankful; but became vain in their imaginations, and their foolish heart was hardened.

1 Corinthians 2:12 Now we have received, not the spirit of the world, but the spirit which is of God; that we might know the things that are freely given to us of God.

Hebrews 8:6 But now hath he obtained a more excellent ministry, by how much also he is the mediator of a better covenant, which was established upon better promises.

1 Corinthians 3:18-19 Let no man deceive himself. If any man among you seemeth to be wise in this world, let him become a fool, that he may be wise. For the wisdom of this world is foolishness with God. For it is written, He taketh the wise in their own craftiness.

1 Corinthians 6:20 For ye are bought with a price: therefore glorify God in your body, and in your spirit, which are God's.

Revelation 14:11 And the smoke of their torment ascendeth up for ever and ever: and they have no rest day nor night, who worship the beast and his image, and whosoever receiveth the mark of his name.

Colossians 3:16 Let the word of Christ dwell in you richly in all wisdom; teaching and admonishing one another in psalms and hymns and spiritual songs, singing with grace in your hearts to the Lord.

Romans 1:5 By whom we have received grace and apostleship, for obedience to the faith among all nations, for his name.

Deuteronomy 30:19 I call heaven and earth to record this day agains you, that I have set before you life and death, blessings and cursing; therefore choose life, that thou and thy seed may live.

Hebrews 4:12 For the word of God is quick, and powerful, and sharper than any two-edged sword, piercing even to the dividing asunder of soul and spirit, and of the joints and marrow, and is a discerner of the thoughts and intents of the heart.

Genesis 2:22 And the rib, which the Lord God had taken from man, made he a woman, and brought her unto the man.

Genesis 2:24 Therefore shall a man leave his father and his mother, and shall cleave unto his wife: and they shall be one flesh.

Romans 8:26 Likewise the spirit also helpeth our infirmities: for we know not what we should pray for as we ought: but the spirit itself maketh intercession for us with groanings which cannot be uttered.

Jeremiah 32:33 And they have turned unto me the back, and not the face: though I taught them, rising up early and teaching them, yet they have not hearkened to receive instruction.

Jeremiah 23:16-17 Thus saith the Lord of hosts, Hearken not unto the words of the prophets that prophesy unto you: they make you vain: they speak a vision of their own heart, and not out of the mouth of the Lord. They say still unto them that despise me, The Lord hath said, Ye shall have peace; and they say unto every one that walketh after the imagination of his own heart, No evil shall come upon you.

Jeremiah 23:25-26 I have heard what the prophets said, that prophesy lies in my name, saying, I have dreamed, I have dreamed. How long shall this be in the heart of the prophets that prophesy lies? yea, they are prophets of the deceit of their own heart.

Matthew 13:15 For this people's heart is waxed gross, and their ears are full of hearing, and their eyes they have closed; lest at any time they should see with their eyes, and hear with their ears, and should understand with their heart, and should be converted, and I should heal them.

Matthew 23:23 Woe unto you, scribes and Pharisees, hypocrites! For ye pay tithe of mint and anise and cummin, and have omitted the weightier matters of the law, judgement, mercy, and faith: these ought ye to have done, and not to leave the other undone.

Matthew 24:11-12 And many false prophets shall rise, and shall deceive many. And because iniquity shall abound, the love of many shall wax cold.

Mark 7:9 And he said unto them, Full well ye reject the commandment of God, that ye may keep your own tradition.

Luke 16:13 No servant can serve two masters: for either he will hate the one, and love the other; or else he will hold to the one, and despise the other. Ye cannot serve God and mammon.

2 Corinthians 11:13-14 For such are false apostles, deceitful workers, transforming themselves into the apostles of Christ. And no marvel; for Satan himself is transformed into an angel of light.

2 Peter 2:1-4 But there were false prophets also among the people, even as there shall be false teachers among you, who privily shall bring in damnable heresies, even denying the Lord that bought them, and bring upon themselves swift destruction. And many shall follow their pernicious ways; by reason of whom the way of truth shall be evil spoken of. And through covetousness shall they with feigned words make merchandise of you: whose judgment now of a long time lingereth not, and their damnation slumbereth not. For if God spared not the angels that sinned, but cast them down to hell, and delivered them into chains of darkness, to be reserved unto judgment.

Ephesians 6:18 Praying always with all prayer and supplication in the Spirit, and watching thereunto with all perseverance and supplication for all saints.

Philippians 4:6 Be careful for nothing; but in every thing by prayer and supplication with thanksgiving let your requests be made known unto God.

Matthew 5:44 But I say unto you, Love your enemies, bless them that curse you, do good to them that hate you, and pray for the which despitefully use you, and persecute you.

Matthew 21:22 And all things, whatsoever ye shall ask in prayer, believing, ye shall receive.

Matthew 26:41 Watch and pray, that ye enter not into temptation: the spirit indeed is willing, but the flesh is weak.

Mark 11:24-26 Therefore I say unto you, What things soever ye desire, when ye pray, believe that ye receive them, and ye shall have them. And when ye stand praying, forgive, if ye have ought against any: that your Father also which is in heaven may forgive you your trespasses. But if ye do not forgive, neither will your Father which is in heaven forgive your trespasses.

Luke 21:36 Watch ye therefore, and pray always, that ye may be accounted worthy to escape all these things that shall come to pass, and to stand be the Son of man.

John 17:9-10 I pray for them: I pray not for the world, but for them which thou hast given me; for they are thine. And all mine are thine, and thine are mine; and I am glorified in them.

John 17:15-21 I pray not that thou shouldest take them out of the world, but that thou shouldest keep them from the evil They are not of the world, even as I am not of the world. Sanctify them through thy truth: thy word is truth. As thou hast sent me into the world, even so have I also sent them into the world. And for their sakes I sanctify myself, that they also might be sanctified through the truth. Neither pray I for these alone, but for them also which shall believe on me through their word. That they all may be one; as thou, Father, art in me, and I in thee, that they also may be one in us: that the world may believe that thou hast sent me.

Romans 12:11 Rejoicing in hope; patient in tribulation; continuing instant in prayer.

1 Thessalonians 5:16-23 Rejoicing evermore. Pray without ceasing. In everything give thanks: for this is the will God in Christ Jesus concerning you. Quench not the Spirit. Prove all things; hold fast that which is good. Abstain from all appearance of evil. And the very God of peace sanctify you wholly; and I pray God your whole spirit and soul and body be preserved blameless unto the coming of our Lord Jesus Christ.

1 John 5:5-8 Who is he that overcometh the world, but he that believeth that Jesus is the Son of God? This is he that came by water and blood, even Jesus Christ; not by water only, but by water and blood. And it is the Spirit that beareth witness, because the Spirit is truth. For there are three that bear record in heaven, the Father, the Word, and the Holy Ghost: and these three are one And there are three that bear witness in earth, the Spirit, and the water, and the blood: and these three agree in one.

Part III ~ Trinity of the Kingdom, Scriptures

Matthew 6:33 But seek ye first the kingdom of God, and his righteousness; and all these things shall be added unto you.

Daniel 4:3 How great are his signs! And how mighty are his wonders! His kingdom is an everlasting kingdom, and his dominion is from generation to generation.

Revelation 1:8 I am the Alpha and Omega, the beginning and the ending, saith the Lord, which is, and which was, and which is to come, the Almighty.

Genesis 1:1-2 In the beginning God created the heaven and the earth. And the earth was without form, and void; and darkness was upon the face of the deep. And the Spirit of God moved upon the face of the waters.

Genesis 1:7-8 And God made the firmament, and divided the firmament: and it was so. And God called the firmament Heaven. And the evening and the morning were the second day.

Genesis 2:4 These are the generations of the heavens and of the earth when they were created, in the day that the Lord God made the earth and the heavens.

Genesis 2:1 Thus the heavens and the earth were finished, and all the host of them.

Genesis 1:28 And God blessed them, and God said unto them, Be fruitful, and multiply, and replenish the earth, and subdue it: and have dominion over the fish of the sea, and over the fowl of the air, and over ever living thing that moveth upon the earth.

Revelation 21:1 And I saw a new heaven and a new earth: for the first heaven and earth were passed away; and there was no sea.

*Daniel 7:14*And there was given him dominion, and glory, and a kingdom, that all people, nations, and languages, should serve him: his dominion is an everlasting dominion, which shall not pass away, and his kingdom that which shall not be destroyed.

Hebrews 10:16-17 This is the covenant that I will make with them after those days, saith the Lord, I will put my laws into their hearts, and in their minds will I write them; And their sins and iniquities will I remember no more.

Revelation 3:12 Him that overcometh will I make a pillar in the temple of my God, and he shall go no more out: and I will write upon him the name of my God, and the name of the city of my God which is new Jerusalem, which cometh down out of heaven from my God: and I will write upon him my new name.

Revelation 20:5-6 But the rest of the dead lived not again until the thousand years were finished. This is the first resurrection. Blessed and holy is he that hath a part in the first resurrection: on such the second death hath no power, but they shall be priests of God and of Christ, and shall reign with him a thousand years.

1 Corinthians 15:52 In a moment, in the twinkling of an eye, at the last trump: for the trumpet shall sound, and the dead shall be raised incorruptible, and we shall be changed.

1 Thessalonians 4:14-17 Then we which are alive and remain shall be caught up together with them in the clouds, to meet the Lord in the air: and so shall we ever be with the Lord.

1 Corinthians 4:20 For the kingdom of God is not in word, but in power.

Matthew 6:5-13 And when thou prayest, thou shalt not be as the hypocrites are: for they love to pray standing in the synagogues and in the corners of the streets, that they may be seen of men. Verily I say unto you, They have their reward. But thou, when thou prayest, enter into thy closet, and when thou hast shut thy door, pray to thy Father which is in secret; and thy Father which seeth in secret shall reward thee openly. But when ye pray, use not vain repetitions, as the heathen do: for they think that they shall be heard for their much speaking. Be not ye therefore like unto them: for your Father knoweth what things ye have need of, before ye ask him. After this manner therefore pray ye: Our Father which art in heaven, Hallowed be thy name. Thy kingdom come. Thy will be done in earth, as it is in heaven. Give us this day our daily bread. And forgive us our debts, as we forgive our debtors. And lead us not into temptation, but deliver us from evil: For thine is the kingdom, and the power, and the glory, for ever. Amen.

Matthew 13:44 Again, the kingdom of heaven is like unto treasure hid in a field; the which when a man hath found, he hideth, and for joy thereof goeth and selleth all that he hath, and buyeth that field.

Psalm 145:13 Thy kingdom is an everlasting kingdom, and thy dominion endureth throughout all generations.

Exodus 17:6 Behold I will stand before thee upon the rock of Horeb, and thou shalt smite the rock, and there shall come water out of it, that the people may drink. And Moses did so in the sight of the elders of Israel.

Ephesians 2:4 But God, who is rich in mercy, for his great love wherewith he loved us.

1 Peter 1:3 Blessed be the God and Father of our Lord Jesus Christ, which according to his abundant mercy hath begotten us again unto a lively hope by the resurrection of Jesus Christ from the dead.

Psalm 100:5 For the Lord is good; his mercy is everlasting; and his truth endureth to all generations.

Matthew 5:39 But I say unto you, That ye resist not evil: but whosoever shall smite thee on thy right cheek, turn to him the other also.

Exodus 16:15 And when he children of Israel saw it, they said one to another, It is manna: for they wist not what it was. And Moses said unto them, This is the bread which the Lord hath given you to eat.

Exodus 33:19 And he said, I will make all my goodness pass before thee, and I will proclaim the name of the Lord before thee; and will be gracious to whom I will be gracious, and will show mercy on whom I will show mercy.

Jude 1:21 Keep yourselves in the love of God, looking for the mercy of our Lord Jesus Christ unto eternal life.

1 Chronicles 16:34 O' give thanks unto the Lord; for he is good; for his mercy endureth for ever.

Romans 2:11 For there is no respect of persons with God.

Hebrew 8:13 A new covenant, he hath made the first old. Now that which decayeth and waxed old is ready to vanish away.

2 John 1:3 Grace be with you, mercy, and peace, from God the Father, and from the Lord Jesus Christ, the Son of the Father, in truth and love.

Romans 5:15 But not as the offence, so also is the free gift. For if through the offence of one many be dead, much more the grace of God, and the gift by grace, which is by one man, Jesus Christ, hath abounded unto many.

Isaiah 54:8 In a little wrath I hid my face from thee for a moment; but with everlasting kindness will I have mercy on thee, saith the Lord thy Redeemer.

Romans 6:14 For sin shall not have dominion over you: for ye are not under the law, but under grace.

Romans 4:14-15 For of they which are of the law be heirs, faith is made void, and the promise made of none effect: because the law worketh wrath: for where no law is, there is no transgression.

John 1:14-17 And the Word was made flesh, and dwelt among us, (and we beheld his glory, the glory as of the only begotten of the Father), full of grace and truth. John bare witness of him, and cried, saying, This was he of whom I spake, He that cometh after me is preferred before me: for he was before me. And of his fulness have all we received, and grace for grace. For the law was given by Moses, but grace and truth came by Jesus Christ.

2 Corinthians 9:8 And God is able to make all grace abound toward you; that ye, always having all sufficiency in all things, may abound to every good work.

Psalm 84:11 For the Lord God is a sun and shield: the Lord will give grace and glory: no good thing will he withhold from them that walk uprightly.

Ephesians 2:8-9 For by grace are ye saved through faith; and that not of yourselves: it is the gift of God. Not of works, lest any man should boast.

Ephesians 4:7 But unto every one of us is given grace according to the measure of the gift of Christ.

Hebrews 4:1 Let us therefore fear, lest, a promise being left us of entering into his rest, any of you should seem to come short of it.

Hebrews 4:16 Let us therefore come boldly unto the throne that we may obtain mercy, and find grace to help in time of need.

1 Timothy 1:14 And the grace of our Lord was exceeding abundant with faith and love which is in Christ Jesus.

Ephesians 1:2 Grace be to you, and peace, from God our Father, and from the Lord Jesus Christ.

2 Corinthians 5:7 For we walk by faith, not my sight.

Hebrews 11:6 Without faith it is impossible to please God.

Romans 5:1-2 Therefore being justified by faith, we have peace with God through our Lord Jesus Christ: By whom also we have access by faith into this grace wherein we stand, and rejoice in hope of the glory of God.

Matthew 17:14-20 And when they were come to the multitude, there came to him a certain man, kneeling down to him, and saying, Lord, have mercy on my son: for he is a lunatic, and sore vexed: for ofttimes he falleth into the fire, and oft into the water. And I brought him to thy disciples, and they could not cure him. Then Jesus answered and said, O faithless and perverse generation, how long shall I be with you? how long shall I suffer you? bring him hither to me. And Jesus rebuked the devil; and he departed out of him: and the child was cured from that very hour. Then came the disciples to Jesus apart, and said, Why could not we cast him out? And Jesus said unto them, Because of your unbelief: for verily I say unto you, If ye have faith as a grain of mustard seed, ye shall say unto this mountain, Remove hence to yonder place; and it shall remove; and nothing shall be impossible unto you.

Romans 12:3 For I say, through the grace given unto me, to every man that is among you, not to think of himself more highly than he ought to think; but to think soberly, according as God hath dealt to every man the measure of faith.

Mark 9:17-24 And one of the multitude answered and said, Master, I have brought unto thee my son, which hath a dumb spirit; And wheresoever he taketh him, he teareth him: and he foameth, and gnasheth with his teeth, and pineth away: and I spake to thy disciples that they should cast him out; and they could not. He answereth him, and saith, O faithless generation, how long shall I be with you? how long shall I suffer you? bring him unto me. And they brought him unto him: and when he saw him, straightway the spirit tare him; and he fell on the ground, and wallowed foaming. And he asked his father, How long is it ago since this came unto him? And he said, Of a child. And ofttimes it hath cast him into the fire, and into the waters, to destroy him: but if thou canst do any thing, have compassion on us, and help us. Jesus said unto him, If thou canst believe, all things are possible to him that believeth. And straightway the father of the child cried out, and said with tears, Lord, I believe; help thou mine unbelief.

Matthew 16:19 And I will give unto thee the keys of the kingdom of heaven: and whatsoever thou shalt bind on earth shall be bound in heaven: and whatsoever thou shalt loose on earth shall be loosed in heaven.

Romans 5:1-2 Therefore being justified by faith, we have peace with God through our Lord, Jesus Christ: By whom also we have access by faith into this grace wherein we stand, and rejoice in hope of the glory of God.

Hebrews 11:1 Now faith is the substance of things hoped for, the evidence of things not seen.

John 14:14 If ye shall ask any thing in my name, I will do it.

Mark 10:27 And Jesus looking upon them saith, With men it is impossible, but not with God: for with God all things are possible.

Matthew 6:10 Thy kingdom come. Thy will be done in earth, as it is in heaven.

Luke 12:2 And he said unto them, When ye pray, say, Our Father which art in heaven, Hallowed be thy name. Thy kingdom come. Thy will be done, as in heaven, so in earth.

Romans 8:23-24 And not only then, but ourselves also, which have the firstfruits of the Spirit, even we ourselves groan within ourselves, waiting for the adoption, to wit, the redemption of our body. For we are saved by hope: but hope that is seen is not hope: for what a man seeth, why doth he yet hope for?

Romans 12:6-8 Having then gifts differing according to the grace that is given to us, whether prophecy, let us prophesy according to the proportion of faith; Or ministry, let us wait on our ministering: or he that teacheth, on teaching; Or he that exhorteth, on exhortation: he that giveth, let him do it with simplicity; he that ruleth, with diligence; he that showeth mercy, with cheerfulness.

Romans 11:29 For the gifts and calling of God are without repentance.

1 Corinthians 12:1 Now concerning spiritual gifts, brethen, I would not have you ignorant.

1 Corinthians 12:4-11 Now there are diversities of gifts, but the same Spirit; And there are difference of administrations, but the same Lord; And there are diversities of operations, but it is the same God which worketh all in all. But the manifestation of the Spirit is given to every man to profit withal. For to one is given by the Spirit the word of wisdom; to another the word of knowledge by the same Spirit; To another faith by the same Spirit; to another the gifts of healing by the same Spirit; To another the working of miracles; to another prophecy; to another discerning of spirits; to another divers kinds of tongues; to another the interpretation of tongues;

But all these worketh that one and the selfsame Spirit, dividing to every man severally as he will.

1 Corinthians 12:28-31 And God hath set some in the church, first apostles, secondarily prophets, thirdly teachers, after that miracles, then gifts of healings, helps, governments, diversities of tongues. Are all apostles? are all prophets? are all teachers? are all workers of miracles? Have all the gifts of healing? do all speak with tongues? do all interpret? But covet earnestly the best gifts: and yet show I unto you a more excellent way!

1 Corinthians 14:1 Follow after charity, and desire spiritual gifts, but rather that ye may prophesy.

1 Corinthians 14:12 Even so ye, forasmuch, as ye are zealous of spiritual gifts, seek that ye may excel to the edifying of the church.

Ephesians 4:8 Wherefore he saith, when he ascended up on high, he led captivity captive, and gave gifts unto men.

Hebrews 2:4 God also bearing them witness, both with signs and wonders, and with divers miracles, and gifts of the Holy Ghost, according to his own will?

1 Timothy 4:14-16 Neglect not the gift that is in thee, which was given thee by prophecy, with the laying on of hands of the presbytery. Meditate upon these things; give thyself wholly to them; that thy profiting may appear to all. Take heed unto thyself, and unto the doctrine; continue in them: for in doing this thou shalt both save thyself and them that hear thee.

2 Timothy 1:6-8 Wherefore I put thee in remembrance that thou stir up the gift of God, which is in thee by the putting on of my hands. For God hath not given us the spirit of fear; but of power, and of love, and of a sound mind. Be not thou therefore ashamed of the testimony of our Lord, nor of me his prisoner: but be thou partaker of the afflictions of the gospel according to the power of God.

James 1:17-18 Every good gift and every perfect gift is from above, and cometh down from the Father of lights, with whom is no variableness, neither shadow of turning. Of his own will begat he us with the word of truth that we should be a kind of firstfruits of his creatures.

John 14:12-17 Verily, verily, I say unto you, He that believeth on me, the works that I do shall he do also; and greater works than these shall he do; because I go unto my Father. And whatsoever ye shall ask in my name, that will I do, that the Father may be glorified in the Son. If ye shall ask any thing in my name, I will do it. If ye love me, keep my commandments. And I will pray the Father, and he shall give you another Comforter, that he may abide with you for ever. Even the Spirit of truth; whom the world cannot receive, because it seeth him not, neither knoweth him: but ye know him; for he dwelleth with you, and shall be in you.

Matthew 6:30 Wherefore, if God so clothe the grass of the field, which today is, and tomorrow is cast into the oven, shall he not much more clothe you, O ye of little faith?

Matthew 9:21-22 For she said within herself, If I may but touch his garment, I shall be whole. But Jesus turned him about, and when he saw her, he said, Daughter, be of good comfort; thy faith hath made thee whole. And the woman was made whole from that hour.

Acts 3:16 And his name through faith in his name hath made this man strong, whom ye see and know: yea, the faith which is by him hath given him this perfect soundness in the presence of you all.

Acts 6:7-8 And the word of God increased; and the number of the disciples multiplied in Jerusalem greatly; and a great company of the priests were obedient to the faith. And Stephen, full of faith and power, did great wonders and miracles among the people.

Acts 14:22-33 Confirming the souls of the disciples, and exhorting them to continue in the faith, and that we must through much tribulation enter into the kingdom of God. And when they had ordained them elders in every church, and had prayed with fasting, they commended them to the Lord, on whom they believed.

Acts 14:27 And when they were come, and had gathered the church together, they rehearsed all that God had done with them, and how he had opened the door of faith unto the Gentiles.

Acts 15:8-9 And God, which knoweth the hearts, bare them witness, giving them the Holy Ghost, even as he did unto us. And put no difference between us and them, purifying their hearts by faith.

Acts 16:5 And so were the churches established in the faith, and increased in number daily.

Romans 1:8 First, I thank my God through Jesus Christ for you all, that your faith is spoken of throughout the whole world.

Romans 1:17 For therein is the righteousness of God revealed from faith to faith: as it is written; the just shall live by faith.

Romans 3:22-24 Even the righteousness of God which is by faith of Jesus Christ unto all and upon all them that believe: for there is no difference. For all have sinned, and come short of the glory of God. Being justified freely by his grace through the redemption that is Christ Jesus.

Romans 5:1-2 Therefore being justified by faith, we have peace with God through our Lord Jesus Christ. By whom also we have access by faith into this grace wherein we stand, and rejoice in hope of the glory of God.

1 Corinthians 1:10 Now I beseech you, brethren, by the name of our Lord

Jesus Christ, that ye all speak the same thing, and that there be no divisions among you; but that ye be perfectly joined together in the same mind and in the same judgment.

Galatians 2:16 Knowing that a man is not justified by the works of the law, but by the faith of Jesus Christ, even we have believed in Jesus Christ, that we might be justified by the faith of Christ, and not by the works of the law: for by the works of the law shall no flesh be justified.

Isaiah 56:5 Even unto them will I give in mine house and within my walls a place and a name better than of sons and of daughters: I will give them an everlasting name, that shall not be cut off.

1 Corinthians 12:1 Now concerning spiritual gifts, brethren, I would not have you ignorant.

1 Corinthians 12:4-6 Now there are diversities of gifts, but the same Spirit. And there are differences of administrations, but the same Lord. And there are diversities of operations, but it is the same God which worketh all in all.

Ephesians 4:9-12 Now that he ascended, what is it but that he also descended first into the lower parts of the earth? He that descended is the same also that ascended up far above all heavens, that he might fill all things. And he gave some apostles; and some, prophets; and some, evangelists; and some, pastors and teachers; For the perfecting of the saints, for the work of the ministry, for the edifying of the body of Christ.

1 Corinthians 12:27-31 Now ye are the body of Christ, and members in particular. Now God hath set some in the church, first apostles, secondarily prophets, thirdly teachers, after that miracles, then gifts of healings, helps, governments, diversities of tongues. Are all apostles? Are all prophets? are all teachers? are all workers of miracles? Have all the gifts of healing? do all speak with tongues? do all interpret? But covet earnestly the best gifts: and yet show I unto you a more excellent way.

1 Corinthians 12:7-11 But the manifestation of the Spirit is given to every man to profit withal. For to one is given by the Spirit the word of wisdom; to another the word of knowledge by the same Spirit; To another faith by the same Spirit; to another the gifts of healing by the same Spirit; To another the working of miracles; to another prophecy; to another discerning of spirits; to another divers kinds of tongues; to another the interpretation of tongues: But all these worketh that one and the selfsame Spirit, dividing to every man severally as he will.

Romans 12:6-8 Having then gifts differing according to the grace that is given to us, whether prophecy, let us prophesy according to the proportion of faith; Or ministry, let us wait on our ministering: or he that teacheth, on teaching; Or he that exhorteth, on exhortation: he that giveth, let him do it with simplicity; he that ruleth, with diligence; he that showeth mercy, with cheerfulness.

Exodus 20:22 And the Lord said unto Moses, Thus thou shalt say unto the children of Israel, Ye have seen that I have talked with you from heaven.

Exodus 20:1-17 I am the Lord thy God, which have brought thee out of the land of Egypt, out of the house of bondage. Thou shalt have no other gods before me. Thou shalt not make unto thee any graven image, or any likeness of any thing that is in heaven above, or that is in the earth beneath, or that is in the water under the earth. Thou shalt not take the name of the Lord thy God in vain; for the Lord will not hold him guiltless that taketh his name in vain. Remember the sabbath day, to keep it holy. Honour thy father and thy mother: that thy days may be long upon the land which the Lord thy God giveth thee. Thou shalt not kill. Thou shalt not commit adultery. Thou shalt not steal. Thou shalt not covet thy neighbour's house, thou shalt not covet thy neighbour's wife, nor his manservant, nor his maidservant, nor his ox, nor his ass, nor any thing that is thy neighbour's.

Hebrews 8:10 For this is the covenant that I will make with the house of Israel after those days, saith the Lord; I will put my laws into their mind, and write them in their hearts: and I will be to them a God, and they shall be to me a people.

Matthew 26:28 For this is my blood of the new testament, which is shed for many for the remission of sins.

Hebrews 9:26-28 For then must he often have suffered since the foundation of the world: but now once in the end of the world hath he appeared to put away sin by the sacrifice of himself. And as it is appointed unto men once to die, but after this the judgment: So Christ was once offered to bear the sins of many; and unto them that look for him shall he appear the second time without sin unto salvation.

Galatians 5:22-23 But the fruit of the Spirit is love, joy, peace, longsuffering, gentleness, goodness, faith, meekness, temperance; against such there is no law.

Ephesians 6:12-13 For we wrestle not against flesh and blood, but against principalities, against powers, against rulers of the darkness of this world, against spiritual wickedness in high places. Wherefore take unto you the whole armour of God, that ye may be able to withstand in the evil day, and having done all, to stand.

Ephesians 6:14-20 Stand therefore, having your loins girt about with truth, and having on the breastplate of righteousness; And your feet shod with the preparation of the gospel of peace; Above all, taking the shield of faith, wherewith ye shall be able to quench all the fiery darts of the wicked. And take the helmet of salvation, and the sword of the Spirit, which is the word of God: Praying always with all prayer and supplication in the Spirit, and watching hereunto with all perseverance and supplication for all saints; And for me, that utterance may be given unto me, that I may open my mouth boldly, to make known the mystery of the gospel, For which I am an ambassador in bonds: that therein I may speak boldly, as I ought to speak.

James 3:6 And the tongue is a fire, a world of iniquity: so is the tongue among our members, that it defileth the whole body, and setteth on fire the course of nature; and it is set on fire of hell.

Job 6:30 Is there iniquity in my tongue? Cannot my taste discern perverse things?

Proverbs 3:33 The curse of the Lord is in the house of the wicked: but he blesseth the habitation of the just.

James 3:9 Therewith bless we God, even the Father; and therewith curse we men, which are made after the similitude of God.

2 Corinthians 5:10 For we must all appear before the judgment seat of Christ; that every one may receive the things done in his body, according to that he hath done, whether it be good or bad.

Matthew 15:4 For God commanded, saying, Honour thy father and mother: and, He that curseth father or mother, let him die the death.

Romans 13:1 Let every soul be subject unto the higher powers. For there is no power but of God: the powers that be are ordained of God.

John 2:21 But he spake of the temple of his body.

1 Corinthians 6:19 What? know ye not that your body is the temple of the Holy Ghost which is in you, which ye have of God, and ye are not your own?

Mark 10:30 But he shall receive an hundredfold now in this time, houses, and brethren, and sisters, and mothers, and children, and lands, with persecutions; and in the world to come eternal life.

Matthew 13:37 He answered and said unto them, He that soweth the good seed is the Son of man.

Mark 4:20 And these are they which are sown on good ground; such as hear the word, and receive it, and bring forth fruit, some thirtyfold, some sixty, and some an hundred.

John 4:36 And he that reapeth receiveth wages, and gathereth fruit unto life eternal: that both he that soweth and he that reapeth may rejoice together.

Psalm 105:14-15 He suffered no man to do them wrong: yea, he reproved kings for their sakes; Saying, Touch not mine anointed, and do my prophets no harm.

1 Peter 4:15 But let none of you suffer as a murderer, or as a thief, or as an evildoer, or as a busy body in other men's matters.

Romans 12:14 Bless them which persecute you: bless, and curse not.

Exodus 20:5 Thou shalt not bow down thyself to them, nor serve them: for I the Lord thy God am a jealous God, visiting the iniquity of the fathers upon the children unto the third and fourth generation of them that hate me.

Hebrews 12:14-15 Follow peace with all men, and holiness, without which no man shall see the Lord: Looking diligently lest any man fail of the grace of God; lest any root of bitterness springing up trouble you, and thereby many be defiled.

Acts 26:18 To open heir eyes, and to turn them from darkness to light, and from the power of Satan unto God, that they may receive forgiveness of sins, and inheritance among them which are sanctified by faith that is in me.

Matthew 18:21-22 Then came Peter to him, and said, Lord, how oft shall my brother sin against me, and I forgive him? till seven times? Jesus saith unto him, I say not unto thee, Until seven times: but, Until seventy times seven.

Romans 7:23 For I delight in the law of God after the inward man.

Romans 2:18 And knowest his will, and approvest the things that are more excellent, being instructed out of the law.

Romans 7:25 I thank God through Jesus Christ our Lord. So then with the mind I myself serve the law of God; but with the flesh the law of sin.

Romans 8:2 For the law of the Spirit of life in Christ Jesus hath made me free from the law of sin and death.

Romans 2:28-29 For he is not a Jew, which is one outwardly; neither is that circumcision, which is outward in the flesh: But he is a Jew, which is one inwardly; and circumcision is that of the heart, in the spirit, and not in the letter; whose praise is not of men, but of God.

John 10:10 The thief cometh not, but for to steal, and to kill, and to destroy: I am come that they might have life, and that they might have it more abundantly.

Revelation 22:3 And there shall be no more curse: but the throne of God and of the Lamb shall be in it; and his servants shall serve him.

1 Peter 2:24 Who his own self bare our sins in his own body on the tree, that we, being dead to sins, should live unto righteousness: by whose stripes ye were healed.

Matthew 27:29 And when they had platted a crown of thorns, they put it upon his head, and a reed in his right hand: and they bowed the knee before him, and mocked him, saying, Hail, King of the Jews!

John 20:25 The other disciples therefore said unto him, We have seen the Lord. But he said unto them, Except I shall see in his hands the print of the nails, and put my finger into the print of the nails and thrust my hand into his side, I will not believe.

John 19:34 But one of the soldiers with a spear pierced his side, and forthwith came there out blood and water.

John 17:4 I have glorified thee on the earth: I have finished the work which thou gavest me to do.

Luke 23:46 And when Jesus had cried with a loud voice, he said, Father, into thy hands I commend my spirit: and having said thus, he gave up the ghost.

Genesis 1:27 So God created man in his own image, in the image of God created he him; male and female created he them.

Isaiah 53:4-5 Surely he hath born our griefs, and carried our sorrows: yet we did esteem him stricken, smitten of God, and afflicted. But he was wounded for our transgressions, he was bruised for our iniquities; the chastisement of our peace was upon him; and with his stripes we are healed.

Psalm 103:1-5 Bless the Lord, O my soul; and all that is within me, bless his holy name. Bless the Lord, O my soul, and forget not all his benefits: Who forgiveth all thine iniquities; who healeth all they diseases; Who redeemed thy life from destruction; Who crowneth thee will loving kindness and tender mercies; Who satisfieth thy mouth with good things; so that thy youth is renewed like the eagle's.

Proverbs 9:11 For the length of days shall be multiplied, and the years of thy life shall be increased.

Ephesians 6:3 That it may be well with thee, and thou mayest live long on the earth.

Romans 8:32 He that spared not his own Son, but delivered him up for us all, how shall he not with him also freely give us all things?

John 16:23-24 And in that day ye shall ask of me nothing. Verily, verily, I say unto you. Whatsoever ye shall ask the Father in my name, he will give it you. Hitherto have ye asked nothing in my name: ask, and ye shall receive that your joy may be full.

John 15:7 If ye abide in me, and my words abide in you, ye shall ask what ye will, and it shall be done unto you.

Jeremiah 30:17 For I will restore health unto thee, and I will heal thee of they wounds saith the Lord.

Deuteronomy 30:19 I call heaven and earth to record this day against you, that I have set before you life and death, blessings and cursing; therefore, choose life, that both thou and thy seed may live.

Psalm 91:16 With long life will I satisfy him, and shew him my salvation.

Psalm 103:3-4 Who forgiveth all thine iniquities; who healed all thy diseases. Who redeemeth thy life from destruction; who crowneth thee with loving kindness and tender mercies.

Proverbs 4:10 Hear, O my son, and receive my sayings; and the years of thy life shall be many.

Exodus 15:26 I am the Lord that healed thee.

Genesis 6:3 And the Lord said, My spirit shall not always strive with man, for that he also is flesh: yet his days shall be an hundred and twenty years.

Genesis 15:15 You shall be buried in a good old age.

Exodus 23:25-26 I will take sickness away from the midst of you and the number of your days I will fulfill.

Deuteronomy 7:15 And the Lord will take away from thee all sickness, and will put none of the evil diseases of Egypt, which thou knowst, upon thee; but will lay them upon all them that hate thee.

Romans 8:11 The same Spirit that raised me from the dead now lives in you and that Spirit will quicken your mortal body.

John 6:63 It is the spirit that quickeneth; the flesh profiteth nothing: the words that I speak unto you, they are spirit, and they are life.

Proverbs 4:20-22 My son, attend to my words; incline thine ear unto my sayings. Let them not depart from thine eyes; keep them in the midst of thine heart. For they are life unto those that find them and health to all their flesh.

Luke 22:44 And being in an agony he prayed more earnestly: and his sweat was as it were great drops of blood falling down to the ground.

Part IV ~ Additional Scriptures

Matthew 21:22 And all things, whatsoever ye shall ask in prayer, believing, ye shall receive.

Matthew 6:5 And when thous prayest, thous shalt not be as the hypocrites are: for they love to pray standing in the synagogues and in the corners of the streets, that they may be seen of men.

Matthew 6:7-8 But when ye pray, use not vain repetitions, as the heathen do: for they think they shall be heard for their much speaking. Be not ye therefore like unto them; for your Father knowth what things ye have need of, before ye ask him.

Matthew 6:9-13 Our Father which are in heaven, hallowed be thy name, Thy kingdom come, Thy will be done in earth, as it is in heaven. Give us our daily bread. And forgive us our debts, as we forgive our debtors. And lead us not into temptation, but deliver us from evil: For thine is the kingdom, and the power, and the glory, for ever. Amen.

Matthew 5:39 But I say unto you, That ye resist not evil: but whosoever shall smite thee on thy right cheek, turn to him the other also.

Luke 6:29 And unto him that smitten thee on the one cheek offer also the other; and him that taketh away thy cloak forbid not to take thy coat also.

Isaiah 56:5 Even unto them will I give in mine house and within my walls a place and a name better than of sons and of daughters: I will give them an everlasting name, that shall not be cut off.

Ephesians 4:4-7 There is one body, and one Spirit, even as ye are called in one hope of your calling. One Lord, one faith, one baptism, One God and Father of all, who is above all, and through all, and in you all. But unto every one of us is given grace according to the measure of the gift of Christ.

1 Corinthians 12:1 Now concerning spiritual gifts brethren, I would not have you ignorant.

1 Corinthians12:4-6 Now there are diversities of gifts, but the same Spirit. And there are differences of administrations, but the same Lord. And there are diversities of operations, but it is the same God which worth all in all.

1 Corinthians 12:27-31 Now ye are the body of Christ, and members in particular. And God hath set some in the church, first apostles, secondarily prophets, thirdly teachers, after that miracles, then gifts of healings, helps, governments, diversities of tongues. are all apostles? are all prophets? are all teachers? are all workers of miracles? Have all the gifts of healing? do all speak with tongues? do all interpret? But covet earnestly the best gifts: and yet show I unto you a more excellent way.

Ephesians 4:9-12 Now that he ascended, what is it but that he also descended first into the lower parts of the earth? He that descended is the same also that ascended up far above all heavens, that he might fill all things. And he gave some, apostles; and some, prophets; and some, evangelists; and some, pastors and teachers; For the perfecting of the saints, for the work of the ministry, for the edifying of the body of Christ.

1 Corinthians 12:7-11 But the manifestation of the Spirit is given to every man to profit withal. For to one is given by the Spirit the word of wisdom; to another the word of knowledge by the same Spirit; To another faith by the same Spirit; to another the gifts of healing by the same Spirit; To another the working of miracles; to another prophecy; to another discerning of spirits; to another divers kinds of tongues; to another the interpretation of tongues: But all these worketh that one and the selfsame Spirit, dividing to every man severally as he will.

Romans 12:6-8 Having then gifts differing according to the grace that is given to us, whether prophecy, let us prophesy according to the proportion of faith; Or ministry, let us wait on our ministering; or he that teacheth, on teaching; Or he that exhorteth, on exhortation: he that giveth, let him do it with simplicity; he that ruleth, with diligence; he that showeth mercy, with cheerfulness.

Exodus 20:22 And the Lord said unto Moses, Thus thou shalt say unto the children of Israel. Ye have seen that I have talked with you from heaven.

Hebrews 8:10 For this is the covenant that I will make with the house of Israel after those days, saith the Lord; I will put my laws into their mind, and write them in their hearts: and I will be to them a God, and they shall be to me a people.

Hebrews 8:13 A new covenant, he hath made the first old. Now that which decayeth and waxeth old is ready to vanish away.

Romans 7:6 But now we are delivered from the law, that being dead wherein we were held; that we should serve in newness of spirit, and not in the oldness of the letter.

Romans 1:5 By whom we have received grace and apostleship, for obedience to the faith among all nations, for his name.

Galatians 5:22-23 But the fruit of the Spirit is love, joy, peace, longsuffering, gentleness, goodness, faith, meekness, temperance: against such there is no law.

John 4:34 Jesus saith unto them, My meat is to do the will of him that sent me, and to finish his work.

Philippians 2:13 For it is God which worketh in you both to will and to do of his good pleasure.

1 Peter 3:18 For Christ also hath once suffered for sins, the just for the unjust, that he might bring us to God, being put to death in the flesh, but quickened by the Spirit.

Luke 22:44 And being in an agony he prayed more earnestly: and his sweat was as it were great drops of blood falling down to the ground.

1 Peter 2:24 Who his own self bare our sins in his own body on the tree, that we, being dead to sins, should live unto righteousness: by whose stripes ye were healed.

Matthew 27:29 And when they had platted a crown of thorns, they put it upon his head, and a reed in his right hand: and they bowed the knee before him, and mocked him, saying, Hail, King of the Jews!

Psalm 22:16 For dogs have compassed me; the assembly of the wicked have enclosed me: they pierced my hands and my feet.

Luke 24:39-40 Behold my hands and my feet, that it is I myself: handle me, and see; for a spirit hath not flesh and bones, as ye see me have. And when he has thus spoken, he showed them his hands and his feet.

John 19:34 But one of the soldiers with a spear pierced his side, and forthwith came there out blood and water.

John 17:4 I have glorified thee on the earth: I have finished the work which thou gavest me to do. which thou gravest me to do.

Luke 23:46 And when Jesus had cried with a loud voice, he said, Father, in to thy hands I commend my spirit: and having said thus, he gave up the ghost.

1 Peter 4:15 But let none of you suffer as a murderer, or as a thief, or as an evildoer, or as a busybody in other men's matters.

Romans 12:14 Bless them which persecute you: bless, and curse not.

Ephesians 6:10-13 Finally, my brethren, be strong in the Lord, and in the power of his might. Put on the whole armor of God, that ye may be able to stand against the wiles of the devil. For we wrestle not against flesh and blood, but against principalities, against powers, against the ruler of the darkness of this world, against spiritual wickedness in high places. Wherefore take unto you the whole armor of God, that ye may be able to withstand in the evil day, and having done all, to stand.

Ephesians 4:29 Let no corrupt communication proceed out of your mouth, but that which is good to the use of edifying, that it may minister grace unto the hearers.

Matthew 5:44 But I say unto you, Love your enemies, bless them that curse you, do good to them that hate you, and pray for them which despitefully use you, and persecute you.

Matthew 15:4 For God commanded, saying, Honour thy father and mother: and, He that curseth father and mother; let him die in death.

1 Corinthians 6:19 What? Know ye not that your body is the temple of the Holy Ghost which is in you, which ye have of God, and ye are not your own?

John 4:36 And he that reapeth receiveth wages, an gathereth fruit unto life eternal: that both he that soweth and he that reapeth may rejoice together.

Psalm 105:14-15 He suffered no man to do them wrong: yea, he reproved kings for their sakes, Saying; Touch not mine anointed, and do no my prophets no harm.

Hebrews12:14-15 Follow peace with all men, and holiness, without which no man shall see the Lord: Looking diligently lest any man fail of the grace of God; lest any root of bitterness springing up trouble you, and thereby many be defiled.

Acts 26:18 To open their eyes, and to turn them from darkness to light, and from the power of Satan unto God, that they may receive forgiveness of sins, and inheritance among them which are sanctified by faith that is in me.

Matthew 18:21-22 Then came Peter to him, and said, Lord, how oft shall my brother sin against me, and I forgive him? till seven times? Jesus saith unto him, I say not unto thee, until seven times: but, until seventy times seven.

Romans 7:22 For I delight in the law of God after the inward man.

Romans 2:18 And knowest his will, and approvest the things that are more excellent, being instructed out of the law.

Romans 7:25 I thank God through Jesus Christ our Lord. So then with the mind I myself serve the law of God; but with the flesh the law of sin.

Romans 8:2 For the law of the Spirit of life in Christ Jesus hath made me free from the law of sin and death.

John 10:10 The thief cometh not, but for to steal, and to kill, and to destroy; I am come that they might have life, and that they might have it more abundantly.

Revelation 22:3 And there shall be no more curse: but the throne of God and of the Lamb shall be in it; and his servants shall serve him.

Proverbs 3:5 Trust in the Lord with all thine heart; and lean not unto thine own understanding.

Psalm 91:11 For he shall give his angels charge over thee, to keep thee in all thy ways.

John 14:27 I leave with you, my peace I give unto you: not as the world giveth, give I unto you. Let not your heart be troubled, neither let it be afraid.

Exodus 23:25 And ye shall serve the Lord your God, and he shall bless thy bread, and thy water; and I will take sickness away from the midst of thee.

3 John 1:2 Beloved, I wish above all things that thou mayest prosper and be in health, even as thy soul prospereth.

1 Corinthians 2:6 That your faith should not stand in the wisdom of men, but in the power of God.

Leviticus 26:2 Ye shall keep my Sabbath and reverence my sanctuary: I am the Lord.

Genesis 2:1-3 Thus the heavens and the earth were finished, and all the host of them. And on the seventh day God ended his work which he had made; and he rested on the seventh day from all his work which he had made. And God blessed the seventh day, and sanctified it: because that in it he had rested from all his work which God created and made.

Matthew 11:28 Come unto me, all ye that labour and are heavy laden, and I will give you rest.

Mark 2:27-28 And he said unto them, The Sabbath was made for man, and not man for the Sabbath. Therefore, the Son of man is Lord also of the Sabbath.

Leviticus 23:24 Speak to the children of Israel, saying, In the seven month, in the first day of the month, shall ye have a Sabbath, a memorial of blowing the trumpets, an holy convocation.

Colossians 2:12-17 Buried with him in baptism, wherein also ye are risen with him through faith of the operation of God, who hath raised him from the dead. And you, being dead in your sins and the uncircumcision of your flesh, hath he quickened together with him, having forgiven you all trespasses; Blotting out the handwriting of ordinances that was against us, which was contrary to us, and took it out of the way, nailing it to his cross: And having spoiled principalities and powers, he made a shew of them openly, triumphing over them in it. Let no man therefore judge you in meat, or in drink, or in respect of any holy day, or of the new moon, or of the Sabbath days: things to come; but the body is Christ.

Hebrews 4:3-11 For we which have believed do enter into rest, as he said, As I have sworn in my wrath, if they shall enter into my rest: although the works were finished from the foundation of the world. For he spake in a certain place of the seventh day on this wise, And God did rest the seventh day from all his works. And in this place again, If they shall enter into my rest. For if Jesus had given them rest, then would he no afterward have spoken of another day. There remaineth therefore a rest to the people of God. For he that is entered into his rest, he also hath ceased from his own works, as God did from his. Let us labour therefore to enter into that rest, lest any man fall after the same example of unbelief.

Scriptures of Love, Sampler

Deuteronomy 6:5 And thou shalt love the Lord the God with all thine heart, and with all thy soul, and with all thy might.

1 John 4:7-16 Beloved, let us love one another: for love is of God; and every one that loveth is born of God, and knoweth God.

John 3:16 For God so loved the world, that he gave his only begotten Son, that whosoever believeth in him should not perish, but have everlasting life.

Matthew 22:37-39 Jesus said unto him, Thou shalt love the Lord thy God with all thy heart, and with all thy soul, and with all thy mind.

1 Corinthians 16:14 Let all your things be done with charity.

1 John 4:8 He that loveth not knoweth not God; for God is love.

Leviticus 19:18 Thou shalt not avenge, nor bear any grudge against the children of thy people, but thou shalt love thy neighbour as thyself: I am the Lord.

1 John 4:19 We love him, because he first loved us.

1 John 4:12 No man hath seen God at any time. If we love one another, God dwelleth in us, and his love is perfected in us.

1 John 4:18 There is no fear in love; but perfect love casteth out fear: because fear hath torment. He that feareth is not made perfect in love.

Mark 12:30 And thou shalt love the Lord thy God with all thy heart, and with all thy soul, and with all thy mind, and with all thy strength: this is the first commandment.

John 14:15 If ye love me, keep my commandments.

1 Corinthians 13:13 And now abideth faith, hope, charity, these three; but the greatest of these is charity.

Galatians 5:22 But the fruit of the Spirit is love, joy, peace, longsuffering, gentleness, goodness, faith, meekness, temperance: against such there is no law.

1 Timothy 1:5 Now the end of the commandment is charity out of a pure heart, and of a good conscience, and of faith unfeigned.

1 Peter 4:8 And above all things have fervent charity among yourselves: for charity shall cover the multitude of sins.

Philippians 1:9 And this I pray, that your love may abound yet more and more in knowledge and in all judgment.

Ephesians 4:32 And be ye kind one to another, tenderhearted, forgiving one another, even as God for Christ's sake hath forgiven you.

John 15:13 Greater love hath no man than this, that a man lay down his life for his friends.

1 John 4:21 And this commandment have we from him, That he who loveth God love his brother also.

John 15:12 This is my commandment, That ye love one another, as I have loved you.

1 Thessalonians 3:12 And the Lord make you to increase and abound in love one toward another, and toward all men, even as we do toward you.

1 John 4:11 Beloved, if God so loved us, we ought also to love one another.

John 15:9-17 As the Father hath loved me, so have I loved you: continue ye in my love.

Galatians 5:14 For all the law is fulfilled in one word, even in this; Thou shalt love thy neighbour as thyself.

Jude 1:21 Keep yourselves in the love of God, looking for the mercy of our Lord Jesus Christ unto eternal life.

Romans 13:8-10 Owe no man any thing, but to love one another: for he that loveth another hath fulfilled the law.

Philippians 2:2 Fulfil ye my joy, that ye be likeminded, having the same love, being of one accord, of one mind.

John 13:34 A new commandment I give unto you, That ye love one another; as I have loved you, that ye also love one another.

Hebrews 10:24 And let us consider one another to provoke unto love and to good works.

1 John 3:18 My little children, let us not love in word, neither in tongue; but in deed and in truth.

1 John 3:11 For this is the message that ye heard from the beginning, that we should love one another.

1 John 2:5 But whoso keepeth his word, in him verily is the love of God perfected: hereby know we that we are in him.

1 John 5:3 For this is the love of God, that we keep his commandments: and his commandments are not grievous.

James 2:8 If ye fulfil the royal law according to the scripture, Thou shalt love thy neighbour as thyself, ye do well.

James 1:12 Blessed is the man that endureth temptation: for when he is tried, he shall receive the crown of life, which the Lord hath promised to them that love him.

Revelation 2:4 Nevertheless I have [somewhat] against thee, because thou hast left thy first love.

Luke 10:27-30 And he answering said, Thou shalt love the Lord thy God with all thy heart, and with all thy soul, and with all thy strength, and with all thy mind; and thy neighbour as thyself.

Ephesians 3:17-19 That Christ may dwell in your hearts by faith; that ye, being rooted and grounded in love.

Scriptures of Healing, Sampler

Proverbs 4:20-22 My son, attend to my words; incline thine ear unto my sayings. Let them not depart from thine eyes; keep them in the midst of thine heart. For they are life unto those that find them, and health to all their flesh.

Isaiah 41:10 Fear thou not; for I am with thee: be not dismayed; for I am thy God: I will strengthen thee; yea, I will help thee; yea, I will uphold thee with the right hand of my righteousness.

Jeremiah 17:14 Heal me, O Lord, and I shall be healed; save me, and I shall be saved: for thou art my praise.

1 Peter 2:24 Who his own self bare our sins in his own body on the tree, that we, being dead to sins, should live unto righteousness: by whose stripes ye were healed.

Jeremiah 33:6 Behold, I will bring it health and cure, and I will cure them, and will reveal unto them the abundance of peace and truth.

Isaiah 53:4-5 Surely he hath borne our griefs, and carried our sorrows: yet we did esteem him stricken, smitten of God, and afflicted. But he was wounded for our transgressions, he was bruised for our iniquities: the chastisement of our peace was upon him; and with his stripes we are healed.

Matthew 8:16-17 When the even was come, they brought unto him many that were possessed with devils: and he cast out the spirits with his word, and healed all that were sick: that it might be fulfilled which was spoken by Esaias the prophet, saying, Himself took our infirmities, and bare our sicknesses.

Galatians 3:13-14 Christ has redeemed us from the curse of the law, being made a curse for us: for it is written, Cursed is every one that hangeth on a tree: That the blessing of Abraham might come on the Gentiles through Jesus Christ: that we might receive the promise of the Spirit through faith.

Proverbs 3:2 For length of days, and long life, and peace, shall they add to thee.

Proverbs 9:11 For by me thy days shall be multiplied, and the years of thy life shall be increased.

Psalm 103:2-4 Bless the Lord, O my soul, and forget not all his benefits.

Psalm 107:20 He sent his word, and healed them, and delivered them from their destructions.

Ephesians 6:3 That it may be well with thee, and thou mayest live long on the earth.

James 5:15 And the prayer of faith shall save the sick, and the Lord shall raise him up; and if he have committed sins, they shall be forgiven him.

Matthew 10:1 And when he had called unto him his twelve disciples, he gave them power against unclean spirits, to cast them out, and to heal all manner of sickness and all manner of disease.

James 5:16 Confess your faults one to another, and pray one for another, that ye may be healed. The effectual fervent prayer of a righteous man availeth much.

3 John 1:2 Beloved, I wish above all things that thou mayest prosper and be in health, even as thy soul prospereth.

Philippians 4:19 But my God shall supply all your needs according to his riches in glory by Christ Jesus.

Matthew 10:8 Heal the sick, cleanse the lepers, raise the dead, cast out devils: freely ye have received, freely give.

Proverbs 17:22 A merry heart doeth good like a medicine: but a broken spirit drieth the bones.

Deuteronomy 7:15 And the Lord will take away from thee all sickness, and will put none of the evil diseases of Egypt, which thou knowest, upon thee; but will lay them upon all them that hate thee.

Hebrews 11:6 But without faith it is impossible to please him: for he that cometh to God must believe that he is, and that he is a rewarder of them that diligently seek him.

Isaiah 54:17 No weapon that is formed against thee shall prosper; and every tongue that shall rise against thee in judgment thou shalt condemn. This is the heritage of the servants of the Lord, and their righteousness is of me, saith the Lord.

Proverbs 16:24 Pleasant words are as a honeycomb, sweet to the soul, and health to the bones.

Matthew 11:28 Come unto me, all ye that labour and are heavy laden, and I will give you rest.

Proverbs 4:20-22 My son, attend to my words; incline thine ear unto my sayings.

Isaiah 57:18 I have seen his ways, and will heal him: I will lead him also, and restore comforts unto him and to his mourners.

2 Corinthians 12:9 And he said unto me, My grace is sufficient for thee: for my strength is made perfect in weakness. Most gladly therefore will I rather glory in my infirmities, that the power of Christ may rest upon me.

Luke 4:18 The Spirit of the Lord is upon me, because he hath anointed me to preach the gospel to the poor; he hath sent me to heal the brokenhearted, to preach deliverance to the captives, and recovering of sight to the blind, to set at liberty them that are bruised.

Hebrews 13:8 Jesus Christ the same yesterday, and to day, and for ever.

Romans 12:1-2 I beseech you therefore, brethren, by the mercies of God, that ye present your bodies a living sacrifice, holy, acceptable unto God, which is your reasonable service. And be not conformed to this world: but be ye transformed by the renewing of your mind, that ye may prove what is that good, and acceptable, and perfect, will of God.

Numbers 6:25-27 The Lord make his face shine upon thee, and be gracious unto thee.

Luke 10:9 And heal the sick that are therein, and say unto them, The kingdom of God is come nigh unto you.

Matthew 13:58 And he did not many mighty works there because of their unbelief.

2 Corinthians 5:7 For we walk by faith, not by sight.

1 Corinthians 12:9 To another faith by the same Spirit; to another the gifts of healing by the same Spirit.

Matthew 4:23 And Jesus went about all   Galilee, teaching in their synagogues, and preaching the gospel of the kingdom, and healing all manner of sickness and all manner of disease among the people.

Jeremiah 30:17 For I will restore health unto thee, and I will heal thee of thy wounds, saith the Lord; because they called thee an outcast, saying, This is Zion, whom no man seeketh after.

Acts 28:27 For the heart of this people is waxed gross, and their ears are dull of hearing, and their eyes have they closed; lest the   should see with their eyes, and hear with their ears, and understand with their heart, and should be converted, and I should heal them.

Acts 4:30 By stretching forth thine hand to heal; and that signs and wonders may be done by the name of thy holy child Jesus.

Matthew 17:20 And Jesus said unto them, Because of your unbelief: for verily I say unto you, If ye have faith as a grain of mustard seed, ye shall say unto this mountain, Remove hence to yonder place; and it shall remove; and nothing shall be impossible unto you.

2 Corinthians 7:1 Having therefore these promises, dearly beloved, let us cleanse ourselves from all filthiness of the flesh and spirit, perfecting holiness in the fear of God.

2 Corinthians 1:3 Blessed be God, even the Father of our Lord Jesus Christ, the Father of mercies, and the God of all comfort.

Acts 10:38 How God anointed Jesus of Nazareth with the Holy Ghost and with power: who went about doing good, and healing all that were oppressed of the devil; for God was with him.

John 14:27 Peace I leave with you, my peace I give unto you: not as the world giveth, give I unto you. Let not your heart be troubled, neither let it be afraid.

Luke 7:7 Wherefore neither thought I myself worthy to come unto thee: but say in a word, and my servant shall be healed.

Isaiah 57:19 I create the fruit of the lips; Peace, peace to him that is far off, and to him that is near, saith the Lord; and I will heal him.

Make life about *God*, for the Father has made it

about you as shown in His *Everlasting Love*.

About the Author

Patricia Marlett is dedicated to write inspirational novels for both the adult and young reader genres. With a contemporary platform, she pens plots that reflect real life events through drama, intrigue, suspense, humor, and love. Faith-inspiring messages are subtly weaved into each of her themes lending to heartfelt expressions from laughter to tears and always with hope and encouragement.

Patricia believes *Everlasting Love, God's Greatest Gift* is the pinnacle of her career, and she always gives honor and glory to God. Her greatest pleasure is writing for the Father, and in *Everlasting Love* she writes about Him. Visit Patricia at her website, www.patriciamarlett.com, to learn more, view her books, and for contact information.

Printed in Great Britain
by Amazon